Global Development of
Community Colleges, Technical Colleges, and Further Education Programs

Global Development of
Community Colleges, Technical Colleges, and Further Education Programs

Edited by Paul A. Elsner,
George R. Boggs, and Judith T. Irwin

Community College Press®
A division of the American Association of Community Colleges
Washington, DC

The American Association of Community Colleges (AACC) is the primary advocacy organization for the nation's community colleges. The association represents more than 1,200 two-year, associate degree–granting institutions and more than 11 million students. AACC promotes community colleges through five strategic action areas: recognition and advocacy for community colleges; student access, learning, and success; community college leadership development; economic and workforce development; and global and intercultural education. Information about AACC and community colleges may be found at www.aacc.nche.edu.

Design: Chaves Design
Editor: Deanna D'Errico
Printer: Kirby Lithographic Company, Inc.

Community College Press
American Association of Community Colleges
One Dupont Circle, NW, Suite 410
Washington, DC 20036

Printed in the United States of America.

Library of Congress Cataloging-in-Publication Data

Global development of community colleges, technical colleges, and further education programs / edited by Paul A. Elsner, George R. Boggs, and Judith T. Irwin.
   p. cm.
   Includes index.
   Summary: "Describes the similarities and differences between community colleges and their equivalent in 23 countries around the world"—Provided by publisher.
   ISBN 978-0-87117-386-7
   1. Community colleges—Cross-cultural studies. 2. Technical colleges—Cross-cultural studies. 3. Continuing education—Cross-cultural studies. I. Elsner, Paul A. II. Boggs, George R. III. Irwin, Judith T. IV. Title.

LB2328.G57 2008
378.1'543—dc22

2008049113

Contents

OCEANIA

CROSS-CONTINENTAL

Preface

Across the globe, countries are expanding and strengthening postsecondary education systems. In the increasingly global society and economy, education and training beyond customary compulsory primary and secondary education is now seen as essential to a nation's competitiveness and the standard of living of its people. The need to open the doors of higher or further education beyond the relatively limited enrollments in elite and selective universities has spawned a movement to develop or expand institutions that are generally less expensive, more accessible, more flexible, and tied closer to business and industry. This book describes the systems that have developed in more than 20 countries to meet these needs.

These institutions go by different names: community colleges, technical colleges, technical universities, polytechnics, further education (FE) institutions, technical and further education (TAFE) institutions, institutes of technology, colleges of technology, and junior colleges. Their evolution has been shaped by the needs that have emerged in various regions, by political and economic pressures, and by the visions of leaders. The institutions vary as to whether they are public, private, or private for profit. The missions vary as to the level of degrees or qualifications they can award and their focus on vocational–technical education or academic liberal arts. In some countries, they are considered part of the higher education system; in others, there is a marked separation between higher education and further education. In some places, they are part of university systems; in others they stand alone. In some countries, students can transfer credits that they earn in these institutions to universities; in others, they cannot. In some countries, the institutions are governed centrally; in others, governance systems are localized. Some focus more on younger students; while others serve adults and their need for lifelong learning.

What, then, defines this sector? Common elements include, for the most part, open access, a nonelitist orientation, a focus on the success of students in their learning, responsiveness to the education needs of local communities and their industries, and a willingness to be creative and to avoid bureaucratic processes. In most countries, the institutions lack the prestige of the elite universities even though the well-being of a country and its people usually depend more on the education levels of the majority rather than of a small minority. In the United States, almost half of all students in higher education are enrolled in community colleges, and some of their alumni have received Nobel prizes or been recognized in other notable ways.

This is the first book to describe this unique sector as it has developed (and is developing) throughout the world. Because of the many differences in governance, funding, and structure, there is much to be learned about the successes and limitations of different systems in different environments. This book will be useful to those who wish to develop or to strengthen the postsecondary education systems in their countries.

George R. Boggs

Acknowledgments

Publication of this book would not have been possible without the assistance of several people in addition to the contributors. Diane Merrell, Gayona Beckford-Barclay, and Laura Phipps Darr provided considerable support with the editing and formatting of the manuscript. James McKenney, Judith Irwin, and Diana Kelley were instrumental in securing contributors for several chapters. Deanna D'Errico, the editor of Community College Press, gave special counsel to this enormous project.

Introduction

Paul A. Elsner

The advent of a global economy has placed extraordinary pressure on education ministries and policymakers to devise strategies and postsecondary education options to educate and train both youth and adults to meet the current and future needs of a global workforce. There are 23 countries highlighted in this book; one common thread that readers will find among them is that all are preoccupied with preparing their citizens for an increasingly complex and technologically driven global economy. The United States is among those countries.

Tough Choices or Tough Times: The Report of the New Commission on the Skills of the American Workforce (National Center on Education and the Economy, 2008), expresses this shared concern from the U.S. perspective:

> When the report of the first Commission on the Skills of the
> American Workforce, *America's Choice: high skills or low wages!*, was
> released in 1990, the globalization of the world's economy was just
> getting underway. That Commission understood the threat in the
> straightforward terms captured in the report's subtitle. A worldwide
> market was developing in low-skill labor, it said, and the work requiring
> low-skills would go to those countries where the price of low-skill labor
> was the lowest. If the United States wanted to continue to compete
> in that market, it could look forward to a continued decline in wages
> and very long working hours. Alternatively, it could abandon low-skill
> work and concentrate on competing in the worldwide market for high-
> value-added products and services. To do that, it would have to adopt
> internationally benchmarked standards for educating its students and
> its workers, because only countries with highly skilled workforces could
> successfully compete in that market.

The challenge of globalization is of paramount consideration for all countries, and developed countries are not immune to swift changes such as the advent of a digitized world and a networked workforce. For example, Australia's economy has moved away from extractive industries and industrial era mechanic and machine trades. Its current workforce demands require more focused standards and a more assertive direction from both its national ministries and its training authorities. For Australia, New Zealand, and other countries, gaining a foothold in Southeast Asia, particularly in China and Japan, and in the Pacific region, is critical.

Like other countries, Australia sees much of its technical training and workforce capacity being tied to international partnerships. In fact, partnership and cooperation is another common thread readers will find across the most of the chapters in this book. Australia, Canada, Denmark, the Dominican Republic, England, Georgia, India, the Netherlands, and the United States are among the countries in which development of technical and community colleges has been assisted by partnership and cooperation between and among countries and organizations including the American Association of Community Colleges, Community Colleges for International Development, and the U.S. Agency for International Development.

Along with the similarities across countries that readers will perceive when reading this book, there are, of course, many differences. For example, the role that history and culture plays in education policy is stronger in some countries than in others. And education is administrated and regulated differently by virtue of the differences in government from one country to another. It is by comparing the differences between countries, however, that the profiles in this book may be of most use to its audience; what works in one country may or may not work in another, but each country stands to learn from another country's experience. In the following section, I summarize some of the issues and conclusions that emerged from my comparison of each country's experience.

There are no universal solutions. Each country reached its workforce and training solutions in characteristic ways that matched the political and government structure in its own country. This variation reminded me that there is no universal definition of excellence, or even guidelines for best practices. Moreover, this book does not suggest that any one country's system is the only answer for meeting complex technological and workforce demands. All the systems represented in this book are worthy, from the start-up initiative for the creation of community colleges in Thailand to the longstanding tradition of junior colleges in Japan. In short, there is no single model that everyone should follow; however, each country's system has features that most all of us would admire or attempt to emulate.

Stakeholders can be better involved. The Netherlands appears to have a thorough compact designed around the participation of parents, the students' aptitudes and interests, and the institutional services provided by its further education institutions. After leaving middle school, students are examined and diagnostically assessed with regard to ability, interests, and personal and career goals. Parents participate with counselors and advisors on the decisions that young people will later confront, whether they are interested in the university, technical education, or successful trade occupations. These decisions are sorted out with parents involved and with solid advisement and data provided by professional staff. By the time a student reaches the age to enter a college, much of the decision making about career goals and aspirations have been responsibly worked out.

In comparison, in the United States, huge numbers of students arrive at community colleges with exploratory aims to succeed without specific goals for career placement. They may find their specific niche but often without the professional planning and guidance one sees in the Dutch system. Although matriculation may be more open in the U.S. community college system, methods of matching students' goals with available options seems much more clearly developed in the Netherlands than in the United States.

National governance affects higher education decisions. Governance and decision-making mechanisms for starting colleges range from powerful central mandates to more decentralized autonomous decision making at the state, provincial, or local and even municipal levels. China, for example, has very specific approval powers for all institutions. The central ministries in China assert full power over certain constitutionally formed universities but encourage direction albeit less control over provincial and local institutions. I was surprised to learn that technical institutes and vocational training centers are sometimes called community colleges but that these institutions bear little resemblance to what other countries call community colleges. The term *community college* is, in fact, actually discouraged by some central ministries. Governance structures can also influence the further education pathways available to students. In Denmark, students have multiple pathways available, including vocational, technical, adult, and university education delivered in several kinds of institutions and at several levels. Also as a result of Denmark's governance structure, money follows the students, regardless of which pathway they choose.

Most countries have central further education policies. Whereas most of the countries represented in this book assert clear and focused national priorities for workforce or technical training, the United States does not. Individual states have their own goals. As a result, there is a lack of consistency regarding accountability standards and, in most cases, how money flows to the community colleges. In contrast, in the United Kingdom, accountability and funding criteria are paramount national considerations. Further education institutions undergo periodic inspection, and institutions can be closed if they do not meet quality and performance goals set down by funding authorities.

Some countries remain in a state of flux. In countries such as South Africa, there have been so many shifts of philosophy, emphasis, and focus that it is difficult to track the historical evolution of mergers and consolidations; philosophies of universities, vocational schools, and technitrons; and an array of complex governance issues. The evolution of education in Spain has been so long and slow that Spain is concerned that its students are not yet being trained at the competitive levels sufficient to succeed against well-developed western European countries. In other countries, evolution has been too slow to stop high-achieving students from moving to those same western European countries for better jobs.

Culture can play a strong role. In French West Africa, the French Colonial culture has had longstanding influence, which has focused more on the cultural assimilation of Africans into the French culture than on setting up an adequate economic development infrastructure and a training apparatus for bringing Africans into successful and gainful employment, as well as creating too few new jobs. As the chapter on French West Africa emphasizes, if more attention had been given to both job creation and prospecting for industries within an economic development framework, countries such as Mali, Burkina Faso, Senegal, and Niger would not have the poverty levels they have. Absent jobs other than in the tourism industry, French West Africans often rely on limited agricultural subsistence and international aid and support.

Strong economic growth exacerbates workforce need. The United Arab Emirates (UAE) is not currently able to meet workforce demands with its own citizens: Native Arabs constitute only about 20% of the workforce; the other 80% is made up of workers from all over the world. To support its robust economy, the UAE employs large numbers of professionals and contract workers for construction, high-tech, and clerical jobs from Canada, Australia, the United States, and Europe; many laborers and less-skilled contract workers come from less-developed African countries. Although its Higher Colleges of Technology (HCT) system is well respected and supported, most of its graduates seek to go into occupations in lesser demand. Explosive growth and development is also a factor in Vietnam, where plans are in place to build 10 technically oriented community colleges to meet workforce needs. Readers will learn that new developments in Vietnam's education system are linked to changing politic ideology.

Workforce demands drive decentralization. In many countries, academic studies have traditionally held primacy over vocational training. But because of the need to prepare citizens to compete in the global economy, countries including Chile and Thailand have found it advantageous to focus more support on local initiatives. This shift away from centrally driven solutions toward local preferences has resulted in deregulation in both countries. Specifically, a 1980s reform in Chile called for transferring financial responsibility to the students and for comprehensive local rather than government regulation for establishing funding and institutions. This governmental posture is in contrast to that of many developed and undeveloped countries; it is therefore interesting to note that Chile's general standard of living is the highest in South America and exceeds that of some developed countries.

Renowned author Thomas Friedman (2007) characterized the world as flat because, among other developments, countries can outsource virtually anything to any place. Moreover, search engines are distributing information more equitably than ever before, so the centers of information and expertise, once controlled by only certain nation states or economic powers, have so decentralized that the world's economies have become much more self-organized than hierarchy controlled. It is obvious to observers of developments in most of the countries surveyed in this book that free market capitalism, availability of markets to virtually anyone in a digital world, and expanding Internet-based commerce calls for new training paradigms. A flatter world must also presuppose more evenly distributed capacity among the world's countries.

As this book shows, all countries are in this challenge together. Thus, this book is intended for not only U.S. community college professionals, but also for policymakers, educators, and ministries throughout the world. The book is not meant to be an exhaustive survey but to provide snapshots of the structure, history, and issues and challenges of further education, community college, and technical college systems across the globe. Above all, this book is intended to serve as a resource for all those engaged in globalizing further education. We hope that readers will be encouraged to use it as a networking tool to share information and practices from their respective countries with one another.

References

Friedman, T. L. (2007, July). *The world is flat: A brief history of the twenty-first century.* New York: Picador.

National Center on Education and the Economy. (2008). *Tough choices or tough times: The report of the New Commission on the Skills of the American Workforce.* http://www.skillscommission.org/pdf/exec_sum/ToughChoices_EXECSUM.pdf

AFRICA

1

Community Colleges and Further Education in French West Africa

Geremie Sawadogo

Technical and vocational schools have long been a staple of the education system in French West Africa (FWA). While they were initially conceived to train workers in the clerical and administrative skills needed by the French colonial administration, these schools, particularly those at the secondary level, slowly became a receptacle for students who were considered to be not smart enough to enter the more prestigious general education stream. As time went by, the perception that these schools were inferior to the French education system grew. However, as the demand for access to education and the need for specialized skills grew, it became increasingly obvious to policymakers and parents in FWA that technical and vocational schools had a crucial role to play in the education and economic development of their countries.

Although the American community college model does not exist in FWA, technical and vocational schools, especially the Institut Universitaire de Technologie in Senegal, have played a similar role. This postsecondary institution grants a 2-year degree in business and administration. Today, as Africa strives to meet the UNESCO goal of education for all, the technical schools are at the forefront of discussions about access to education, especially in rural areas and for marginalized populations, and are recognized for the impact they can have on economic development by equipping Africans with the technical skills and knowledge needed for the 21st century.

In this chapter, I review the historical, cultural, and political rationale that led to the establishment of the technical schools. I discuss their place and effectiveness in eight West African countries (Benin, Burkina Faso, Cote d'Ivoire, Mali, Niger, Mauritania, Senegal, and Togo). I conclude with recommendations for how these institutions can play an even greater role in FWA's economic development. This chapter draws extensively on key reports from UNESCO and UNEVOC, UNESCO's International Centre for Technical and Vocational Education and Training.

The French Colonial Legacy

Understanding the place of technical education in FWA today requires a brief review of colonial French policies in Africa. Although public, or official, schools appeared in Senegal between 1847 and 1895, they did not become common in the rest of the French colonies until late 1896. Only after 1900, with the organization of the federated colonies of French West Africa (*Afrique occidentale française,* or AOF), did France outline its education policies for the region. By a 1903 decree, education in French West Africa was organized into a system of primary schools, upper primary schools, professional schools, and a normal school. Additional decrees were made in 1912 and 1918. Some key schools were established as a result, including the St. Louis Normal School in 1907, the School for Student Marine Mechanics of Dakar in 1912, and the School of Medicine of Dakar in 1916 (Institut Fondamental d'Afrique Noire [IFAN], 1921).

French colonial education policy was intended to expand the influence of the French language and French culture in Africa. In 1931, the French governor-general of FWA stated that

> Colonial duty and political necessity impose a double task on
> our education work: on the one hand it is a matter of training an
> indigenous staff destined to become our assistants throughout the
> domains, and to ensure the ascension of a carefully chosen elite, and
> on the other hand it is a matter of educating the masses, to bring them
> nearer to us and to change their way of life. (IFAN, 1931)

The first schools in FWA were missionary schools. According to Crowder (1968), Scanlon(1965), and Kelly (1984), although they played a key role in introducing Western-style education to the colonies, they failed for several reasons:

- Missionaries were kept out of inland areas, where most of the people practiced Islam and were not interested in being educated by Christians.

- Because French was the only language used in the missionary schools, Africans who were not proficient in French could not be educated.

- The curriculum and textbooks were the same as used in France, and thus had little relevance in Africa. (One history textbook began "Our ancestors the Gauls.")

- The French education system has always been elitist. It separates the most talented from the majority at an early age and does not give high priority to educating the majority.

To address the shortcomings of the missionary schools and to infuse its own political ideology into the schooling process, the colonial government gradually replaced religious learning with a largely secular school system. Education served an entirely different purpose for the government than it had for the missionaries: reducing native resistance to the White outsiders. In 1909, the governor-general urged all colonial governors to reduce the powers of native leaders and to pressure chiefs to send their children to French schools. As the inspector of education for the AOF commented 10 years later, "The first requirement of the education which we give in our colonies should be one of practical utility, first of all for [the French], and then for the natives" (Harrison, Ingawa, & Martin, 1987).

The elitist and political nature of French colonial education policies explains the role that was historically bestowed on FWA's technical and vocational schools. These institutions were primarily conceived to train qualified labor for the colonial economy, with an initial emphasis on clerical and administrative skills and on educating those who were not sufficiently qualified or smart enough to go through the general education cycle (Foster, 1992).

Transitional Phase

A decade after the colonies were granted independence from France, it became obvious that the French education model was no longer meeting their development needs. Too many people, including a growing number of the educated, were unemployed. At the same time, many jobs went unfilled because of a shortage of technical and vocational skills. The economic and financial crisis that struck sub–Saharan Africa in the mid-1980s brought extensive changes to the production system and labor market (Atchoarena & Delluc, 2002).

The end of guaranteed access to public-sector employment meant that more graduates were unemployed. The rate of return for investment in education beyond primary school deteriorated. These factors pointed to an urgent need to strengthen technical and vocational education (TVE).

Most FWA countries used one of two approaches to improve TVE: strengthening separate vocational institutions, usually at the secondary level, or adding prevocational subjects to primary- and secondary-school curricula. Proponents of the second approach asserted that it would benefit dropouts and repeaters (Mazonde, 1997). Unfortunately, the occupational areas addressed by the new curricula were rarely chosen with labor market considerations in mind. As a result, the prevocational subjects seldom kept pace with the demands of the economy (Middleton & Demsky, 1989).

The FWA countries borrowed heavily from France's education model as they developed technical and vocational schools. This often resulted in serious oversights. For example, in France, students who held the technical BAC (baccalaureate) were eligible to enter a 2-year training program that led to the Brévet de Technicien Supérieur (BTS), which opened doors to the job market. In Africa, however, few systems offered the BTS, limiting the training, and therefore the job opportunities, available to students with technical BACs. In rare cases, a BAC holder might be accepted into tertiary education but would be unprepared for the course work, which was designed for students who had obtained the more stringent science BAC rather than a technical BAC.

Although FWA governments promoted technical and vocational schools' importance to national economic development, parents and students continued to perceive TVE as inferior to general education, particularly at the primary and secondary levels. Many believed that these schools existed only to salvage general education failures. Indeed, most technical and vocational school students were from a lower economic class or had primary-school grades that were not high enough to permit them to continue on to general secondary education (Psacharopoulos & Loxley, 1985). The effectiveness of the technical and vocational schools was hampered by their rigidity, their inability to adapt to the changing demands of the labor market, and the continuing perception that they were inferior to other education institutions.

THE CHANGING FORTUNES OF TECHNICAL AND VOCATIONAL EDUCATION

In the 1980s, worldwide unemployment increased alarmingly, and the number of young people excluded from secondary school grew to more than 300 million according to UNESCO (2005). TVE, long considered second-rate, regained some luster. Key organizations worldwide publicly supported the view taken by UNESCO and UNEVOC that TVE could give young people and adults equitable access to learning and life-skills programs and usher developing countries into the 21st century by equipping their citizens with the technical skills needed to work in the knowledge economy.

What Benavot (1983) referred to as the "rise and decline of vocational education" (see also UNESCO, 2005) in Africa resulted in large part from the continuous failures and challenges of general education. According to 2006 statistics from UNESCO, Africa has the lowest rate in the world of primary school completion. While most of the European countries have a 90% or greater completion rate, only 8 of the 45 African countries do. Completion rates are particularly low in six African countries, four of them in FWA: Niger, 21%; Burkina Faso, 27%; Chad, 32%; and Mali, 33%. In most countries in Europe, Asia, North America, and South America, more than 85% of children who complete primary school continue to secondary school. In Africa, only 30% of children who enroll in primary school go on to secondary education or vocational training; only 3% pursue tertiary level education or training.

In the technical area, Africa has only 20,000 scientists and engineers, just .36% of the world's total. Africa publishes only 1.5% of the world's scientific publications and has no recorded patents. According to the United Nations Economic Commission for Africa (2007), the continent loses thousands of specialists (doctors, university professors, and engineers) every year, totaling about 60,000 between 1985 and 1990.

CURRENT CHALLENGES TO TECHNICAL AND VOCATIONAL EDUCATION

The education system in FWA countries typically has four levels: primary education (6 years); junior secondary school (4 years); senior secondary school (3 years); and basic university, which grants the bachelor's degree (3 years). Students are placed in either a general education stream or a TVE stream, sometimes as early as in primary education. Although general education students can move into the technical and vocational stream, the reverse is not true. As a result, technical and vocational students cannot attend school beyond the end of junior secondary school level.

Most of the technical and vocational schools in FWA are in urban areas; however, the skills they teach are more in demand in rural areas, where unemployment and illiteracy are high and access to education is very limited. Students in rural areas face the further disadvantage that the technical and vocational schools use French, rather than local languages, for instruction. Nang Son (2001) identified five characteristics that make FWA's economy and education system bleak:

- High unemployment, especially among young people who have graduated from secondary schools without developing any technical or professional skills.

- Growth in the informal economy and a very dynamic apprenticeship sector.

- Poor organization of apprenticeship programs.

- Lack of coordination between technical schools and universities.

- A belief that technical education is less valuable to Africa's economic development than general education is.

Atchoarena and Delluc (2002) identified three main configurations for governing TVE:

- Technical and vocational schools are overseen by the ministry of education (as in Mali).

- Technical and vocational schools are overseen by a separate ministry for vocational education (as in Benin, Cote D'Ivoire, Senegal, and Togo).

- Vocational schools are attached to the ministry of labor or employment, while technical schools are overseen by the ministry of education.

In many countries, the responsibility for overseeing technical and vocational schools is or has been shared by several ministries—typically the ministries of education, technical training, and labor—which results in a lack of focus and direction, as well as insufficient funding. In Cote d'Ivoire, for example, the ministry of TVE was created in 1970. In 1983, TVE was integrated into the ministry of education; in 1986, it became a separate ministerial unit; and in 1996, it was again incorporated into the ministry of education and scientific research. Since 2000, all TVE has been overseen by the ministry of youth, employment, and vocational education. Most FWA countries exhibit similar ambivalence about the role technical and vocational schools play in their education systems and economic development efforts.

According to Grierson (1997), one of the most obvious shortcomings of formal technical education in FWA is that it lacks relevancy. For instance, education systems have ignored the informal sector, especially the artisans' microenterprises and very successful apprenticeship models the region is famous for. As a result, extensive apprenticeship programs are cropping up at the margins of formal TVE systems. There is wide concern that, for the most part, these apprenticeships do not provide theoretical knowledge relevant to the skills they teach.

In countries throughout FWA, the education system consists of multiple schools that each specialize in a single technical area. Although this model might lead to highly focused training, it is not cost-effective and it cannot take advantage of the teaching and learning synergy that institutions with diverse offerings and a diverse student body can offer. In addition to the limited number of institutions, UNEVOC (2005) identified other factors that limit access to technical education in FWA:

- In many countries, TVE is provided only in French, which many citizens do not speak.

- Women are often denied access to or poorly served by TVE programs.

- The tuition fees charged by training providers make it difficult for those with low incomes to enter TVE programs.

- In most countries, the best vocational schools and training programs are in cities. Rural residents cannot attend them unless they live far from home and thus are absent from work and apart from family and friends.

- Older people are often unable to attend training because of the cost or because the TVE systems in many countries serve only young people.

- In many countries, negative perceptions of TVE make it undesirable for people to attend.

While there has been no conclusive study, research suggests that vocational education in sub–Saharan Africa has had a positive economic effect during certain periods. According to Benavot (1983), between 1955 and 1970, vocational education affected economic growth in less-developed countries slightly more than general education did. Providing the people of FWA with technical skills will combat high unemployment rates and help the countries become globalized.

RECOMMENDATIONS

Revitalizing technical education in FWA will require numerous changes. Among the recommendations made to UNESCO (1999) by the Second International Congress on Technical and Vocational Education were the following:

- Ensure that TVE is accessible and available to all.

- Make TVE systems flexible, innovative, and productive.
- Form new partnerships between education providers and business and industry.
- Foster the development of generic competencies, a strong work ethic, and technological and entrepreneurial skills.
- Impart human values and standards for responsible citizenship.
- Design TVE to provide developmental life experiences that have cultural and environmental aspects as well as economic dimensions.
- Reorient TVE curricula to reflect new subjects and issues of importance.

These are good recommendations, but too broad. FWA countries need to address these areas of TVE: cost, relevance, governance, image, access, and the need for data.

Cost

The cost of TVE remains high compared to the cost of general education. Growing demand and declining resources have created a need for less costly, more efficient, and more appropriate forms of TVE education, which has often resulted in lower quality offerings. Although international agencies such as the World Bank and UNESCO and donor countries including Switzerland, Germany, and France have contributed funds to TVE initiatives in some FWA countries, local businesses remain the best hope for resources. Senegal, Togo, and, to some extent, Cote d'Ivoire have developed successful private-sector funding mechanisms that can serve as examples for the other FWA countries. Furthermore, the regional schools, which were established in the 1970s and 1980s and are now closed due to low enrollment and the failure of member countries to pay their dues, should be reorganized to accept regional intake as a financially viable alternative for running expensive country-specific training centers or schools.

Relevance

There is a growing mismatch between technical and vocational training and the job skills that people need in order to contribute to dynamic competitive markets. This mismatch is a lingering effect of French colonial education policies, but it is also a result of the absence of national debate about the goals and roles of technical and vocational institutions. National conferences on education reform in FWA rarely address technical schools, which are often an afterthought. Discussions of technical education must take into account the skills and competencies that the employers and enterprises of each country, region, and community need. They should also take into account student motivation as it relates to self-employment, in order to ensure that students are placed in the right programs of study. Finally, many countries have used enterprise-based training to reduce education costs and to ensure that students are learning relevant skills. Technical and vocational schools should have specific departments that are responsible for partnerships with business. These departments should analyze the labor market and identify the worker skills that are and will be needed.

Governance, Image, and Access

Problems related to the financial health of the TVE systems and to students' perception of their relevancy and usefulness can be alleviated if FWA governments properly address issues related to their governance and their image. Frequent changes in governance have created an identity crisis for TVE, sending the message that it is disposable and not important. The FWA countries must establish long-lasting ministerial anchors for technical schools. Having stable governance will help the systems gain allies and supporters who can assist in policy advocacy and fundraising.

Advocates, educators, and politicians must work together to repair the image of technical and vocational schools so that people consider them to be as good as general education schools. This can be accomplished by making sure that the training offered reflects labor market needs. It is also important to create pathways and articulation agreements that allow testing and free transfer between technical and vocational programs and universities. Currently, general education students can take tests to attend technical schools, but students in technical schools are rarely permitted to transfer to general education. Creating such pathways will not only make more opportunities available to more students, it will also go a long way toward changing the perception that TVE is inferior to general education.

Need for Accurate and Timely Statistical Data

Given the challenges to governing TVE systems, it is not surprising that there is a lack of accurate and timely statistical data about their enrollment and economic impact. Many have recommended that such data be available. In response, most FWA countries created national observatories in the 1980s to collect data on technical and vocational schools as well as labor statistics, to help the countries make informed planning decisions. However, these observatories cannot be relied upon to produce actionable data. I placed several calls to the observatories in many of the countries reviewed in this chapter, only to be told to call either BREDA (the regional UNESCO office for Africa, in Dakar, Senegal) or UNESCO. Without accurate data about enrollment, occupations, and economic development, FWA cannot succeed in reducing unemployment and meeting the economic demands of the 21st century. The established observatories must gather data and make it available so that planners and educators can respond to students' needs and positively affect national development.

CONCLUSION

The classic novel, *L'aventure ambiguë* (Kane, 1961), required reading for generations of students, depicts a clash between traditional African cultures and those of the West, primarily represented by modern education. At issue is whether the locals should send their children to the foreigners' school. The matriarch of the family, while recognizing the risks, decides to send her children to the foreigners' school, explaining that the school "is the new form of war which those who have come here are waging, and we must send our elite there, expecting that all the country will follow them. . . . If there is a risk, they are best prepared to cope successfully with it, because they are most firmly attached to what they are" (p. 37). Although this story is set in Senegal in the 1940s, the core issues that it depicts are as compelling for TVE in FWA today as they were then.

There is a wide diversity in the types, governance, and funding schemes of technical schools in FWA countries, but the countries share the challenges presented by lingering negative stereotypes, lack of funding, and lack of statistical data. The best way to address these challenges is for governments, employers, business, and educators to work together. Governments and businesses can address questions of funding and which occupational skills technical schools should teach; educators can determine what technical training practices are relevant to their own countries. Government support for and commitment to TVE is lacking in most FWA countries. If citizens see that governments have made TVE a priority, the reputation and image of these institutions will be enhanced.

References

Atchoarena, D., & Delluc, A. (2002). *Revisiting technical and vocational education in sub–Saharan Africa: An update on trends, innovations, and challenges.* Paris: UNESCO, International Institute for Educational Planning.

Benavot, A. (1983, April). The rise and decline of vocational education. *Sociology of Education, 56,* 63–76.

Crowder, M. (1968). *West Africa under colonial rule.* Evanston, IL: Northwestern University Press.

Economic Commission for Africa. (2007). *Strategy to revitalize technical and vocational education and training (TVET) in Africa.* Presentation at the meeting of the Bureau of the Conference of Ministers of Education of the African Union, Ethiopia.

Foster, P. (1992). Vocational education and training: A major shift in World Bank policy. *Prospects, 22*(2), 149–155.

Grierson, J. P. (1997). *Where there is no job: Vocational training for self-employment in developing countries.* St. Gallen, Switzerland: Swiss Centre for Development Cooperation in Technology and Management; University of Edinburgh, Centre of African Studies; and Swiss Agency for Development and Cooperation.

Harrison, C., Ingawa, T. B., & Martin, S. M. (1987). The establishment of colonial rule in West Africa, c. 1900–1914. In J. F. Ade Ajayi & M. Crowder (Eds.), *History of West Africa, Vol.1* (2nd ed., pp. 485–545). Harlow, UK: Longman.

Institut Fondamental d'Afrique Noire (IFAN). (1921). *Bulletin de l'Enseignement en AOF* (No. 25). Dakar, Senegal: Author.

Institut Fondamental d'Afrique Noire (IFAN). (1931). *Bulletin de l'Enseignement en AOF* (No. 74). Dakar, Senegal: Author.

Kane, C. H. (1961). *L'aventure ambiguë* [Ambiguous adventure]. Paris: Julliard.

Kelly, G. P. (1984, July). The presentation of indigenous society in the schools of French West Africa and Indochina, 1918 to 1938. *Comparative Studies in Society and History, 26*(3), 523–542.

Mazonde, I. (1997). *Culture and education in the development of Africa.* UN Workshop on Education, UNESCO, Zambia.

Middleton, J., & Demsky, T. (1989). *Vocational education and training: A review of World Bank investment.* Washington, DC: World Bank.

Nang Son, J. (2001, November/December). L'Afrique et la formation technique et professionnelle à l'aube du 21ème siècle [Africa's vocational and professional training at the beginning of the 21st century]. *D+C Development and Cooperation, 6,* 14–17.

Psacharopoulos, G., & Loxley, W. (1985). *Diversified secondary education and development.* Baltimore: Johns Hopkins University Press.

Scanlon, D. (1965). Traditions of African education. *Classics in Education, 16.*

UNESCO. (1999, July). *Second international congress on technical and vocational education: Final report.* Retrieved July 17, 2008, from http://unesdoc.unesco.org/images/0011/001169/116954E.pdf

UNESCO. (2005, April–June). Vocational education: The come-back? *Education Today, 13,* 74–77.

UNEVOC. (2005). *Improving access to TVET.* Paris: UNESCO.

2

Public Further Education and Training Colleges in South Africa

Glen Fisher and Marianne Scott

S outh Africa does not have a community college system, but its education policies and practices have been influenced by the U.S. and Canadian community college model. In recent years, the post-apartheid government has created a system of further education and training (FET) colleges that have some similarities to North American community colleges and the United Kingdom's FET colleges.

In 1996, the new democratic government appointed a National Committee on Further Education (NCFE) to advise on the development of FET, which constitutes Levels 2, 3, and 4 of South Africa's 8-level National Qualifications Framework (NQF) (Level 1 is general education; Levels 5–8 are higher education). NCFE looked closely at international models, in particular the United Kingdom's further education system, which it used as a model for proposing a funding mechanism. It also considered South Africa's own past support for the community college concept.

The community college concept had been supported in South Africa since the 1980s, and a number of South African colleges had had connections with U.S. and Canadian community colleges. In the late 1980s and early 1990s, South Africa's National Institute for Community Education (NICE) promoted the implementation of community colleges in the country, with support from the U.S. Agency for International Development's (USAID's) Tertiary Education Program Support project (NICE, 1994; Strydom, Bitzer, & Lategan, 1995).

Shortly before its demise in 1994, South Africa's apartheid government proposed an education renewal strategy (ERS) that included transforming some of the country's technical colleges into "edukons"—colleges for advanced or further education. ERS was ostensibly motivated by a quest for efficiency: Because universities and polytechnics had become increasingly expensive, "only students who have a realistic chance of completing their studies successfully should be admitted to these institutions." The country needed "less-costly preparatory study avenues that could lead up to tertiary studies" (Department of National Education [DNE], 1991, pp. 59–60). The edukons would have offered the academic bridging and transfer functions of U.S. community colleges, which on the surface would appear to give Black South Africans, who had been excluded from the country's education system for decades, improved access to higher education.

ERS was criticized in many quarters. Fisher (1993) and others argued that incorporating a college transfer function into the proposed edukons would make only a limited improvement in Black citizens' access to universities—and that to ensure the success of Blacks, South Africa's higher education system must be transformed. Although radical intellectuals who opposed the apartheid education system favored "peoples' education," they believed that the government was using that concept for its own purposes. Edukons might have some of the features of community colleges, they argued, but "the chances of this type of educational reform succeeding seem remote" (Levin, 1991, p. 129). South Africa's employers and worker organizations challenged the proposed community education concept, too. Policymakers from business and labor did not believe that edukons would support their priorities: workforce development and economic growth.

In a country that was undergoing the profound political and social transition from apartheid to a new democratic order, some perceived ERS as an attempt by the old regime to limit the disadvantaged Black majority's access to higher education—and, by extension, to maintain the privileged and elitist status of the universities. Whatever the intent, ERS did not address the need for transformation in higher education, or the social and political imperative for higher education that would serve all of South Africa's people.

Because the term *community college* had developed negative connotations in South African, the post-apartheid government instead adopted the term *further education and training college.* By including the word *training,* the government explicitly recognized that organized labor and the private sector wanted the new system to emphasize training and skills development. South Africa's current system of technical colleges has a long history, dating back to the 19th century. In keeping with the country's dramatic social, and economic transformations, technical and vocational education and training (TVET) institutions have undergone numerous changes.

A History of South Africa's Technical College System

1884–1990

The development of TVET in South Africa has been integrally linked with the country's economic development, beginning with the discovery of diamonds and gold in the late 19th century. These minerals were located in remote parts of the country and were deep in the earth. To mine them, the country had to develop railways to transport the necessary heavy equipment and supplies, it had to develop power sources, and it had to mobilize large numbers of laborers. These developments in turn lead to the creation of new urban centers and the growth of commercial farming and manufacturing.

The first apprenticeship programs were established at railway workshops in Natal in 1884 and in the Cape around 1890. Programs in mining engineering were introduced in the Cape in 1894. Over the next 20 years, some of these programs evolved into South Africa's first universities, in Cape Town, Natal, and the Witwatersrand; others became technical institutes.

Under the government's protectionist policies, the period between the two world wars was one of accelerating industrialization. Technical college enrollment grew rapidly, fueled in part by the Apprenticeship Act of 1922, which required that apprentices attend formal technical classes. Between 1935 and 1955, full-time technical college enrollment grew from about 4,000 to 9,000, but part-time enrollment soared from 16,000 to 55,000 (Malherbe, 1977, p. 174). The great majority of technical college students were White. There was a small number of Indian and coloured[1] students, but Blacks remained largely excluded from TVET. Technical colleges enjoyed considerable autonomy but were closely linked with local employers and communities. "Their organization was flexible and adaptable, so that they could readily meet the educational needs of all ages and all levels in almost every conceivable subject. For the most part it was education provided cafeteria style" (Malherbe, 1977, p. 173).

The assumption of political power by the National Party in 1948, and the introduction of its policies of apartheid and racial exclusion, led to a weakening of the technical college sector. The new government asserted centralized control over the colleges. It also promoted the development of institutions where all instruction was in the Afrikaans language, and school-based TVET was established in the predominantly Afrikaans-speaking rural areas. State funding of technical colleges fell sharply relative to funding for higher education.

A shortage of the skilled personnel needed to meet South Africa's rapidly growing commercial and industrial sectors prompted the passage in 1967 of the Advanced Technical Education Act. This act transformed a number of the larger urban technical

---

[1] *Coloured* is used to describe one of the four main racial groups identified by South African law: Blacks, Whites, Coloureds, and Indians. Coloureds are mixed-race people with negroid ancestry, but not enough to be considered Black. In the interest of clarity, the South African terminology is is maintained in this chapter.

colleges into colleges for advanced technical education (CATEs, later known as technikons). By 1972, the country had six of these colleges, which enrolled more than 16,000 full-time and almost 15,000 part-time students (Malherbe 1977, p. 333).

The late 1970s and the 1980s in South Africa were marked by steadily intensifying political conflict, declining economic growth, and the government's shift away from heavily interventionist economic policies toward a more market-friendly approach. By the beginning of the 1980s, skills shortages had again become a pressing concern for government and the private sector. This time, however, the issue was bound up with the pressures of increasing Black urbanization and with business-sector demands for greater political and economic liberalization. Racial divisions in education and training, and the concentration of technical and vocational skills within the relatively small White population, were increasingly contested on both political and economic grounds.

Historically, South Africa had limited TVET opportunities for Blacks, especially for native Africans. According to Malherbe (1977), from 1946 to 1970, the number of Black Africans enrolled rose from a mere 2,015 to a miserly 3,652. At the end of the 1960s, Coloured enrollment barely exceeded 2,000 part-time and some 200 full-time students, and Indian enrollment was 1,300 full time and 4,500 part time. Total (full- and part-time) White enrollments by this time were approximately 83,000.

Despite their differing political and economic perspectives, both the government and the private sector sought to increase non-White enrollment in TVET. Technical training institutions for Blacks were established in urban townships, in some cases with significant financial support from the private sector (Chisholm, 1984; Swainson, 1991). By the beginning of the 1990s, South Africa had 123 technical colleges. Sixty-seven served White students; 3, Indian students; 8, Coloured students; and 45, Black students. Despite the growth in the number of technical colleges that served Blacks, in 1991, after a decade of so-called reform, fully two thirds of the 76,435 students enrolled in technical colleges were White.

1990–1994

Lifting the ban on the African National Congress (ANC) and other liberation movements in February 1990 began a far-reaching process of change in South Africa, marked most obviously by the 1994 election of an ANC-led democratic government. The consequences are long-term and still playing themselves out in the country's social, economic, and political terrains.

The period from 1990 to 1994 was one of considerable debate across many areas of public policy, including the politically symbolic and fiercely contested arena of education and training. The apartheid government sought to shape education policy through the release of its ERS. At roughly the same time, the National Education Policy Investigation (NEPI), an initiative of the National Education Co-ordinating Committee (NECC), mounted an unprecedented inquiry into almost all aspects of education in post-apartheid South Africa. In consideration of the interests of the ANC, other liberation organizations, and the trade unions, NEPI presented its findings as options for a future democratic government to consider, not as policy choices or recommendations.

The private sector was also closely engaged in the education and training debate. It did not put forward its views in a single overarching policy statement, but its statements and actions demonstrated strong support for improving the quality of South Africa's basic education and for improving both the scale and the quality of TVET. The Congress of South African Trade Unions (COSATU) was a powerful advocate for building the skills of the existing workforce, work-seekers, and the unemployed. The international community's contribution to South Africa's political transition during this period took the form of reports and proposals on primary and higher education (USAID) and human resources (Commonwealth Expert Group). A variety of special interests in education and training attempted to stake out positions in the evolving policy arena (see NEPI, 1993a, p. 40).

There was some common ground among the various policy interventions, stakeholders, and policy actors (see NEPI, 1993a, pp. 39–47). These included broad agreement on the need for a unified national education system and policy framework; the need for improvements in the quality of basic education and in the range and relevance of vocational education and training; the importance of adult education and training; and improved access to and opportunities for success within higher education by Black citizens, particularly the African majority. However, agreement on broad principles masked significant differences of approach. Key among these were competing interpretations of the meaning of, and the priority to be accorded to, equity, equality, and redress; the centralization or decentralization of educational control; access to education and the nature of curricula; education financing and management; the organization of higher education; and the nature of democratic policymaking in a post-apartheid state.

The key state and private sector proposals for a national training strategy (NTS) were outlined by the National Training Board (NTB) and the Human Sciences Research Council (HSRC), which proposed the introduction of a competency-based modular training system, the establishment of industry training boards, and the creation of a sense of partnership between the training system's main stakeholders (see Pittendrigh, 1991). Although the national training strategy proposals emerged from an extensive process of consultation between government and employers, they were developed without the participation of trade unions, including the largest confederation, COSATU, which had put forward detailed and comprehensive proposals of its own.

COSATU envisaged a national system of TVET in which financing came from the state and employers, unions were actively involved in the management of industry-based training, and training was linked to a comprehensive qualifications framework that would allow learners to move up the occupational ladder. Employers, on the other hand, favored more flexible and diversified forms of training. Their views about the role that the state, employers, and workers should play in financing and managing training differed considerably from COSATU's. Under the Further Education and Training Act of 1998 (Act 98 of 1998; DOE, 1998), South Africa's technical colleges were renamed FET colleges. The FET colleges were and are the responsibility of the national department of education (DOE).

It is beyond the purview of this chapter to explore in more detail the intricacies of the education and training policy debates of this period. It is important to note, however, the thrust of the debate, against what might be called a broad democratic movement, including by NEPI, toward the coordination of education and training within an integrated system of qualifications and provision and its alignment with economic policy and a national growth and development strategy. Training policy, in particular, drew on a rich and vibrant process of debate and engagement between the state, employers, and organized labor, whereas state policy on education was largely a closed affair, conducted within the state education apparatus (see NEPI, 1993b). The actual playing out of these debates within the technical colleges sector, declared FET colleges in 2002 by the FET Act of 1998, provides an interesting illustration of the long and winding road from education and training research and analysis, to policy development and policy implementation, over the past 15 years.

Colleges were and remain the responsibility of DOE. Although the policies of state, employers, and organized labor converged over systems coordination and the integration of education and training during the transitional period of 1990–1994, it has been argued that the then-government's Education Renewal Strategy and its proposals for the development of technical colleges as edukons were developed with relatively closed educational discourse and in isolation from the vocational education and training debates that were occupying the minds of employers, unions, and other government departments.

As will be seen in the following section, in the first term of office of the new post-apartheid government, the commitment to coordinating and integrating the development of new education and training policies and human resource development strategies was followed through, albeit in different forms and with different emphases. (For a thorough examination of the competing vocational education and training policy proposals of the former government, the private sector, COSATU, and the ANC, see NEPI, 1993b.) Yet, from the vantage point of the present, one of the ironies of the post-apartheid period is that the separate development of the colleges sector, symptomatic of a wider dichotomy between education and training, has, in the actual implementation of policy, persisted, long outliving its apartheid-era origins.

1994–1998

The ANC put forward its education and training policies both before and after the historic 1994 election (see ANC, 1992, 1994, 1995). The ANC's commitment to uniting education and training in a single system was at the heart of its proposals:

> For education and training to make a significant contribution to social and economic development, they need to be seen as an integrated whole. Until now, the two have been strictly separated, since education has been seen primarily as an academic activity and training has been seen primarily as a vocational activity. As is increasingly recognized here and abroad, this is a false dichotomy that does not correspond to the structure of knowledge, the needs of the workplace or the requirements of ordinary life in society. (ANC, 1995, p. 34)

Although preelection plans to combine DOE and the department of manpower were dropped after the new government came to power, the government did move toward integrating education and training: DOE and the South African Department of Labour (DOL) jointly sponsored the creation of NQF and the establishment of the South African Qualifications Authority.

In March 1997, DOL published a green paper, *Skills Development Strategy for Economic and Employment Growth in South Africa* (hereinafter referred to as the DOL green paper). In keeping with the ANC's policies, the DOL green paper stressed the need for integration and coordination of training and education and for partnerships between government, business, labor, and communities. The substance of the paper, however, was focused on skills development within the context of employment. It portrayed DOL's skills development strategy as complementary to DOE's FET strategy, but it included little discussion of how the strategy would work in practice, other than the suggestion that the "technical college sector represents a critical supplier of the country's mid-to-high level technical skills" (DOL, 1997, p. 77). Observing that graduates from the colleges were often unable to find employment within industry, the DOL green paper suggested this unsatisfactory situation could be remedied if the colleges delivered learnerships (i.e., apprenticeships). Observing, however, that graduates from the colleges were often unable to find employment within industry, the DOL green paper suggested that the delivery of learnerships by colleges, and the introduction of a revised funding mechanism that incorporated some form of "conditional link to industry" could help to remedy an unsatisfactory situation.

Stating that colleges "are the obvious institutions" to respond to the need for "improved institutional technical education and training," the DOL green paper suggested that the government use a portion of DOE's budget for technical colleges to support the "structured learning" component of the new learnerships, provided that "the technical colleges [improved] the quality and relevance [of] their outcomes in relation to industry" (DOL, 1997, pp. 77–78). To receive such funding, a technical college must make a contract with both employer and learner and register that contract with what is now called a Sectoral Education and Training Authority (SETA).

In 1995, the ANC had proposed the establishment of two national commissions, one on higher education and one on further education. While DOL was creating its skills development strategy, DOE established the NCFE in September 1996, which presented its final report to the minister of education in August 1997. In September 1998, the ministry of education released a white paper (Education White Paper 4) on transforming FET. The paper explicitly stated that DOE and DOL had "a joint responsibility for providing education and training pathways for young people and adult workers, and for developing more effective linkages between training and work," and, because DOL's skills development strategy and the ministry of education's new FET framework were complementary, that the two departments should "work in close collaboration" (Ministry of Education, 1998, pp. 16–17).

The two departments' approaches to the question of the colleges' role in delivering learnerships had some critical differences. Most obviously, DOL looked to the education budget to supplement the funding of the skills strategy, while DOE hoped to identify mechanisms for colleges to access additional funding through DOL's skills levy. In addition, DOL unambiguously focused on ensuring that colleges improved the relevance and quality of their programs in relation to the requirements of industry.

Education White Paper 4 also emphasized the need for partnerships:

> We will build new partnerships with the social partners, communities, NGOs and others, to promote the development of new, more responsive programmes and curricula, build capacity and mobilise resources and expertise for the development of the new FET system. In particular, we will deepen the relationship between FET and the Skills Development Programme of the Ministry of Labour. . . . A high-priority initiative, in collaboration with the provincial education departments, the Department of Labour and the new National Skills Authority and Sectoral Education and Training Authorities, will be promoted, to fast-track a systematic preparation for the introduction of learnerships in FET colleges and other programmed envisaged by the Skills Development Act. (Ministry of Education, 1998, pp. 37, 40)

The ministry would allocate earmarked funding for the development of college-industry linkages and partnerships, with the aim of developing new programs and curricula and modernizing existing programs to meet the needs of the labor market. Such initiatives would aim particularly to promote linkages with industry that combined theory and practice and offered learners practical and on-the-job training. In 1998, DOL followed up with a raft of legislation that created the basis for introducing a national skills levy, establishing 25 SETAs and launching a system of learnerships and skills programs to replace South Africa's declining apprenticeship system.

Policy Implementation, 1999–2004

Notwithstanding the positive messages about collaboration in the implementation of policy, the goal of closer coordination and integration has remained elusive, while the national human resource development strategy (i.e., of which FET policy, higher education policy, and DOL's skills strategy are all elements) has effectively lapsed. Although SETAs were rolling out 5-year plans meant to be supporting the implementation of DOL's skills development strategy, the equal buy-in of employers, organized labor, and government was absent. DOE also did not participate in the development of these 5-year plans.

As for the introduction of learnerships in colleges, early on a number of collaborative pilot schemes were initiated, with some success, while some colleges took the initiative and introduced learnerships more or less independently and usually funded through the SETAs or other forms of funding. Because the legislative framework did not provide for colleges to offer these learnerships using funding from DOE in fear of being accused of double-dipping into state funds, colleges then established separate section 21 (not-for-profit) companies in order to create the legal framework for the delivery of more responsive programs such as learnerships. Clear guidelines from DOE were never issued, and in some cases provincial education departments actively discouraged offering programs outside of the official DOE curriculum, in spite of the specific reference to fast-track the introduction of learnerships in FET colleges (see DOE, 1998, p. 40).

Without clear official direction, the provision of so-called nonformal programs, that is, learnerships and skills programs other than those approved and funded by DOE, expanded unevenly but more rapidly than overall enrollment growth. Unweighted FTEs for nonformal programs was 8,169 out of a total of 122,742 in 1998, increasing to 19,995 out of 143,913 in 2002. Reform and modernization of the dated official curriculum was placed on hold, and, as will be seen in the next section, other key elements of Education White Paper 4 were also delayed, while DOE, which is charged with practical administration, focused its attention on the reorganization of the institutional landscape of colleges. (See Fisher, Jaff, & Scott, 2003, for an analysis of the uneven process of FET policy reform from 1999 onward.) One unintended consequence of this situation was that in many colleges a growing institutional divide emerged between those programs and teaching departments that offered the by now outdated national curriculum of the minister of education, primarily to full-time young learners, and those that engaged directly with industry and some SETAs in the provision of training for workers and employees.

As has been noted, TVET at the beginning of the 1990s remained heavily skewed toward Whites, while the technical colleges sector itself was relatively small and fragmented, with some 76,000 students enrolled across 123 racially divided institutions. Alongside this provision was a system of employer-provided training, much of it informal and uncertified, and constrained by the weak state of the economy. Training for the unemployed was provided by Department of Manpower training centers, the quality and effectiveness of which was variable and uncertain, however (NEPI, 1993a, 1993b).

Again, the FET system as a very important tier of the South African education and training system needed dedicated focus, leadership, and resources. The private sector realized the significance of this sector and through the National Business Initiative (NBI) brought collective action to this arena from as early as 1997 by participating actively in the development of policy for the sector. To support the successful implementation of this policy, through the Business Trust, businesses invested ZAR 85 million for 5 years (1999–2004) in the sector by establishing the Colleges Collaboration Fund (CCF), managed by NBI.

The CCF program was initiated as an independent business-funded initiative in support of DOE, but it was ultimately was drawn a service-level agreement with DOE, supporting DOE in relandscaping the sector from 150 small and medium-sized technical colleges to 50 large multicampus FET colleges. CCF produced three sets of comprehensive data based on situational analyses of the FET sector. These informed the first period of policy implementation. CCF also provided extensive capacity building in the sector: to the management of these institutions, to the provincial departments that had executive authority over these colleges, to emerging middle managers of mainly historically disadvantaged background through an exchange program with UK colleges, supported by the British Council. A significant contribution to FET came in the form of support to the newly merged institutions addressing change management and also strategic planning for every institution at the end of 2003.

In spite of the availability of significant financial resources and expertise, however, the implementation of policy was very slow. It could be argued that the political will to transform these institutions as critical to the skills development challenges in South Africa was not evident. In the first 5 years, many significant areas of policy implementation had not been addressed, and few plans for future implementation were evident.

In their analysis of the policy framework for FET in South Africa, Fisher and Jaff (2003) cited the perspective of Ashton and Green (1996), who argued that a policy framework for education and training that aims at improving the national skills base and at placing a country on the path to a high-skill, high-wage economy requires the following: an effective integration of education and training policies with national trade and investment and labor market policies, a robust institutional framework, and strong political and social consensus, especially between government and business elites. Fisher and Jaff used this wider sense of a system for skill formation, linked to policies for economic growth and development to inform their discussion of the policy framework for FET in South Africa, and the implementation thereof. They argued further that in 5 years of FET college policy implementation, much of it was focused on the transformation of the institutional landscape of the colleges sector and on college capacity building, to the neglect of other elements of the FET and skills policy frameworks, resulting in uneven developments in the sector.

Based on the evidence gathered, Fisher and Jaff (2003) pointed to the fact that the question of delivery by FET colleges cannot be answered only at the college level, but must also be answered in terms of the immediate policy and institutional contexts, especially as relates to the development of new programs and qualifications; the implementation of new funding and quality assurance regimes; and the integration and linkages between FET policy, other education and skills policies and their institutional arrangements, the articulation of these with current skills requirements, and the targeted economic development and skills paths.

The key features of the new FET system toward a progressive approach to system change, as Education White Paper 4 sought to map out, are about creating a new governance framework; changing learning and teaching through NQF by looking at qualifications, programs, and curriculum; developing a new funding system as a lever for system change; and promoting and ensuring quality. Education White Paper 4 proposed a new FET framework that would be founded on the principle of cooperative governance, with a "strong steering, coordinating and developmental role" (Ministry of Education, 1998, p. 27) for government, substantial authority for colleges, and partnerships between government, organized business and labor, and communities. A national board for FET was to be established as a major statutory body to advise the minister of education, and provincial advisory bodies were also to be set up.

Cooperative governance during this period is reflected primarily in the various committees and subcommittees of the Heads of Education Department Committee that are concerned with FET, as well as in three ad hoc but important exercises that played a significant part in shaping the new FET college sector over the past 4 years. The first was the National Landscape Task Team, appointed by the minister of education to advise on the restructuring of the college landscape. Its report (DOE, 2001) laid the basis for the merger mentioned earlier. With this foundation, the appointment of college councils and principals in terms of the FET Act of 1998 could proceed.

DOE then established the Merger Operations Task Team to oversee and support the process of mergers, the declaration of colleges as FET institutions, and the appointment of councils and principals. A smaller task team of national and provincial representatives, with CCF support, was responsible for drafting an initial proposal and financial estimates for the development of a new FET funding regime in 2003. With the merger and declaration of colleges and the appointment of new governance and management structures, the devolution of greater authority to colleges could follow, as envisaged in Education White Paper 4 and in the FET Act of 1998. These cooperative governance structures and key initiatives demonstrated that DOE's will to play a strong steering, coordinating, and developmental role certainly existed, and visible results could be produced.

Partnerships were another element in the new governance arrangements. According to Fisher and Jaff (2003), "There is little doubt that the partnership with business through the Business Trust and through the close working relationship between the Department and the CCF has provided critical technical and financial support to the change strategy of the Department, and is a tangible expression of the commitment to partnerships in the White Paper." Partnerships between colleges and business, government departments, and communities were also growing. However, it was clear that more could be done by the national and provincial education departments to collaborate with DOL and other government departments to encourage the development of mutually beneficial partnerships and to create an appropriate enabling environment, especially with respect to factors such as governance, programs, staffing, infrastructure, and funding. (With the endorsement of DOE and DOL, NBI subsequently secured the support of business leaders and leading companies for the establishment of strategic partnerships between the colleges and key industry sectors.)

As has been mentioned, the other element in the new governance framework is the National Board for Further Education and Training (NBFET) and the related provincial structures. NBFET was established, not as a statutory body, but by ministerial appointment according to the terms of the National Education Policy Act of 1996 (Act 27 of 1996; DOE, 1996).

> The perception is common amongst observers that the Board lacks status and recognition and has not played a particularly effective role and that its profile and influence with key stakeholders, including the Department of Education itself as well as organized business and labor, has been limited. Provincial advisory boards, where they have been established, would seem to be faced with the same difficulties.
>
> The key consequence, from the perspective of the new governance framework, is that FET lacks a credible, high-level, and knowledgeable advisory forum capable of forging consensus among key stakeholders on the development of the FET system and of providing robust and independent advice to the minister. Moreover, NBFET in some respects parallels the National Skills Authority established by DOL, but there would appear to be little structured or systematic communication or cooperation between the two bodies. According to Ashton and Green (1996), the lack of an effective national forum for forging consensus and shaping the national agenda is a critical weakness in the development of the national system for skill formation. (Fisher & Jaff, 2003)

The second pillar of the FET policy framework focused on programs and qualifications. DOE programs offered at that time by colleges in terms of NATED 190 and 191 (i.e., departmental regulations approved by the minister of education to establish approved education and training programs for public institutions) were widely criticized as out of date and as failing to provide the educational and generic underpinnings required, not only by the wider social and individual aims of FET policy but by the modern workplace. (DOL's green paper on the skills development strategy provides a broad definition of skill, which complements that found in Education White Paper 4.) The modernization of these programs commenced during this period was put on hold until the landscaping was in place. Along with the lack of cooperation between the DOL and DOE, clear guidelines on the implementation of learnerships, and the development and motivation of college educators, this area of implementation did not receive the attention that it should have.

Quality assurance was the third pillar of the FET policy framework outlined in Education White Paper 4. Work in this area commenced at a time when the entire quality assurance and accreditation architecture was under review by the two sponsoring government departments (DOE & DOL, 2002) and was contested by stakeholders. The notion of a funding system as the fourth pillar for system change extended well beyond a new funding formula; it included the development of reliable management information systems, the building of planning and managerial capacity in the national and provincial education departments, and the building of college systems and capacity accompanied by the phased delegation of budgets to colleges. Some progress was made. Proposals for significant new public investments in colleges, and the outlines of a new program-based funding regime, including funding envelopes for capital investment, staff development, student financial aid, and innovation, were under consideration in the DOE.

Work on a new FET Management Information System was ongoing but not ready for underpinning the new funding and planning mechanisms. The planning and managerial systems and capacity in the education departments to implement the new funding regime are still to be developed. These constraints and time lags indicated that it would probably take some time before a new planning and funding cycle could be implemented and before the new funding would begin to flow to the FET system and to have significant impact on its quality and performance.

Reflecting on the systemic nature of policy implementation in the FET sector over the first 5 years and asking whether the changes that had taken place amount to real and sustainable system change, Fisher and Jaff (2003) concluded that

> at one level, the evidence has shown that implementation of FET policy over the past 5 years cannot be regarded, at the present moment, as amounting to system change, although in some important respects it has begun to lay the foundations for this. At the same time, key elements of the policy framework have yet to be addressed, and the

mechanisms for funding, planning and steering FET colleges as a system are not in place.

Significant time and effort had been invested by DOE and the colleges and, through CCF, by the private sector. The most significant investments were visible in the new institutional landscape of FET colleges. However, it was clear that, from a wider perspective, the limitations to the steering, coordinating, and developmental role of DOE were not in the capacity or will to mobilize around policy objectives, but in the failure or inability to "develop a sustainable capacity to guide and monitor the overall development of the FET system on an ongoing basis" (Fisher & Jaff, 2003).

Employers have necessarily had a strong interest in the provision of TVET throughout the history of South Africa's industrialization. In particular, the involvement of employers, through NBI, in the development of the new post-1994 FET policy framework and private sector investment of ZAR 85 million in CCF, ensured that employers would seek to play a continuing and proactive role in creating systemic change for sustainable impact. Partnerships seemed to be the most appropriate vehicle for ensuring responsiveness, as was called for in Education White Paper 4. Embracing the concept of partnerships, NBI developed a business case for a high-level strategic and developmental partnership between industry and the new FET college sector. The partnership would assist business leaders in playing a pivotal role in supporting DOE in capacitating and shaping the development of a new sector of leading-edge FET colleges that would meet the intermediate and higher skills needs of the economy and of society.

Leadership is essential if colleges are to be assisted in playing a larger and more strategic national role in skills development and uplifting communities, if government is to be supported at the highest levels in its efforts to build the sector, and if employers are to share collectively both in the benefits of a new system and in making the necessary investments of time and resources. The Colleges-Industry Partnership (CIP) initiative seeks to promote practical working relationships between colleges and companies that will build the capacity of colleges to respond to industry, national and provincial FET demands, and continuous engagement of business leaders with the FET college sector in addressing the skills challenges of South Africa.

As has been stated, a real breakdown of relationships between the government and its colleges on the supply side, and the parties such as business and communities on the demand side, occurred during the 1980s. Although some examples of localized linkages between colleges and local communities were evident, the parties lost the ability to work together on finding solutions at a systemic level for the mid- to higher-level education and training needs and actually testing and learning from joint practice. During his 2004 and 2005 state-of-the-nation addresses, President Thabo Mbeki referred to the importance of the FET colleges to the skills development challenges of South Africa. A new minister of education was appointed, and a serious reshuffle of top senior positions in DOE occurred. It was clear that new political focus was to be given to this sector. At the beginning of 2005, the president and the minister of education announced a ZAR 1.5 billion (which later became ZAR 1.9 billion) new investment by government over a 3-year period into the recapitalization of the FET college sector.

An initial ZAR 50 million was granted to DOE by the Department of Finance to prepare for the rollout of this investment from 2006 onward. It was envisaged that the investment would kick-start the FET colleges on the road toward responsiveness: responding to the government's economic growth and development strategy via big investment in infrastructure and other areas and responding to business by investing in solutions to its ever-changing and growing skills needs. The recapitalization would focus mainly on helping colleges develop their human resources, programs, curriculum, infrastructure, equipment, administration systems, and site or building upgrades and acquisitions.

TECHNICAL COLLEGES FROM 2005 ONWARD

By providing public education and training, FET colleges have played and will continue to play an important part in South Africa's social, cultural, and economic development. According to Mayer and Altman (2005), South Africa's unemployment crisis could be partly contributed to a lack of skilled labor. To resolve the crisis, the government had to institute policies that support skills training and education, because both DOL and DOE had recognized that, as public institutions, FET colleges have a critical part in providing skills development at intermediate and higher levels.

The government of South Africa has sound reasons for investing in TVET that addresses the country's economic needs, including the need for a skilled and well-trained workforce. Both public and private TVET providers have a role to play. However, because South Africa has a history of limiting access to TVET and now faces pressures from the global marketplace, a strictly market-led approach presents dangers. If public policy does not support TVET, South Africa will not have enough skilled workers to meet the economy's needs.

The point of departure for policy implementation should have been with Education White Paper 4. It provided a comprehensive policy framework identifying key leaders for systems change that should have ensured the effective integration of education and training where the supply side speaks to the demand side of the labor market and economic growth. Because of DOE's use of CCF to focus mainly on creating a new landscape of the FET college sector in the first 5 years, many other significant policy implementation areas, such as curriculum reform and a new funding strategy to drive the system's change, were placed on hold. This meant that little or no expression of those areas could happen, and FET colleges were left to devise their own institutional arrangements to address delivery in a policy implementation vacuum. College councils and CEOs were tasked with areas of governance that again had to happen without any policy implementation framework.

The other significant consequence was that, with the focus on the restructuring of the new landscape, the paralysis that had become evident between the two departments (DOE and DOL) deepened, which did not speak to the integration of education and training as intended, and a strong education supply side focus remained and grew in DOE. Under the leadership of the minister of education and because of demand-side pressure for responsiveness to economic growth and social improvement, the impetus behind education policy was again the direction outlined in Education White Paper 4.

As was stated before, in an important show of implementing education policy, the government committed ZAR 1.9 billion in capital funding to the FET colleges for 2006–2008. In 2005, the government began the significant and necessary process of modernizing the national DOE curriculum. This modernization responds to South Africa's critical shortage of artisans, technical workers, and skilled people for other key sectors by developing apprenticeship programs and other curricula for the 21st century.

As in other countries, South Africa's employers must respond to technological innovations, global competitiveness, productivity issues, and structural changes in different sectors of the economy. The government must continually review and update education and training programs that serve employers' needs, and it must take a dynamic approach to doing so. To best serve the economy, the government must take a supply-and-demand approach to training and education in the 21st century. If it does not, increasingly greater numbers of potential workers will lack the skills that employers need. FET colleges must provide programs that meet the needs of learners, the labor market that will employ these learners, and the communities they serve. If the colleges are not able to continually transform themselves in order to provide such programs, the students they train will have qualifications but will lack the skills they need in order to be employable.

At the end of 2005, the minister of education and a number of prominent business leaders developed a proposal to create a joint business–government initiative for college excellence and priority skills acquisition (CEPSA). The initiative will mobilize business leaders and company support to develop centers of technical and vocational excellence, within the framework of government's recapitalization of the FET college sector. CEPSA will also make a contribution to the delivery of the Joint Initiative for Priority Skills Acquisition launched and led by the deputy president of South Africa in support of the government's Accelerated and Shared Growth Initiative for South Africa.

According to the minister of education, South Africa's FET college system should "equip youth and adults to meet the economic and social needs of the 21st century, provide relevant further education and training that speak to the needs of industry and communities, focus on the job creation and skills agenda that are key to SA's future success, [and] support a massive and rapid growth in intermediate skills" (Pandor, 2005). This speaks to South Africa's need for further education for school leavers and adults;

community and socioeconomic development; and technical, vocational, and career skills development.

Business is part of society, not separate from it, and operates best when society is stable and prosperous. South Africa's business community is increasingly recognizing that it must act in a way that is responsible to society, and that its employees are more than workers: They are citizens, parents, and human beings with talents and abilities that should be developed. Business has a particularly direct interest in TVET, and its involvement is integral to its success. South Africa's business community wants colleges to play a role in further education and community development, and to provide structured programs in which learners can gain the basic knowledge and skills that they need to be productive workers. To be meaningful, any relationship between business and the FET college sector must recognize that business is part of society and thus has a legitimate interest in and a legitimate role to play in TVET. Business also has a broader interest in education and training in so far as it contributes to a sustainable and economically successful society.

Work is a key part of life, and education that prepares people for life is incomplete if it does not prepare them for work. In addition to learning the skills they will need to take on specific roles, tasks, and responsibilities, students must also be prepared to deal with the constant changes in the workplace that result from a business's need to constantly adjust to the marketplace. The business and education sectors must work together to determine how training will meet industry needs. If training practices and curricula are created without input from the business community, FET college graduates will lack the skills they need if they are to be employable.

Initial partnerships between FET colleges and industry have proven to be of real value and have provided lessons for the future. If such partnerships are to be successful, the partners must be prepared to learn and to move beyond entrenched stereotypes. The national and provincial departments of education, FET colleges, and employers have engaged in more critical dialogue, and there is a growing recognition that the issues are complex. The parties' roles, responsibilities, and interests in the partnership are shaped and have become defined. FET college programs have been designed, and a process of making these programs more relevant to industry needs is happening.

With government, business, and other partners actively involved, South Africa will be able to create FET colleges that are responsive to the country's economic and other growth needs. The colleges that succeed will be the ones that understand the relationship between education, training, and work. They will systematically engage in open, responsive partnerships that help them produce programs and qualifications that are "fit for purpose," that is, relevant to learners and responsive to the economy.

Conclusion

Under South Africa's apartheid regime, education was a key instrument for subjugating the oppressed majority. With the election of a democratic government in 1994, education policy reform became a national priority. Jansen (2001) argued that the new government emphasized symbolic rather than substantive reform. One of the characteristics of the immediate post-apartheid period—a time of major social and political transition in South Africa—was that, although the government was quick to develop education policy, there were significant delays in policy implementation. When new education policy was implemented, it was often done so in a piecemeal, haphazard, and contradictory way, coupled with the persistence of education discourses from the struggle era—and from the apartheid education bureaucracy.

A classic example of the latter is the persistence of the language of "general, pre-vocational and vocational" education and training over a 15-year period, from the apartheid government's Education Renewal Strategy of 1991 to DOE's 2005 program and curriculum policy statements. This language, and the conceptual and policy distinctions that it seeks to make, have persisted alongside—and remained unaffected by—major developments in government's training strategy, including the development under DOL and SETA of a new framework of skills programs and learnerships, tied to a notionally overarching NQF.

As political pressures grow stronger, South Africa's need for accelerated and shared economic growth will be the real driver for education and training reform. Although the government has demonstrated a great commitment to the FET colleges, it is not clear whether the colleges will be able to produce the skills needed to support South Africa's economic growth. Political and economic pressures are expected to lead to the promotion of public, private, and corporate education and training institutions that can deliver on the economic imperatives and address the challenges presented by unemployment and poverty. By developing sustainable relationships with employers and cooperative agreements with private and corporate providers, the FET system will become relevant and responsive to the needs of democracy in South Africa in the next decade.

References

African National Congress. (1992). *Ready to govern: ANC policy guidelines for a democratic South Africa adopted at the national conference 28–31 May 1992.* Retrieved September 25, 2008, from http://www.anc.org.za/ancdocs/policy/readyto.html

African National Congress. (1994, January). *A policy framework for education and training* [Discussion document]. Johannesburg, South Africa: Department of Education, African National Congress.

African National Congress. (1995). *1995 ANC policy framework: A policy framework for education and training.* Manzini, Swaziland: Macmillan Boleswa Publishers.

Ashton, D., & Green, F. (1996). *Education, training and the global economy.* Cheltenham, UK: Edward Elgar.

Chisholm, L. (1984) Redefining skills: South African education in the 1980s. In P. Kallaway (Ed.), *Apartheid and education* (pp. 387–409). Johannesburg, South Africa: Ravan Press.

Department of Education (DOE). (1996). *National Education Policy Act, 1996 (Act No. 27 of 1996).* Pretoria, South Africa: Government Printer. Available from the Department of Education Web site: http://www.education.gov.za/index.aspx

Department of Education (DOE). (1998). *Further Education and Training Act, 1998 (Act No. 98 of 1998).* Pretoria, South Africa: Government Printer. Available from the Department of Education Web site: http://www.education.gov.za/index.aspx

Department of Education (DOE). (2001). *National Landscape Task Team report.* Pretoria, South Africa: Government Printer.

Department of Education & Department of Labour. (2002). *Report of the study team on the implementation of the National Qualifications Framework.* Pretoria, South Africa: Authors.

Department of Labour. (1997, March). *Skills development strategy for economic and employment growth in South Africa* [Green paper]. Pretoria, South Africa: Author. Retrieved September 30, 2008, from http://www.polity.org.za/polity/govdocs/green_papers/skills.html

Department of National Education (DNE). (1991). *Education renewal strategy* [Discussion document]. Pretoria, South Africa: University of South Africa.

Fisher, G. (1993). *Access to post-secondary education in South Africa: Taking the community college route* [Working paper]. Pretoria, South Africa: National Education Policy Investigation.

Fisher, G., & Jaff, R. (2003, October 13). *Work in progress and progress towards the world of work: Education, training and skill formation in South Africa. The case of further education and training colleges.* Paper presented at the annual Further Education and Training Convention, Midrand, Johannesburg, South Africa.

Fisher, G., Jaff, R., & Scott, M. (2003). *Some policy implications of recent research and experience: Accelerating the development of the FET colleges sector.* Johannesburg, South Africa: National Business Initiative.

Jansen, J. D. (2001). Rethinking education policy making in South Africa: Symbols of change, signals of conflict. In A. Kraak & M. Young (Eds.), *Education in retrospect: policy and implementation since 1990* (pp. 41–57). Pretoria, South Africa: HSRC Publishers.

Levin, R. (1991). People's education and the struggle for democracy in South Africa. In E. Unterhalter, H. Wolpe, T. Botha, S. Badat, T. Dlamini, & B. Khotseng (Eds.), *Apartheid education and popular struggles* (pp. 117–130). Johannesburg, South Africa: Ravan Press.

Malherbe, E. G. (1977). *Education in South Africa: Vol. 2. 1923–1975.* Cape Town, South Africa: Juta and Company.

Mayer, M. J., & Altman, M. (2005, March). South Africa's economic development trajectory: Implications for skills development. *Journal of Education and Work, 18*(1), 33–56.

Ministry of Education. (1998, September 25). A programme for the transformation of further education and training: Preparing for the twenty-first century through education, training and work (Education White Paper 4). *Government Gazette, 399*(19281). Pretoria, South Africa: Department of Education. Retrieved May 7, 2008, from http://www.info.gov.za/whitepapers/1998/19281.pdf

National Education Policy Investigation (NEPI). (1993a). *Education planning, systems and structure.* Cape Town, South Africa: Oxford University Press and National Education Co-ordinating Committee.

National Education Policy Investigation (NEPI). (1993b). *The national education policy investigation: The framework report and final report summaries.* Cape Town, South Africa: Oxford University Press and National Education Co-ordinating Committee.

National Institute for Community Education (NICE). (1994). *NICE response to ANC education and training framework: A framework for the provision of adult basic and further education.* Braamfontein, South Africa: Author.

Pandor, N. (2005, November 7). *Address by the Minister of Education, Ms Naledi Pandor, MP, at the Limpopo FET Colleges Summit, Polokwane.* Retrieved September 30, 2008, from http://www.info.gov.za/speeches/2005/05110811151001.htm

Pittendrigh, A (1991). *The NTB/HSRC investigation into a national training strategy for the RSA.* Pretoria, South Africa: Human Sciences Research Council.

Strydom, A. H., Bitzer, E. M., & Lategan, L. O. K. (1995). *Community colleges for South Africa.* Bloemfontein, South Africa: University of the Orange Free State.

Swainson, N. (1991). Corporate intervention in education and training, 1960–89. In E. Unterhalter, H. Wolpe, T. Botha, S. Badat, T. Dlamini, & B. Khotseng (Eds.), *Apartheid education and popular struggles* (pp. 95–115). Johannesburg, South Africa: Ravan Press.

AMERICA

3

Community Colleges and Further Education in Canada

Michael L. Skolnik

Canada is a bilingual, multicultural country with about 33 million people living in 10 provinces and 3 territories. It is the second largest country in the world in area, spanning almost 10 million km². More than 43% of the population lives in six major metropolitan areas (Toronto, Montreal, Vancouver, Ottawa, Calgary, and Edmonton), and a large proportion lives within 300 km of the U.S. border.

Politically, Canada is a federation in which education is within the jurisdiction of the provinces. There is no federal department of education; no integrated national education system; and no national legislation pertaining to the establishment, governance, or missions of higher education institutions. However, the federal government has had a significant influence on the development of postsecondary education because of its responsibility for national economic policy and its superior capacity for raising revenue. In the 1960s, the federal government provided much of the funding used to establish community colleges, and for a time it shared operating costs with the provinces. It still funds postsecondary education by paying for occupational retraining and for the acquisition of official languages, by providing student financial assistance, by awarding research grants, and by supporting programs for aboriginal students.

Despite federal financial support, the provinces fully control the governance, mission, structure, and content of postsecondary education. Community colleges serve as instruments of provincial social and economic policy. In contrast to universities, which have considerable autonomy, colleges are subject to a great deal of direction and regulation by provincial governments.

Canada's terms for postsecondary schools differ from the ones used in the United States. Canadian *colleges* are similar to U.S. *community colleges:* They offer postsecondary programs that are mainly or entirely below the baccalaureate level, for which completion of secondary school is a requirement for admission, as well as a variety of other programs for adults, industry, and communities. *University* refers to a postsecondary institution whose programs are primarily at the baccalaureate or higher level. "Going to college" means attending a community college, not a university. Only five colleges use the term *community college* in their names, although two of these are multicampus provincial college systems. The term *institute* appears in the names of a dozen college-type institutions. Therefore, the most accurate descriptor for this sector of Canadian postsecondary education is "colleges and institutes," although in this chapter I will use the term *colleges* to refer to all these institutions. Because most colleges do not award associate degrees, *degree* generally refers to a baccalaureate or higher degree.

The Origins and Varieties of Canada's Provincial Colleges

Canada's community colleges originated during two distinct periods. The first was prior to the 1960s, when a variety of nonuniversity postsecondary institutions were created and developed through what Campbell (1971) called "a process of quiet evolution" (p. 3). The second period was largely between the early 1960s and the early 1970s, when most provinces created systems of community colleges with precise mandates and comprehensive arrangements for funding, governance, and programming.

It is unclear just when the first period started, or which institution could be considered Canada's first community college. Smyth (1970) traced Ontario's community colleges to the mechanics institutes that were first established in 1830. Campbell (1971) identified Victoria College in British Columbia as the country's first junior college. Under an affiliation with McGill University in Montreal, Victoria College began offering lower division arts and science courses in 1903. It later changed its affiliation to the University of British Columbia, and in 1962 it became the independent University of Victoria. Dennison and Gallagher (1986) identified Lethbridge Junior College, established in Alberta in 1957, as Canada's first community college, but said that a case could be made for Lakehead College of Arts, Science, and Technology in Ontario having been first. That college was formed in 1956 from Lakehead Technical Institute, which began in 1948. Regardless of which was first, Canada had 49 junior colleges by 1958–1959. More than half were in Quebec, 40 were controlled by churches, and only 2 called themselves junior colleges (Campbell, 1971).

In the pre-1960 period, colleges were established by municipalities, churches, or other interested groups. In the second period, provincial governments provided the will, direction, and design for emerging systems of community colleges. In most cases, the blueprint for these new systems came from a royal commission or other comprehensive study of provincial needs and resources. In one of the first of such studies, the president of the University of British Columbia recommended a plan for addressing that province's postsecondary education needs, including the establishment of six community colleges (Macdonald, 1962). In Quebec, a royal commission on education advised creating colleges as part of an overhaul of the entire education system (Royal Commission of Inquiry, 1963–1966). Between 1963 and 1973, six provinces enacted legislation pertaining to the establishment, funding, and operation of new systems of community colleges.

According to Dennison and Gallagher (1986), although the timing and nature of the new college systems differed among the provinces, some common factors contributed significantly to their development. The first and most urgent was a projected increase in the numbers of secondary school graduates seeking postsecondary education. In 1960, enrollment in colleges and universities totaled 120,000, but it was projected to increase to 250,000 by 1967 and to more than 350,000 by 1970 (Dennison & Gallagher, 1986). In addition to increasing university capacity, Canada needed to create intermediate-level institutions, between high school and university, that would train workers in changing technologies. Another factor that contributed to community college development was that many of the people who sought postsecondary education to prepare for work in the modern economy did not need and were not prepared for a university education.

Finding the resources for an unprecedented expansion of postsecondary education would be difficult. A historian of postsecondary education in Ontario made an observation that also fit other provinces: "It was clear that the province could bankrupt itself in a vain attempt to provide the most expensive of postsecondary facilities [i.e., universities] to all comers, regardless of evidence of ability to benefit from them" (Fleming, 1971, p. 492).

Another factor for developing community colleges was the strong influence of human capital theory on government and public opinion (Dennison & Gallagher, 1986). A number of studies showed that society could expect high returns from increased investment in higher education. One study attributed about a third of the 25% per capita income gap between the United States and Canada to the fact that postsecondary participation was substantially lower in Canada than in the United States (Skolnik, 2005b).

Differences among provincial governments' economic, social, cultural, and political needs resulted in differences among college systems. Gallagher and Dennison (1995) categorized the different systems into five models. The first model was the one used in Ontario, the most populated province, and Prince Edward Island, the least populated. In these provinces, colleges were distinct and separate from universities and did not offer university transfer. Their main role was to prepare young people who were not eligible for university admission to enter the workforce. In introducing the legislation for Ontario's colleges, the minister of education rejected the idea of offering "university-parallel courses" (Davis, 1966, p. 14). To emphasize that difference from U.S.

community colleges, the government used the term *colleges of applied arts and technology,* although they soon came to be called community colleges.

The second model, used in Alberta and British Columbia, was of comprehensive community colleges that, like California's, combined university transfer programs with technical–vocational programs. Colleges in British Columbia also provided second-chance opportunities for adults, whereas in Alberta, "most second-chance students were still directed to government-run vocational centers established throughout the province" (Gallagher & Dennison, 1995, p. 385).

The third model was adopted in Manitoba, New Brunswick, Newfoundland, and the Yukon and Northwest Territories. As in Ontario and Prince Edward Island, the colleges offered postsecondary vocational–technical education and did not offer university transfer. However, they emphasized shorter-term work-entry training programs over advanced technological education. Newfoundland later incorporated university transfer into the mandate of its colleges, but in a more limited form than British Columbia and Alberta had.

The fourth model, unique to Saskatchewan, had a combination of colleges without walls in rural areas and technical institutes in urban areas. The rural colleges operated as brokers, arranging for other institutions and community agencies to provide education services. This practice was intended to meet the adult education and community development needs of small, widely dispersed communities whose populations were declining. It was "effectively set aside in the late 1980s when four previously independent technical institutes were reconstituted as a new multicampus Saskatchewan Institute of Applied Science and Technology and the more rural community colleges began to provide, as well as broker, educational services" (Gallagher & Dennison, 1995, pp. 385–386).

Perhaps the most distinctive model was the fifth: Quebec established colleges of general and vocational education that borrowed from European experience. After completing Grade 11, secondary students would enter one of two streams: a 3-year career preparation stream or a 2-year university preparation stream, required for attending a Quebec university. Although the Quebec colleges did not originally emphasize adult education or short-term vocational training, most soon became active adult education centers.

Nova Scotia did not create a system of community colleges when all the other provinces did. At the time, it had more universities per capita than any other province, and 70% of the population lived within 50 km of a university. Nova Scotia also had two institutes of technology, a land survey institute, an agricultural college with both university-level and vocational courses, and a junior college operated by one of the provincial universities. In 1974, the junior college campus of St. Francis Xavier University merged with the Nova Scotia Eastern Institute of Technology, creating University College Cape Breton (changed to Cape Breton University in 2005), which offered both university and college programs. In 1988, the government created Nova Scotia Community College, which now has 19 campuses in 14 communities.

COLLEGE AND ENROLLMENT NUMBERS

There are 150 colleges in Canada. Full-time enrollment in their postsecondary programs in 2004–2005 was 514,000 (Statistics Canada, 2007, Table D 1.4). To put these numbers in perspective, the comparable figures for universities were 90 institutions and full-time enrollment of 757,000 (Table D 1.5). Thus, colleges constituted about 40% of total postsecondary enrollment. Of course, colleges serve many other learners than those in postsecondary programs. The Association of Canadian Community Colleges (AACC) estimated that in 2002 the total number of people served by Canada's colleges in all programs—including general adult education, apprenticeship, literacy, and contract training for industry—was about 2.5 million (Brown, 2002).

COLLEGE CHARACTERISTICS AND RECENT DEVELOPMENTS

One of the most fundamental characteristics of Canada's community colleges is the comprehensiveness of their curricula. The range of subject matter, program structure and duration, method and format of instruction, location and scheduling, and target clientele is enormous and continually increasing. The colleges appear to thrive on this diversity. However, because they never have enough funding to serve all the people that they might, the colleges must make difficult decisions about which activities they will and will not expand or strengthen.

Such decisions are considerably influenced by the provincial governments, which often impose more intrusive and detailed regulations and policy guidelines on the colleges than they would apply to their university systems. However, provincial governments have learned that too much explicit direction can be stultifying and have been granting more latitude to colleges, subject to provincial oversight and with explicit provision for the government to limit the powers of local boards. This approach is evident in the 2002 Ontario Colleges of Applied Arts and Technology Act, which replaced earlier legislation pertaining to Ontario's colleges. Government oversight of colleges includes increasingly sophisticated annual performance indicators and, in some provinces, the use of performance funding.

The colleges have typically lacked the participatory decision-making structures that the universities have, with the exception of shared governance elements that were introduced into British Columbia's colleges through 1991 legislative amendments. Lately, college faculty in a few other provinces have participated slightly more than before in making decisions about academics. However, because some in Canada charge that university governance structures impede universities' ability to be more entrepreneurial, it is unlikely that colleges will become more like universities in this way in the near future. An exception is where the mandate of a college is changed to allow it to become a substantial provider of bachelor's programs, as happened recently with Grant MacEwan College in Edmonton.

Undoubtedly, the factor that has had the greatest influence in shaping Canada's colleges in the past decade or so is globalization. In the new global economy, the enterprises that the colleges have traditionally trained students to work in must be more and more innovative and efficient. Provincial governments expect colleges to provide more and better services to these enterprises, thus contributing to the global competitiveness of their local economies. Serving as engines of economic growth is nothing new for Canada's colleges: It has always been one of the most important elements of their missions. With increasing pressure from government, colleges have greatly expanded some of the economic services they provide.

One such service, which most Canadian colleges provide, is customized contract training for particular enterprises and industries. For example, the petroleum industry in Alberta pays Keyano College in Fort McMurray to train workers in extraction technology for the oil sands. The east coast shipping industry pays the School of Maritime Studies in St. John's, Newfoundland, to train pilots on a ship's bridge simulator. After workforce preparation, contract training "ranks as the second most important role for colleges in economic development" (Ivany, 2004, p. 6). Contract training for industry typically accounts for 20% to 30% of a college's revenue (Gadd, 2005). Sometimes colleges provide their industry and government clients with services that go beyond training to include designing and developing programming and infrastructure. Some clients are overseas: In 2000, Newfoundland's College of the North Atlantic won an $800 million contract to establish a new college for the government of Qatar.

In many cases, partnerships between colleges and industry involve other activities that are of mutual benefit. These include the opportunity for college faculty to gain experience with the newest technology, as in the partnership between Niagara College in Ontario and the automobile manufacturing industry. Industry often contributes funds for state-of-the-art technology. For example, Sheridan College Institute of Technology and Advanced Learning in Ontario built its Centre for Advanced Manufacturing and Design Technologies with the combined financial assistance of the provincial government, the city of Brampton, and local industry. This 18,000 sq.-ft. center trains students and workers in the latest design and manufacturing technologies, thus addressing the shortage of skilled labor in Ontario and making Ontario industry more globally competitive.

Doing applied research can produce significant economic benefits for colleges, which have substantially expanded applied research programs in recent years. Research is a natural complement to instructional activity in areas where colleges have the necessary technology and faculty expertise. At Southern Alberta Institute of Technology, for example, researchers helped a local manufacturer develop a new type of highly efficient water boiler. Twelve students were involved in developing the prototype, and six were hired by the firm. Red River College in Manitoba provides applied research for the aviation and aerospace industry. According to one estimate, more than half of Canada's community colleges have formal applied research programs, and another 30% conduct some project-based research (Ryval, 2005). As of June 2005, the Canada Foundation for Innovation (CFI) had provided 30 colleges with more than $30 million in funding (CFI, 2005). CFI is an independent corporation created by the government to strengthen the capacity of Canadian universities, colleges, research hospitals, and nonprofit research institutions to carry out world-class research and technology development. An indication of how applied research has been recognized as a role of colleges is that the 2002 Ontario Colleges Act, unlike previous legislation, lists applied research, as well as forming partnerships with industry, as a core function of the colleges.

Colleges' increasing involvement in applied research reflects the high level of their faculty members' technical expertise and the sophistication of many of their occupational education programs. Many university graduates enroll in these programs to acquire job skills. One college in Ontario, for example, has developed more than 40 programs that cater specifically to university graduates. One in six applicants for the college's occupational education programs is a university graduate.

Community colleges and universities have been collaborating in other innovative ways. Some now offer joint baccalaureate programs that combine courses from both institutions. For example, the University of Guelph and Humber College Institute of Technology and Advanced Learning established a campus in Toronto where they offer programs designed by faculty members from both institutions. Graduates earn both a Humber diploma and a baccalaureate. Of the first six programs offered at the joint campus, four were in areas where the university had not had its own programs. Another area of significant collaboration between community colleges and universities is nursing education. Most provinces now require registered nurses to have a baccalaureate in nursing, and many new nurses, including the vast majority in Ontario, graduate from programs that are delivered jointly by colleges and universities.

Canada's colleges now offer some baccalaureate programs on their own. This practice started in the late 1980s, when a handful of community colleges in British Columbia, most of which were far from a university, were given the authority to offer baccalaureate programs while maintaining their community college focus. These institutions were renamed "university colleges" to indicate their combined mandate. Community colleges in Ontario, British Columbia, and Alberta may now apply to a provincial board to offer baccalaureate programs in applied fields of study. As of October 2005, about 40 colleges had been approved to offer more than 100 baccalaureate programs. Under recent legislation in Alberta, colleges may apply to the ministry for approval to offer baccalaureate programs in traditional academic areas. The first college to obtain such approval, Grant MacEwan College in Edmonton, now offers a Bachelor of Commerce and a Bachelor of Arts with eight different majors.

Before long, nearly half the colleges in Canada may offer baccalaureate programs. There are two reasons for this revolutionary development, both related to globalization: to expand access to bachelor's degrees and to offer postsecondary education that combines the advanced liberal and theoretical education of a university with the high-level technical and applied education of a college. It is believed that in an increasingly competitive global labor market, a baccalaureate will be a more desirable credential than a college diploma is. It is also thought that combining the features of college and university educations will enhance the competitiveness of Canadian industry.

The movement toward colleges offering baccalaureate education has been less controversial in Canada than in the United States, perhaps because Canadian programs have been restricted largely to applied fields of study and can thus be seen as extensions of the colleges' traditional role of providing career education. Nevertheless, this development raises many questions about the future of Canada's colleges, especially about whether it will compromise their historic commitment to serving academically and economically disadvantaged students (Skolnik, 2005a).

THE CURRENT CHALLENGE: BALANCING SOCIETAL AND ECONOMIC ROLES

From the time of their establishment, Canada's colleges have had to balance two roles: (1) serving as engines of economic growth by training skilled workers and (2) contributing to the betterment of communities and society by providing opportunities for people to change and enrich their lives. The greatest challenge they face today is to continue balancing these roles. In recent years, pressure to emphasize the economic role has increased substantially. Canadians have many concerns about what might result from a growing imbalance in the roles, including that offering baccalaureate programs may mean that colleges provide less service to those who are at the greatest educational disadvantage. It is generally much easier for colleges to obtain government and other external funding for high-end activities than for literacy and basic skills education, so it is feared that people who need those basic skills will suffer. Colleges' international activities used to have a considerable philanthropic component, but those activities now appear to be driven more by commercial concerns. As Levin (2001) noted, in the 1990s in both Canada and the United States, "the mission of the community college had less emphasis on education and more on training; less emphasis on community social needs and more on the economic needs of business and industry; less emphasis upon individual development and more on workforce preparation and retraining" (p. 171).

On the other hand, Canadian colleges seem to be continuing to fulfill their traditional role of serving society. They are still behaving philanthropically in some of their overseas activities (Gupta, 2004), responding to the education needs of large numbers of immigrants (ACCC, 2004), and developing and offering innovative programs for aboriginal students. The enthusiasm with which Canadian colleges have embraced the principles of the learning college is indicative of their strong commitment to maintaining what Dennison (1995) described as "an environment in which learning is revered and in which opportunities for personal advancement abound" (p. 282).

REFERENCES

Association of Canadian Community Colleges (AACC). (2004, March). *Responding to the needs of immigrants: Final report.* Ottawa, ON: ACCC & Skills Development Canada.

Brown, G. (2002). Knowledge and innovation through workplace learning. *College Canada, 7*(1), 3.

Campbell, G. (1971). *Community colleges in Canada.* Toronto, ON: Ryerson Press.

Canadian Foundation for Innovation. (2005). *Projects funded* [Database]. Retrieved October 16, 2005, from www.innovation.ca/projects

Davis, W. G. (1966, June). Statement by the minister in the legislature, 21 May 1965. In Ontario Department of Education, *Colleges of Applied Arts and Technology Basic Documents* (pp. 5–16). Toronto: Ontario Department of Education.

Dennison, J. D. (1995). Conclusion. In J. D. Dennison (Ed.), *Challenge and opportunity: Canada's community colleges at the crossroads* (pp. 275–284). Vancouver: University of British Columbia Press.

Dennison, J. D., & Gallagher, P. (1986). *Canada's community colleges: A critical analysis.* Vancouver: University of British Columbia Press.

Fleming, W. G. (1971). *Ontario's educative society: Vol. 4. Post-secondary and adult education.* Toronto, ON: University of Toronto Press.

Gadd, J. (2005, September 26). Industry links: The rise of teaching on demand. *The Globe and Mail,* p. E4.

Gallagher, P., & Dennison, J. D. (1995). Canada's community college systems: A study of diversity. *Community College Journal of Research and Practice, 19*(5), 381–394.

Gupta, M. (2004). Canadian colleges and institutes foster relationships with the private sector in support of socioeconomic development in developing countries. *ACC International, 9*(2), 4–7.

Ivany, R. (2004). Economic development and a new millennium mandate for Canada's community colleges. *College Canada, 9*(1), 5–7.

Levin, J. S. (2001). *Globalizing the community college: Strategies for change in the 21st century.* New York: Palgrave.

Macdonald, J. B. (1962). *Higher education in British Columbia and a plan for the future.* Vancouver: University of British Columbia Press.

Royal Commission of Inquiry. (1963–1966). *Report of the Royal Commission of Inquiry on Education in the Province of Quebec* (Vols. 1–5). Quebec: Government of Quebec.

Ryval, M. (2005, September 26). Applied research: Industrial strength problem solving. *The Globe and Mail,* pp. E1–E2.

Skolnik, M. L. (2004). The relationship of the community college to other providers of postsecondary and adult education in Canada and implications for public policy. *Higher Education Perspectives 1*(1), 36–59. Retrieved May 1, 2008, from https://jps. library.utoronto.ca/index.php/hep/article/viewFile/574/653

Skolnik, M. L. (2005a). The community college baccalaureate in Canada: Addressing accessibility and workforce needs. In D. L. Floyd, M. L. Skolnik, & K. P. Walker (Eds.), *The community college baccalaureate: Emerging trends and policy issues* (pp. 49–72). Sterling, VA: Stylus Publishing.

Skolnik, M. L. (2005b). From the 1960s to the 2000s: Reflections on the difficulty of maintaining balance between the university's economic and non-economic objectives in periods when its economic role is highly valued. In G. A. Jones, P. L. McCarney, & M. L. Skolnik (Eds.), *Creating knowledge, strengthening nations: The changing role of higher education* (pp. 106–126). Toronto: University of Toronto Press.

Smyth, D. M. (1970). *Some aspects of the development of Ontario colleges of applied arts and technology.* Unpublished master's thesis, University of Toronto.

Statistics Canada. (2007). *Education indicators in Canada 2007. Report of the Pan-Canadian Education Indicators Program.* Ottawa, Canada: Statistics Canada & Council of Ministers of Education.

4

The Chilean Experience in Technical and Further Education: Public Policies and Private Providers

Marcelo Von Chrismar, Cristóbal Silva, Mary Crabbe Gershwin, Shelley L. Wood, and Philip Cary

Chilean students begin their education with 8 years of primary school, followed by 4 years of compulsory secondary education. Secondary education is taught in two branches: humanistic–scientific (EMHC) and technical–professional (EMTP). Students completing the former are granted a degree leading to higher education studies. EMTP students complete 2 years of a basic core curricula and 2 years of specialization in a trade. Since 1981, academic and vocational education at the postsecondary level has been provided through universities, professional institutes, and technical training centers. Despite a traditional belief in the primacy of academic over vocational studies, Chile has actively taken steps to bring vocational education to its people to aid the country's commercial advancement, the focus of this chapter.

HISTORY OF TECHNICAL EDUCATION IN CHILE

Technical training in Chile began in 1797 with the founding of the San Luis Academy, "the only attempt that we know of in the Colony, of a school oriented toward the worker or laborer, industry and commerce of the country. It was ahead of its time by almost a half a century to similar institutions in America" (Labarca, 1939, p. 58). In 1849, in response to pressing needs for technical and scientific development voiced by the National Society of Agriculture, the recently created University of Chile opened the School of Arts and Trades, Chile's first formal technical education institution. This school rapidly expanded to include Copiapó, La Serena, and Antofagasta. New industrial schools were created in Concepción, Temuco, and Valdivia to train people to support industrial development in all regions of the country. In 1947, all these original arts and trades schools became branches of the new Universidad Técnica del Estado.

Technical Training Institutes

Chile's first technical institute, the Commercial Institute of Santiago, was founded in 1898 (Labarca, 1939). By 1925, there were 11 technical institutes in cities throughout the country. Industrial and mining schools began training mechanical engineers and electricians for the armed forces, annexed to the School of Arts and Trades, which in 1900 started sending promising students abroad. Mining practices schools were created in Copiapó, La Serena, and Santiago. The first school of agriculture was established in 1857 with the support of the National Agricultural Society (Campos, 1960).

Chile's technical training institutes also had private origins. The Catholic Church played a key role, participating in the educational development of the country since the pioneering days of the Colony. The Don Bosco Brothers (Salesianos) offered free professional training to disadvantaged youth starting in Concepcion around 1887 (Campos, 1960). The first private initiative in postsecondary technical education was the 1888 founding of the Universidad Católica de Chile, which was both a university and a polytechnic school. According to Abdón Cifuentes, one of the university's founders,

> It is accurate and correct to establish on a large scale and in a scientific manner the teaching of the arts and social sciences to the people, it is appropriate to open new and varied vocational and labor activities, and it is correct to augment the means to earn a living for those thousands upon thousands of youth whom might be literary bumpkins, but true geniuses in industry. Fewer walking encyclopedias and more work, less rhetoric and more industry, fewer sophists and more engineers, less theory and more applied sciences, this is what this new hard working country needs to increase its wealth, prosperity and well being. (cited in Krebs, Muñoz, & Valdivieso, 1994, p. 17)

Development of Public and Government Support

Not all sectors of Chilean society in the 19th century favored establishing vocational education. Technical institutes, programs, and curricula met with strong resistance from the *estado docente* (roughly translated, academicians or faculty), the guiding paradigm for all public education policies until the end of the 20th century. The constitution declared education to be a state priority. The Chilean education model did not consider technical or vocational education sufficiently worthy to merit public interest.

Valentín Letelier, a highly influential figure in Chilean public education policy in the 19th and 20th centuries, believed that all vocational training "has a direct profit motive, tending individuals to sell their souls" (cited in Correa, 1981, p. 166). According to the historian Luis Galdames (1937), a follower of Letelier's, this view largely explains the "social devaluation of technical training and corresponding professions" (p. 236). Galdames said that Letelier's actions, particularly during his tenure as dean of the University of Chile, showed an attitude somewhat more flexible than his opinions, but he also recognized that Letelier's ideas were generally pushed to extremes by his followers, and "in countries like Chile and the rest of Ibero-America, where the industrial or merchant work was deemed fruitful, but not honorable, that concept grew stronger under the protection of the master, with an evident prejudice toward private and public economies."

As a result of these perceptions, technical training in Chile developed little until the middle of the 20th century. In 1907, all the industrial schools combined had no more than 200 students (Campos, 1960). In 1920, only 4.5% of educated people in Chile had received technical training. In 1932, the philanthropist Federico Santa María created two secular private institutions, the School of Arts and Trades and the José Miguel Carrera College of Engineers. They were later combined into the Federico Santa María Technical University, which is still operating and offers 3-year technical programs.

But it was not until the government of Pedro Aguirre Cerda (1938–1941) and the creation of CORFO (Corporación de Fomento de la Producción), combined with a great industrial push in Chile, that technical training became a government priority. By 1956, state technical and vocational education institutions enrolled 70,663 students (Campos, 1960). In 1947, the government merged several independent vocational mining, engineering, arts, and trade schools into the Industrial Engineering School in Santiago and the Technical Pedagogic Institute with the goal of creating a new public university. The Universidad Técnica del Estado was exclusively oriented toward technical education (Bernasconi, 2003).

At the same time, several diverse and relatively autonomous private centers developed under the academic supervision of the University of Chile, which reserved the right to issue diplomas and certificates. The Universidad Católica de Chile was one of the most active of these centers, developing courses in electronics and telegraphy that were taught at the Electro Technical Institute (renamed the Industry, Commercial, and Polytechnic Institute in 1920). The institute offered 3-year programs that trained students to become assistant electricians, industrial engineers, or construction engineers. The institute was a notable success until 1950, when the Universidad Católica de Chile created the new Facultad de Tecnología (Krebs et al., 1994).

Beginning in the 1960s, universities that offered short-term technical and professional education, including Universidad Técnica del Estado, Universidad Federico Santa María, and Universidad Católica de Chile, lengthened those programs, making them increasingly similar to the traditional academic programs. At the same time, new educational initiatives were launched, based on short worker-training courses. These courses evolved into today's vocational-type tertiary education institutions, two leading examples of which are the Instituto Nacional de Capacitación and Departamento Universitario Obrero Campesino at Universidad Católica de Chile, both of which are discussed in more detail later in the chapter.

REFORM OF POSTSECONDARY EDUCATION

Until the late 1970s, the Chilean higher education system comprised nine universities, seven of them private and two of them state owned. Although all of the universities had a public orientation, having been either created or recognized by a special law and completely financed by the government, they were all completely autonomous, both economically and academically, and had no legal obligation to make their academic or financial results public. The seven private universities were highly selective and educated only 7% of Chile's 20- to 24-year-olds (Bernasconi & Rojas, 2004).

In 1980, Chile passed a new constitution that limits government involvement in civil matters. Services traditionally administered by the state, such as social security, health, and education, were transferred to private institutions. In education, the state sets minimal standards, but responsibility was transferred to nongovernment providers that have a full guarantee of educational freedom. Legislation passed in 1981 established reforms of the higher education system with four elements:

- Transfer of financial responsibility for education from the state to the students

- Diversification of education institutions according to levels and categories

- Total freedom from government interference for newly created private institutions

- A high level of discrimination in the way financial support from the state is assigned

In 1990, the Ley Orgánica Constitucional de Enseñanza was passed, gathering all substantial characteristics and structures of the 1980 amendment. The state ceased to create universities by law and instead limited itself to maintaining on public record for 6 to 11 years the operational statutes of those institutions that organize and monitor private entities. This monitoring is done by an autonomous public ministry of education, the Consejo Superior de Educación.

Three types of institutions make up Chile's postsecondary education system: universities, professional institutes (IPs), and technical training centers (CFTs). The hierarchy of the institutions is determined by the type of degrees they can grant. In ascending order of difficulty, they are as follows:

- CFTs grant a *título técnico de nivel superior,* equivalent to a license, degree, or diploma granted by a typical 2-year U.S. community college program.

- IPs grant a *título técnico* and professional degrees that do not require students to earn a baccalaureate. These correspond to a 4-year degree in the United States.

- Universities grant professional degrees, with or without a baccalaureate, upon completion of a program that lasts from 5 to 7 years. Universities also grant other academic degrees recognized by law, including master's degrees and

PhDs. Universities are the only education institutions that grant the 17 professional degrees that require at least a baccalaureate, including medicine, law, and architecture.

In the Chilean system, the professional qualification is given by education institutions. Three certification levels or degrees enable the graduate to exercise a technical or professional activity: mid-level technician, higher-level technician, and the professional degree. Mid-level technician is a certificate given by some high schools, and it is a vocational program with differences in the last levels. The higher-level technician and professional degrees correspond to certificates granted by higher education institutions. The exception is the license to practice law, which is granted by the Supreme Court.

Peculiarities of the Reformed System

Some of the characteristics of Chile's postsecondary education system have been generated through regulatory exceptions or political decisions, or because authorities have accepted or tolerated practices that are common in private institutions. For example, some traditional public and private universities that were created before 1981 were grandfathered into the new system. There are new ones, several of which grew from those that were already in existence. These 25 universities maintain traditional functions, as they were either created or recognized by the state through special laws. Among some of their privileges, these institutions still receive important and direct financial support from the state, which is not available for the rest of the institutions. At the same time, the students who enroll in any of the universities belonging to this group are entitled to economic support from the state under exceptionally favorable terms and conditions, either as a scholarship or subsidiary loan. A recent law established a state-guaranteed credit system that benefits some private institutional students, however, with less favorable conditions than the aforementioned.

Thus, Chile has two coexisting subsystems of higher education that operate independently from one another: the one with the 25 traditional universities, which enrolls 41% of the students within the system, and the rest of the higher education institutions, composed of 204 entities that enroll 59% of the students. This dichotomy, which is not articulated in the general structure of the reforms, is one of the most relevant elements in the segmentation of the system.

Another peculiarity of the postsecondary education system in Chile is that universities must by law (as of 1990) be nonprofit private corporations. In contrast, IP and CFT institutions can be established as for-profit corporations. However, in practice, most of the universities that were formed after 1981, which are privately owned, follow indirect control formulas and complex legal strategies that allow their owners to make a profit. The most common strategy used is the establishment of real estate holding companies that then rent the infrastructure back to the universities for academic operations.

A third peculiarity of the system is that all state institutions devoted to vocational or technical education, which were originally derived from Universidad Técnica del Estado and that were originally established as IPs in 1981, were transformed into universities in the 1990s. In this way, the state is currently in charge of universities, and most postsecondary technical education is provided by private IPs and CFTs. In any case, some public universities, such as the Universidad de Santiago, and some private ones as well, offer technical programs or short-term professional programs, generally of 3 years' duration. Recently, some public universities and traditional private universities have organized, principally through profit organizational structures, small Technical Formation Centers.

Enrollment Issues

Postsecondary education coverage in Chile accounts for 37% of the population between 18 and 24 years old, surpassing 700,000 students. Higher education of technicians is provided by the three institutional categories already mentioned (universities, IPs, and CFTs). Percentages of students enrolled are distributed unevenly, with a majority in the shorter programs at the CFTs: universities (14.1%), IPs (23.6%), and CFTs (62.3%). The total enrollment for short 2-year programs reaches 20% of the entire system.

Enrollment in programs leading to certification at this level has been highly variable. After a strong push in the 1980s representing 80% of the postsecondary system, it plummeted to about only 10%. However, after 2000, enrollment stabilized at 20.2% of the total for tertiary education in the country. The decline in postsecondary technical education enrollments is primarily due to a cultural belief in the superiority of academic, university education. As a result, there exists a complete lack of promotional or public policy incentives to aid technical education. Several examples illustrate this point:

- Donations to CFTs (unlike to universities) are not tax deductible.
- Financing for students (who are typically from the lower economic strata) is provided primarily by private agents with some minor government support available.
- Lack of articulation between technical education programs has hindered students' possibilities to transfer or work toward further professional degrees.

Some of the primary institutions specifically dedicated to technical training closed, in part because of the lack of institutional capacity. When the main state public institutions refocused on university studies leaving the vocational sector, many small for-profit schools took on the burden of technical education. In fact, 47.7% of the 117 CFTs enroll fewer than 250 students.

Another important weakness in technical training is the overlapping curricula with middle school professional technical education. This type of secondary education, which educates 40% of middle-school-aged students, boasts free education and graduates that are claimed to be superior to those achieving next level of education and, in some cases, to those achieving professional education levels. While it is improbable that middle school students in Chile are achieving skill levels beyond those offered at the postsecondary level, technical colleges have often responded by overreaching and promising to fulfill ever higher academic and technical goals for their students. These goals are difficult to achieve in 2-year programs and thus harm the reputation of the institutions.

World Bank Initiatives

World Bank financing is providing access to grants and funding through the MECESUP (Improvement of the Quality and Equitable Access in Higher Education) program. Between 2000 and 2004, 69 projects for more than $23 million were approved to support effectiveness, quality, and innovation in thematic areas of national importance or projects fostering improvements in productivity, such as those for upgrading teachers, curricula, and management practices. It is worth noting that 98% of the resources of the MECESUP program were reserved for 25 traditional universities.

The government developed another program called Chile Califica, also with World Bank funding, which focused on the creation of inter-institutional networks for the development of projects leading to comprehensive articulation between different levels of formal education and training programs. From the standpoint of financial student aid, the government has begun to award limited partial scholarships. In addition, a law was recently passed establishing a new system for student aid with state guarantee for students attending public and private universities, IPs, CFTs, and the Armed Forces Schools Network. These scholarships are aimed at students with academic merit and economic necessity. The new student aid system began operation in 2006.

It is important to highlight, however, that the World Bank–funded initiatives do not appear to have gone much further than wishful thinking. Evidence of this can be found in the conclusions arrived at by the commission in charge of evaluating the MECESUP program for the World Bank: "the articulation problem in higher education, or lack thereof, continues largely unchanged and MECESUP, even though in its initial objectives mentioned the intention to undertake the issue, in practice has done nothing" (Ministerio de Educación, 2004, p. 78).

INACAP and DuocUC

Two institutions mentioned earlier in the chapter are worthy of further attention. The first is INACAP (Instituto Nacional de Capacitación), the largest public technical institute, as well as the largest higher education institution, in Chile. The second is DuocUC (Departamento Universitario Obrero Campesino/Universidad Católica).

They are significant not only for the numbers of students they serve but also because they represent the two new models that have emerged in the field of professional and technical higher education in Chile.

In 1960, SERCOTEC (Technical Cooperation Service) was established as a professional training department of the state and charged with improving the Chilean workforce. By 1966, the importance given to workforce development by this department led to the creation of an autonomous organization. Renamed INACAP in 1973, training centers were established in Santiago and the regions with the cooperation of the governments of France, Germany, Denmark, England, Belgium, and Switzerland. However, the educational reforms of 1980 discontinued funding, forcing INACAP to begin financing its own professional education and training. In 1981, INACAP was granted formal recognition as a CFT, by which it could deliver technical diplomas in higher education and professional diplomas for 4-year IP programs. INACAP currently has more than 70,000 students in 25 branches from Arica and Punta Arenas. A group of students at the Universidad Católica de Chile, supported by faculty and union and labor groups, began organizing in the labor community. Their goal was to provide access to higher education for the average citizen in Chile. The university embraced this goal by making it one of the principles in its mission statement. The initiative was officially established in 1968 with the challenge of extending university work into the agricultural and workforce sectors. DuocUC began to offer educational programs for administrative assistance, handicrafts, gardening, electrical installation, community development, and other workforce areas. Without much formal structure, DuocUC took hold quickly and enrollment boomed. This accelerated development inspired the university to grant it special autonomous status to meet its specific mission more effectively, as well as obtain its own financial resources without having to rely on the university budget.

In the reforms of 1980, DuocUC adapted its academic structure to new regulations, creating the Professional Institute DuocUC and the Technical Training Center DuocUC, which received official recognition 1982 and 1983, respectively. Today DuocUC is one of the most important higher education institutions in the country, with a total of 42,000 full-time students and more than 40 programs at the technical level (2-year programs) and 30 at the professional level (4-year programs). Academic programs are oriented toward helping students acquire specific competencies required by industry and labor markets, supported by a competency-based curricula model that incorporates broad core competencies: ethics, math skills, communication in Spanish and critical thinking, computer literacy, entrepreneurship, and functional English fluency.

Since 2000 the DuocUC institutional response in vocational training has focused on information technology and teaching of English as a foreign language (TEFL). DuocUC currently has the largest TEFL program in Chile, if not South America, with more than 20,000 full-time TEFL students, all in programs in which English is a mandatory requirement for graduation. DuocUC also offers online programs, which are perceived as a competitive resource for international partner institutions looking to provide academic alternatives at lower costs as part of international academic exchange programs. In addition, a comprehensive ethics program provides students with high behavioral standards.

Reasons for Success

INACAP and DuocUC have developed similar strategies to ensure their continuous growth and development. In spite of unfavorable government policies for the vocational sector, enrollments have thrived at these institutions. Reasons for their success are summarized as follows.

They are nonprofit private institutions. Even though this status does not entail receiving any special treatment from the state, or any special legal status, it allows these entities to allocate profits, earned through highly efficient operations, to financing development projects. Both institutions place special emphasis on maintaining an excellent infrastructure and procuring and maintaining state-of-the-art technologies and equipment.

Size is an advantage. INACAP is the largest higher technical education institution in the country in terms of enrollment, whereas DuocUC is the largest in terms of the three geographical regions in which it operates. In the IP education sector, these institutions enroll more than 60% of IP students. As the weakness of many smaller institutions that have not reached a critical level of development attests, size is an important advantage for these institutions. In DuocUC's case, that advantage is reflected in the growth achieved between 2000 and 2005, 82%, compared to 35% across the higher education system.

An integrated operational model allows for articulation between technical and professional levels. Representing both institutional categories, these institutions make use of the same infrastructure, resources, and staff to develop curricula for each level according to homogeneous standards. However, this means more than taking advantage of economies of scale. Where the lack of articulation with other educational levels has been a weakness of the CFTs, INACAP and DuocUC have developed curricula that allows for direct articulation between professional and technical levels, ensuring that students from short study programs have opportunities to continue studying in the higher levels.

DuocUC and INACAP have followed different paths in their strategy of articulation toward the college level, however. While INACAP recently acquired a private university, integrating in one organization the three levels admitted in the system, DuocUC has undertaken a strategy to reach articulation agreements with some of the most renowned universities of the country. Both are achieving success through implementation of their respective models.

Strict internal mechanisms are in place to ensure homogeneous standards of quality. Both institutions operate a multisite system distributed over a wide geographic area. However, they each apply the principle of internal control in different ways. At DuocUC, each site (or campus) serves an average of 4,000 students, and all campuses are located in the most populated cities. Each site purposefully focuses its academic offerings to a specific industrial area, thus concentrating resources. INACAP, having smaller centers, focuses on wider geographical coverage in all regions of the country. In spite of their differences, both institutions devote most of their efforts to establishing programs and control mechanisms that enable each center to express the same educational attributes, regardless of location and size. The sites operate independently from one another but are centrally managed as part of a hierarchical system, which is in permanent communication with the sites.

Providing low tuition and adequate financing for students ensures long-term growth and survival. By strictly observing quality and operational controls, these institutions are able to offer average tuition lower than that offered by other prestigious universities. The average tuition in these institutions varies from USD 1,000 to USD 2,000, while in a midsize university tuition can easily reach USD 4,000. Furthermore, both institutions have developed their own scholarship programs and financing agreements with banks. They have also obtained direct support from companies for the partial financing of their workers' and families' studies. This has enabled access to higher education for lower-income social groups historically excluded from traditional institutions, the segment of general population growing fastest within the system. The importance of this factor will become more apparent in the next section.

The strategies that guide these institutions, along with the principle of consistently providing high-quality education, have earned both institutions a prominent status and a high level of credibility within Chile's higher education system. Recently, both institutions were granted institutional accreditation for 6 years, over a maximum of 7, by the Comisión Nacional de Acreditación, the public agency responsible for the quality assurance process in the country. Currently INACAP and DuocUC are the only IP and CFT institutions to have achieved such accreditation.

CHALLENGES AND OPPORTUNITIES FOR TECHNICAL EDUCATION IN CHILE

In spite of declining enrollments in the vocational sector, Chile has experienced a strong increase in higher education coverage, in general, in terms of percentage of population. Nevertheless, this coverage varies significantly depending on the socioeconomic level of the population. There are evident differences among the quintiles of the population, for example, high enrollment of those aged 18–25 in the high-income bracket, and low enrollment of those in the lowest income levels.

By 2010, enrollment in postsecondary technical education is anticipated to increase substantially, and the increased student population is expected to come from the lower-income quintiles, which will require more financial assistance than is currently planned. Likewise, we anticipate an increase in the need for remedial offerings as more low-income students enter for training. As is evidenced in U.S. postsecondary education, we also expect to see the use of additional student services, including those aimed at retaining those at risk for attrition.

Employer demand for skilled workers is rising around the globe. It is our conviction that implementation of public policies in Chile that specifically focus on the development of technical education is urgently needed. We must meet demands for human capital to enable the economy to be competitive with the most advanced countries. Likewise, there should be increased opportunities for upward social mobility, ensuring levels of fairness in accordance with a modern and politically stable country.

In order to materialize such policies, the state must be effectively involved in higher technical education. It can certainly begin, as it has, by strengthening programs and initiatives launched by public universities. But this alone will not have a significant impact in the midterm. Currently, the traditional academic institutions do not have adequate expertise to manage technical and vocational training models of education. Also, since their institutional priorities are oriented elsewhere, technical education will not receive the attention needed to develop and thrive.

A more effective means would be to make use of the institutions that for decades have been able to develop the sector in spite of difficulties. The strategy of institutional diversification seemed to give good results at the beginning of the reforms started in the 1980s, achieving the important development reached by the IPs and CFTs. There are many weak institutions, but others have been able to overcome obstacles and remain strong. Instead of creating new institutions, it would be interesting to consider the possibility of transferring the experience of the most successful entities to those with lower levels of consolidation.

The development of vocational higher education represents an important opportunity to overcome the persistent inequalities still present in Chilean society. Fostering the rapid education of high-level technicians (through 2-year programs) would help to decrease the deficit of trained labor force. At the same time, incrementing and improving financing policies to establish substantial incentives to enable the aforementioned (loans and scholarship policies) would result in a safer leverage instrument for smaller suppliers. Furthermore, it is a fact that societal benefits are greater when vocational and higher education is offered to population levels that have a deficient secondary education and also lack the resources to reach university.

Chile is currently constrained by an academic degree and professional title structure that is inflexible. If articulation plans between the levels were developed, students who have discontinued university studies could acquire some demonstrable and profitable competence in the labor market. Likewise, those who have achieved technical degrees could seek further professional levels in the university. The establishment of official systems that grant formal recognition to different models and levels of certification for knowledge and labor competencies should be synchronized with formal education systems at all levels.

Finally, to increase quality and productivity in the higher education system, and put it at the level demanded by an economy based on the intensive use of knowledge, it is necessary to adapt Chilean systems to those validated internationally in the more advanced countries. It is also necessary to further develop the emerging internationally validated procedures for quality assessment and assurance, promote the transference of best practices and efficient management models, and increase relationships within the global higher education market.

Conclusion

The modern economy is based on knowledge, and the greatest wealth of nations is measured by their ability to produce and use this intangible commodity. Countries with a higher level of development have obtained an edge by focusing their policies on the increase of human social capital. A significant feature of a high level of national social capital is demonstrated first by high levels of literacy in the general population, and second, by broad support of higher education. Chile, in spite of being a highly productive country, with relatively high levels of school enrollment and productivity, continues to show major deficiencies in higher education. In terms of quality and student access for all economic sectors, prevailing policies have worked more against than in favor of higher education in the area of technical education.

The history of postsecondary technical education has been mixed with a typical struggle between demands in the labor market for advanced technical skills versus cultural prejudices against vocationally oriented education. Both INACAP and DuocUC have created sustainable, high-quality education despite the obstacles. Upcoming and current changes are promising, yet it remains to be seen whether Chile will be willing to recognize the sources of expertise in implementing new policies.

References

Bernasconi, A. (2003). *Organizational diversity in Chilean higher education: Faculty regimes in private and public universities.* Unpublished doctoral dissertation, Boston University.

Bernasconi, A., & Rojas, F. (2004). *Informe sobre la educación superior en Chile 1980–2003* [Report on higher education in Chile 1980–2003]. Santiago, Chile: Editorial Sudamericana.

Campos, F. (1960). *Desarrollo educacional 1810–1960* [Development of education 1810–1960]. Santiago, Chile: Editorial Andrés Bello.

Correa, G. V. (1981). *Historia de Chile 1891–1973* (Vol. 1) [History of Chile 1891–1973]. Santiago, Chile: Santillana del Pacifico.

Galdames, L. (1937). *Valentín Letelier y su obra 1852–1919* [Valentín Letelier and his work 1852–1919]. Santiago, Chile: Imprenta Universitaria.

Krebs, R., Muñoz, M., & Valdivieso, P. (1994). *Historia de la Pontificia Universidad Católica de Chile* [History of the Catholic University of Chile]. Santiago, Chile: Universidad Católica de Chile.

Labarca, A. (1939). *Historia de la enseñanza en Chile* [History of teaching in Chile]. Santiago, Chile: Imprenta Universitaria.

Ministerio de Educación Chile. (2004). *Informe final de evaluación programa MECESUP* [Final evaluation report of the MECESUP program]. Santiago, Chile: Author.

Universidades Tecnológicas de Mexico: Technical Institutions Extend Higher Education to the People

Bertha Landrum, David Valladares Aranda, and Arturo Nava Jaimes

M exico's system of public 2-year technical institutions of higher education (*universidades tecnológicas*, or UTs) originated in 1991. A major purpose of these new educational institutions was to improve and increase the opportunities for high school graduates, 9 out of 10 of whom were the first in their families to participate in higher education. After 15 years of remarkable development, in 2005 Mexico had 60 UTs in 26 states and, with a population of approximately 66,000 students, the UTs have gained recognition for the professional abilities of the graduates. Gradually, the UTs see increasing demand and recognition by the business community for graduates of the programs.

The UTs developed during a pronounced period of change in Mexican higher education, marked by substantial growth in student enrollments, a shift to technological institutions, efforts to reach underserved populations, and extensive growth in women's enrollments. Within the decade, UTs are expected to

- Continue to provide a higher education experience to a segment of society that otherwise would not have access.
- Offer programs that have a high level of applicability and that employers judge to be of high quality.
- Offer a degree recognized by other institutions of higher education (i.e., for transferability).
- Show that graduates are incorporated into the labor market.

The authors would like to thank Veronica Murillo for assisting with the translation of Arturo Nava Jaimes's monograph.

- Show accountability and transparency in managing the finances and other resources of the institutions.

The system also envisions a change in the educational model of curriculum development that moves from program development along traditional lines to a process of delineating competencies for each program that students are expected to achieve. This change should lead not only to employer confidence in employing graduates but also to greater recognition and respect for UTs by residents in the community.

Mexico, Briefly

Mexico shares the North American continent with Canada and the United States. Mexico came under Spanish rule early in the 16th century when Hernan Cortez conquered the territory that had been occupied by the Aztec. Mexico proclaimed independence from Spanish rule on September 16, 1810, but its struggle for independence continued until 1821. Emperor Napoleon III of France, the nephew of Napoleon Bonaparte, attempted to install Maximilian, a Hapsburg heir, as emperor of Mexico in 1862 following a military attempt by European powers to collect foreign debts. Napoleon's forces were defeated on May 5, 1862, at Puebla, Mexico, by General Ignacio Zaragosa and Brigadier General Porfirio Diaz. Porfirio Diaz was later elected president of Mexico. Both Cinco de Mayo, or May 5, and September 16, the Day of Independence, are celebrated as holidays.

Mexico is now a federal republic with 31 states. The official language is Spanish, but several regional indigenous languages are spoken. The population is more than 108 million. Mexico has a free market economy with a growing private business community. Since it joined the North American Free Trade Agreement in 1994, Mexico's trade with the United States has tripled. Economic challenges include supporting economic growth, improving international competitiveness, and reducing poverty. The role of higher education is seen as immensely important to future economic growth.

A Decade of Change in Mexican Higher Education

Mexican higher education changed significantly in the 1990s. Change occurred in "organization, scale, geographical distribution and performance" (Rodriguez-Gomez & Casanova-Cardiel, 2005) of higher education institutions. The UTs were an integral part of this decade of change. Rodriquez-Gomez and Casanova-Cardiel identified seven main areas of transformation:

1. Enrollment growth. In 1990, 13.5% of the 18- to 23-year-old cohort was enrolled in the Mexican higher education system. In 2000, 20% of this cohort was enrolled in higher education institutions.

2. Enrollment shift to technological institutions. Almost 100 technology-oriented institutions (institutes and UTs) were created in the 1990s. The technological

subsystem grew by more than 60%, increasing from 20% to 36%, while university enrollments remained steady.

3. Growth of private higher education. During the 1990s, private higher education grew 2.5 times. In particular, private graduate student enrollment expanded by 4.5 times. These private institutions emphasize training for professional and semiprofessional careers, but, unlike most public universities, they do not support research projects, emphasize academic subjects, or make efforts to reach cultural groups. About 20% of Mexico's 700 private higher education institutions are universities.

4. Reaching underserved populations. Prior to 1990, 23% of students enrolled in baccalaureate-type programs attended institutions in Mexico City. As of 2000, that enrollment was 21.5%. In contrast, student enrollment increased 2 times or more in the states of Aguascalientes, Baja California Sur, Campeche, Chiapas, Hidalgo, Morelos, Oaxaca, Quintana Roo, Tabasco, Tlaxcala, and Yucatan. Other states showed smaller increases.

5. Student program choices moved toward business and administrative services. Enrollment in agricultural and science programs increased, while enrollment in health sciences, education, and humanities remained stable. By 2000, about 50% of students were enrolled in social, business, and public administration programs, including programs in law, accounting, and administration.

6. Growth of postgraduate programs. Before 1990, enrollment in master's degree, doctoral degree, and specialty postgraduate programs slightly exceeded 40,000 annually. In 2003, enrollment in these programs was 138,287. This increase was a result of policies to further professionalize higher education and reflects the role of the labor market in rewarding the pursuit of further education as a means to gain employment. Nonetheless, only about 15% of baccalaureate-type degree completers pursued a postgraduate degree.

7. Role of women pursuing higher education. The numbers of women pursuing higher education, particularly in teacher training and technology programs, increased, while the numbers of men seeking higher education did not grow. By 2000, the number of women in higher education equaled the number of men; women constituted about 70% of enrollments in health sciences, social and administrative science, education, and humanities.

Other changes during the 1990s in Mexican higher education were evident in policies concerning financing, evaluation, accreditation, quality, and coordination. However, major emphasis was directed toward student enrollment growth and improving the quality of faculty.

CREATING THE UT SYSTEM

The development of the UTs emanated from a strategic objective of the National Program for the Development of Higher Education, 2001–2006, to improve the opportunities for graduates of high schools to participate in higher education. As an outgrowth of that strategic objective, a system for developing new, individual UTs across the nation was designed. Thus, the development of a new UT occurs as a result of an agreement between the Mexican federal government and each state government based on five feasibility studies. These feasibility studies address the following:

- An analysis of the surrounding region for the proposed institution regarding the economic and workforce situation as compared with other areas of the state, neighboring states, and the country. This study includes a review of the economic prospects and sites, standard of living of the residents, condition of the state educational system, currency of technological capacity, and the justification for a new UT.

- A more localized study that looks at cultural, current, and historical economic and sociopolitical issues. This study includes a review of local economic and business activities and the expectations that a UT would fulfill.

- A labor market study reflecting the human resource requirements of the public and private sectors. This study is used to determine educational programs and to gain industry participation in the academic processes of the university.

- A study of the expectations of students completing high school that provides information on students' interest in attending a UT, the social and economic situation of families, and the educational background of parents and their expectations of further education for their children.

- A review of the current supply and demand for higher education in the region through a historical analysis of student enrollment in higher education. Also this study considers projections of demand and enrollments 5 and 10 years into the future.

The feasibility studies provide a basis for creating and operating a UT and its educational programs. Once the formation of the institution is authorized, an agreement of coordination is signed between the secretary of public education and the state government. The state provides the land (a minimum of 20,000 hectares) along with an assurance that the land and the composition of the soil are suitable for construction. The plan for financing a UT calls for the federal government to provide 50% of first-year start-up costs via the Office of the General Coordination of Universidades Tecnológicas, and the remaining 50% is provided by the state. Each UT exists in Mexican law as a single legal entity with the ability to own property and possess wealth in order to ensure the financial viability of the institution.

Factors Shaping UTs in the Next 10 Years

The point of view of the Coordinator General of the UTs is that they operate in a social context, but the way in which the university affects society and vice versa is not always clear (Nava Jaimes, 2005). What seems clear is that institutions of higher education will shape, transform, create, influence, and change social realities as a result of lively exchanges, confrontations, and dialogues.

In 10 years, by 2015, the institutions will be a product of actions taken now and the social context in which they occur. Today, the issues are ones of consolidation and development. Five of these issues are outlined as follows:

- Students. The UTs offer higher education to a sector of society that otherwise would not have access to it.

- Academics. Programs offered have a high degree of applicability and the external evaluation of student results indicates an acceptable level of quality. Faculty also benefit from opportunities to come together in their academic areas.

- Society. The goal is to obtain increased recognition of the degrees awarded by the UTs. This is an area that needs more dedication of time and work. This is also an area where the professions exert a cultural and status element rather than a rational view of the realities of what is needed to perform in certain careers.

- Labor. It is sometimes the case that institutions of higher education fail to satisfy the skills requirements needed in the labor market. The UTs have worked to minimize this situation by linking with business and industry. These collaborative efforts have enabled graduates to move more quickly into the workforce. In a study of 89,643 graduates, 76% secured their first career positions within 6 months (Nava Jaimes, 2005).

- Finance. The need for resources to operate UTs with efficiency and quality depends on providing clear and transparent fiscal data that show how resources are used.

A review of UT programs by the Interinstitutional Committee for the Evaluation of Higher Education determined that 158 programs were operating at highest quality levels (Nava Jaimes, 2005). Also, UTs have supported the development of programs of continuing education, which were reviewed by international teams and found to be promising. These favorable reviews have generated action plans to work to fulfill the recommendations for development.

For the future of the UTs, the system has selected a process of continuous development rather than sporadic efforts that are not administratively connected. The objectives for the future, in the judgment of the coordinator general, will center on the following considerations.

- The technological revolution and the spectacular and dramatic impact on the content of programs and the performance requirements for technical careers.
- Insufficient economic growth to reduce unemployment.
- The inevitable slowness of change in educational processes, especially at the primary and secondary education levels.
- Activating the accreditation process in an environment of an abundance of degrees and of doctoral programs of low quality in a world that expects professional competence.

The UT administration is particularly concerned about the ability to arrive on time to incorporate the so-called third industrial revolution of technology along with the concomitant social–labor changes. These technologies, according to the Office of the Coordinator General, may include artificial intelligence, genetic engineering, robotics, new materials, laser exploitation, and fiber optics. Additional challenges include responding to globalization, environmental deterioration, social inequities, deformation of values, and the culture of minimum effort.

Thus, the vision for the UTs for the coming decade will be a higher education system that offers high-quality education that fulfills the expectations of students and the community and responds in an effective way to the needs of the business community with competent graduates. Within the UTs the future looks to greater cohesiveness of academic faculty and closer relationships with the social fabric of the cultural and business communities. Evaluation processes will be further developed along with methods of external accreditation reviews. Another major goal is for the UT system to be flexible, innovative, and integrated with other systems of higher education, with transparent processes in both finances and methods of operation.

The UT system looks to the possible reengineering of the educational model, with greater applicability of the educational programs, not only to the business community, but with greater acceptance from the public. This recognition, if achieved, will probably be based on professional competencies wherein graduates of the UTs will have the abilities to perform the tasks of a professional occupation. It is most important that the students become the competent workers of the future. Basing future curricula on competencies will surpass the concepts of traditional credentials and enable the student to reply to an employer with what he or she can do rather than what he or she studied. This qualitative jump requires UTs to organize programs with flexibility, address new and forgotten populations through programs of professional certification, and offer companies a new worker with the abilities to plan, solve problems, show creativity, communicate, collaborate, and innovate.

Universidad Tecnológica del Sur de Sonora

Universidad Tecnológica del Sur de Sonora (UTS), was selected as an example of a 2-year technical institution of higher education partly due to its newness, but also as an example of how it has developed its mission and its relationship to the communities it serves. UTS was proclaimed an approved and new institution of 2-year technical higher education on August 30, 2002, and commenced operations on September 2, 2002—a rapid deployment in a very few days.

UTS is located in the center of the Yaqui Valley, a place of ancestral history and culture. The major endeavor is to continue the development of the valley but while using new techniques, methods, equipment, and tools. UTS was developed in accordance with feasibility studies focusing on the needs of the southern region of Sonora. Based on these studies, the state decided to locate UTS in Ciudad Obregon, the principal city in the county of Cajeme, to serve students in the 12 southern counties of the state. This region has a population of 900,000 people, 40% of Sonora's population.

The primary mission of the institution is to serve the people and the communities of the region. Therefore, in what has been a principally agricultural and sea fishing economy, UTS endeavors to bring new knowledge and skills to enable the development of a broader economy. UTS will thus enable young people to remain in the area and contribute to the development of the communities and the standard of living.

The four major programs are as follows: production and process technology, marketing and commerce, computer science and information technology, electronics and automated systems. In 2005, 541 students were enrolled in the four programs. These students represent a steady growth in enrollment since 2002: 138 students were enrolled 2002–2004; 86.7% graduated, and 61.2% became employed in the area of their major. Of the 2005 class, 123 were scheduled to graduate (Valladares Aranda, 2005).

Additional program areas involve preparing students for CISCO and Microsoft certifications and Java and Solaris languages. Ten professors have achieved certification in these specialties, and 80 information technology students have completed their certification exams. To support these programs, the college has maintained relationships with 80 large, medium, and small corporations in the area. The Language Center is another specialty program area at UTS, featuring language schools in English and French. For the French language program, a relationship with the University of Regina in Canada resulted in internships for faculty in 2004 and 2005.

An innovative project of UTS is the Software Site, an in-house company of the university that employs students as interns in software development for and with local corporations. The project enables companies to develop software and applications for a lower cost and provides the students with work experience. The institution has been working with industries to certify labor force capabilities, using agreed-upon standards of performance.

Another direction of UTS has been to focus on the quality of education, giving primary attention to the process of teaching and of continuing education. As a part of this effort, UTS has established a process for evaluating instructor performance and provide faculty development. This is a challenging task for an institution where of 61 professors, 24 are full-time and 37 are part-time. Professors are evaluated in seven areas:

- Punctuality and attendance
- Timely delivery of information to Department of Academic Services
- Teaching performance
- Participation in related activities
- Development of knowledge in teaching area
- Cooperation in university affairs
- Involvement in activities that complement the subject area taught

The faculty improvement program depends in some degree on the cooperation of major universities in the state of Sonora and across Mexico. From August to December 2005, 28 professors were enrolled in programs of advanced technology, representing 45.9% of the professors in the areas of information technology and engineering (Valladares Aranda, 2005).

The development of programs at UTS in 3 short years exemplifies the pressure on these institutions to rapidly develop new programs for the 21st century while responding to local economic development goals for change. At the same time, the UTS is working to bring along the industries of the area and the residents of the surrounding communities to a common vision of development for the future.

REFERENCES

Nava Jaimes, A. (2005, December). *Las universidades tecnológicas: Un modelo prometedor.* Unpublished monograph, National Program of Education, Federal District, Mexico.

Rodriguez-Gomez, R., & Casanova-Cardiel, H. (2005). Higher education policies in Mexico in the 1990s: A critical balance. *Higher Education Policy, 18*, 51–65.

Valladares Aranda, D. (2005, November). *The beginning of the UTS in Cajeme in the 21st century.* Unpublished manuscript, Universidad Tecnológica del Sur de Sonora, Mexico.

Community Colleges in the United States of America

George R. Boggs and Judith T. Irwin

The United States of America (the United States) is a complex country because of its size and the racial and ethnic diversity of its people. It is one of the largest countries in the world in terms of land mass. At roughly 9.6 million km², it is about the same size as China, although with nearly 300 million people, it is far behind China in population. Continental United States, encompassing 48 of 50 states, borders Canada to the north and Mexico to the south. It is bound by the Pacific Ocean on the west and the Atlantic Ocean on the east, with much of the population living near these two coasts. The remaining states are Hawaii, a group of islands in the Pacific Ocean, and Alaska, located in the Arctic Circle in northwestern North America and separated from the contiguous states by Canada.

Geographically, the United States is a country of contrasts. Within its borders are beaches, deserts, mountains, and plains. Its national and state parks are stunning in their beauty. Its lakes and rivers have historically served as important transportation arteries, as well as sources of recreation. The country is a mixture of densely populated urban areas and large areas of low population.

The U.S. government is a representative democracy, or federal republic. The country is divided into independent entities called states, each with its own capital and elected policymakers. There is a division of powers between the state governments and the national or federal government, with the nation's capitol located in Washington, DC. Political subdivisions of the states include counties, boroughs, townships, cities, villages, and towns. There are more than 10,000 cities, towns, and villages in the United States.

To a great degree, the history of the United States was shaped by immigration. The United States has historically been seen as the country of "the American Dream," where success is not bound by class distinctions. The country is a melting pot of cultures. According to the most recent census, 80.4% of the population is White, 12.8% is Black, 4.2% is Asian American, 14.1% is Hispanic, and 1% is Native American (U.S. Census Bureau, 2005). Hispanics and Asian Americans are the most rapidly growing populations. Although the United States does not declare English as its official language, it is the de facto official language; however, because of the large immigrant populations, a sizable percentage of the population (18%) speak a language other than English at home (U.S. Census Bureau, 2003).

Public elementary and secondary schools are funded at the county or city level, generally by taxes on property. States have recently begun to exert more control over funding, and the federal government, which historically has not been involved in education, passed the No Child Left Behind Act of 2001 to improve the quality of primary education throughout the country. There are also numerous private elementary and secondary schools, often religiously affiliated, that are funded through tuition and private donations.

The Structure of the Higher Education System

The U.S. higher education system offers a great variety of options. Institution types range from community colleges, to small liberal arts colleges, to state universities, to major research universities, to proprietary (for-profit) institutions. Although the earliest colleges were greatly influenced by European models of higher education, the United States has created its own very diverse system of postsecondary and higher education.

Postsecondary education institutions in the United States generally are of three broad types, each of which includes both public and private institutions:

- Two-year colleges, usually referred to as community, junior, or technical colleges.
- Four-year colleges, which offer either 4 years of general undergraduate education or a combination of general and pre-professional education.
- Comprehensive universities, which offer both undergraduate and graduate education as well as professional degrees.

The federal government does not exercise control over or serve as the primary funder of higher education institutions. Each state is responsible for most aspects of education within its borders. The states have limited authority over private colleges and universities. Most postsecondary institutions are either established by the state (public colleges and universities) or receive their charters from them (private colleges and universities). State governments have the legal authority to regulate and approve their continued operations, even though independent nongovernment bodies carry out the accreditation.

Origins and Development of the Community College Movement

From relatively modest 19th-century beginnings, community colleges are now educating nearly half of all students in the higher education system. These institutions were established to provide everyone with an opportunity to pursue postsecondary education. Community colleges are regionally accredited institutions that grant associate degrees and certificates, as well as bachelor's degrees at an increasing number of colleges. The community college mission is to provide access, serve all segments of society, provide a comprehensive educational program, serve the community, focus on teaching and learning, and foster lifelong learning. The egalitarian and open-access mission of community colleges and their community-responsive curricula reflect the democratic ideals and values of the United States (Boggs & Cater, 1994). Policymakers refer to these institutions as the economic engines of the United States because of the positive effects of their workforce education and training programs.

In about 1835, private academies, the forerunners of U.S. community colleges, began to appear (Palinchak, 1973). These academies, with elements of both secondary and postsecondary curricula, offered vocational courses and a variety of courses that could transfer into a university curriculum. Such institutions included 2-year "normal schools" or teachers' colleges, as well as institutions for women and Blacks. Although these institutions have either disappeared or changed to 4-year status, they proved the value of higher education below the baccalaureate level.

By the latter part of the 19th century, some higher education leaders, influenced by the German system, argued that the first 2 years of collegiate education should be left to the secondary schools. This model would free universities from undergraduate education and would allow them to concentrate on upper-division, graduate, and professional curricula. In the view of these educators, some students from the "junior colleges," as they were beginning to be called, would transfer to the university for additional study, while others would end their education at grade 14 (Boggs & Cater, 1994). Although this idea did not influence the structure of universities other than the University of Chicago, which created junior college and senior college divisions, it did stimulate the creation of the first community colleges.

In 1901, under the guidance of William Rainey Harper, the president of the University of Chicago, and J. Stanley Brown, the principal of Joliet High School, Joliet Junior College was established near Chicago, Illinois. Most community college historians point to the founding of Joliet Junior College as the beginning of the community college movement in the United States, a movement that would open access to higher education and training opportunities to students who would not otherwise have had a chance because of economic, mobility, and social barriers. Joliet is the oldest community college that is still in operation. Other areas of the United States soon followed this model. In

1907, California approved legislation that allowed local school districts to offer the first 2 years of college work.

In 1917, the North Central Association of Schools and Colleges established specific standards for the accreditation of public and private junior colleges. These standards, governing areas such as admissions policies, faculty qualifications, and minimum funding levels, not only brought a degree of uniformity to these new institutions, but also invited them to participate in a unique system of institutional self-regulation and quality assurance (Vaughan, 2006). Today, all U.S. community colleges are accredited by one of the same six regional agencies that accredit 4-year colleges and universities. Most community colleges offer associate degrees (after completion of the first 2 years of a university education) and a variety of certificates of completion. Community colleges in some states can now offer bachelor's degrees, usually in select disciplines.

The coming of the Great Depression in the 1930s brought an unexpected boost to the community college movement (Brint & Karabel, 1989). The pressures of economic hard times and the resulting high unemployment among all ages, combined with the number of college-age youth, led the states to establish 65 public junior colleges between 1933 and 1939. These institutions opened the doors for thousands of students at a cost they could afford and offered employment opportunities once they completed their studies.

A second significant growth period for community colleges began at the conclusion of World War II. Millions of returning veterans were eager to move back into the workforce, but they needed affordable education and training opportunities The Servicemen's Readjustment Act of 1944, commonly called the GI Bill of Rights, provided the financial aid that allowed hundreds of thousands of returning veterans to consider the possibility of higher education.

Out of concern for the capacity of the higher education sector to accommodate the enrollment demand caused by the GI Bill, then-President Harry Truman established a Commission on Higher Education in 1946. The Truman Commission Report, issued in 1947, changed the course of higher education from "merely being an instrument for producing an intellectual elite" to becoming "the means by which every citizen, youth, and adult, is enabled and encouraged" to pursue higher learning (President's Commission, 1947). The Commission's report marked the first general use of the term *community college* and recommended that they expand nationally to provide universal access to postsecondary education.

The greatest expansion of community colleges took place between 1960 and 1970. During that decade, more than 450 new community colleges opened their doors to accommodate the education and training needs of the baby boom generation (the children of the returning World War II soldiers). As a result, about 45% of all 18-year-olds enrolled in a community college (Phillippe & González Sullivan, 2005).

With the approval of the Higher Education Facilities Act of 1963 and the Higher Education Act of 1965, the U.S. federal government dramatically expanded its direct aid to community colleges and their students. Through the Facilities Act, communities were given the means to construct new campuses and enlarge existing facilities. Through the Higher Education Act and its subsequent reauthorizations, the federal government provided a range of direct grants and loans to students based on financial need as a means of lessening the barrier of cost to higher education access (Vaughan, 2006).

Beginning with the Navajo Community College in 1971, the federal government began to support the development of tribally controlled community colleges. These efforts culminated in 1978 with the adoption of the Tribally Controlled Community College Assistance Act and the resulting expansion of community colleges to previously underserved communities throughout the western United States (Vaughan, 2006). The 31 tribal colleges operating today are relatively small, receiving funds primarily from the U.S. Bureau of Indian Affairs. A few offer bachelor's degrees, but most offer the associate degree as their highest credential (Phillippe & González Sullivan, 2005).

Whereas the early junior colleges focused on the transfer mission, that of providing students with the first 2 years of a baccalaureate education before moving to university, some states developed technical colleges to prepare students to enter the workforce. Over the years, these two types of institutions began to evolve into today's comprehensive community colleges. The technical colleges gradually began to offer transfer courses, and the junior colleges began to offer vocational courses. The colleges also began to offer a variety of remedial or developmental education courses to prepare students for college-level work, community service courses to meet the needs of community members, and contract education courses to serve local industry. Depending upon their location, these institutions may today be called community colleges, technical colleges, technical community colleges, or even junior colleges. However, no matter what they are named, these institutions are commonly referred to as community colleges. They are considered a part of the higher education system, generally affected by the same laws and regulations that affect 4-year colleges and universities.

As of 2006, there were 1,202 regionally accredited community colleges in the United States, including 991 public institutions, 180 independent institutions, and 31 tribal colleges. Approximately 6.6 million students take courses leading to the associate degree, and an additional 5 million students take noncredit courses (AACC, 2007). Essentially, community college programs serve three purposes, the first being to provide the first 2 years of a 4-year college education. The goal for these students is to earn an associate degree and then transfer to a 4-year university to obtain a bachelor's degree. Today, however, many students transfer to a 4-year university without earning an associate degree from the community college.

The second purpose is to provide certificates and degrees for students so they can immediately enter the workforce upon graduation. There are many programs that provide students with a combination of liberal arts courses and courses more focused on technical or occupational skills. Through these kinds of programs, students can obtain associate degrees or certificates in fields such as allied health and computer sciences. These degrees are not designed so that students can transfer to other 4-year colleges; however, students who wish to continue on to obtain a 4-year university degree often are able to transfer their credits from these programs. According to 2004 data, the five most popular community college programs in the United States are registered nursing, law enforcement, licensed practical nursing, radiology, and computer technologies (McPhee, 2004). The average lifetime earnings for a graduate of a community college with an associate degree are $1.6 million, or about $.4 million more than a high school graduate earns (Phillippe & González Sullivan, 2005).

The third purpose of community college programs is to focus on a wide variety of community-based educational needs that are not met at the level of higher education. This is done in collaboration with employers in the community who need specific skills for their workers. Community colleges typically see this as part of their role and responsibility in the economic development of their community. This is considered noncredit work, because the education does not lead to a formal college degree. Noncredit courses are also generally offered in subjects such as remedial education, English as a second language, community service, professional development, and personal growth.

COMMUNITY COLLEGE VALUES

There are four enduring values that, taken together, separate community colleges from other institutions of higher education: access, community responsiveness, focus on learning, and innovation. Community colleges provide access to the most diverse student body in higher education: 43% of community college students are age 21 or younger; 42% are between ages 22 and 39; and 16% are 40 or over. Of the students attending community colleges, 35% are minorities, 39% are first-generation college students, and 17% are single parents. Sixty percent of community college students are women (AACC, 2008). Community colleges are considered more affordable than universities, and students no longer have to go away to college because campuses are located within commuting distance of more than 90% of the U.S. population. And a growing number of community colleges are making learning even more accessible by delivering courses through distance education.

Community colleges often develop unique education and training programs to meet the needs of local business and industry. These institutions have traditionally responded to the educational needs of their communities, developing important vocational programs, partnering with local institutions and agencies, providing contract education, and offering both credit and noncredit community service programs. Some colleges provide facilities and support services to incubate new entrepreneurial businesses; others are seen as cultural centers for their communities. Community colleges also develop unique training programs to meet the needs of the local business and industry. For example, the Community College of Southern Alabama has a paper technology program to meet the needs of the pulp industry in that region. Napa Valley College in California has a viticulture program to support the local wine industry. The Maricopa County Community Colleges in Phoenix, Arizona, have computer chip manufacturing programs to support the needs of the technology industry in that area of the country.

When new immigrants enter a community, it is the community college that provides courses in English language and citizenship. When a factory closes down in a community, it is the community college that retrains the workers who are displaced. When community leaders want to attract new businesses, the ability of the local community college to provide the needed training for new workers is an important service to the community. Ninety-five percent of businesses and organizations that employ community colleges graduates are satisfied and recommend community college workforce and education programs (Zeiss, 1997).

Community college faculty staff and administrators care about the success of their students. Class sizes are generally much smaller than those found in the lower-division classes in 4-year colleges and universities, which leads to more one-on-one interactions between students and professors. The faculty, unlike those in universities, is not expected to do discipline-area research or to publish (although some do). Instead, the focus is on teaching and learning. Faculty members have at least a master's degree in the field in which they teach, although an increasing number have doctoral degrees. They are typically involved in setting up the courses and the standards for academic achievement. These decisions are often made within the framework of the specific academic disciplines. With some disciplines, such as nursing or paralegal studies, national certification examinations set standards and accredit each program.

Students who transfer from community colleges to 4-year colleges and universities to earn bachelor's degrees generally do at least as well as the students who start at the universities in terms of grade point average and degree completion. Distinguished graduates include Richard Carmona, the former surgeon general of the United States; Craig Venter, the scientist who mapped the human genome; Gaddi Vasquez, the former director of the U.S. Peace Corps; and Eileen Collins, the first woman U.S. space shuttle commander. Many community college graduates say that their best teachers were at the community college and that they would not have been able to pursue a higher education without community colleges.

Community college leaders often form partnerships with other educational institutions, local business and industry, or local government agencies to provide facilities and educational programs for students and community members. This innovative spirit extends into the classroom, where faculty and staff are among the first to experiment with self-paced instruction, distance learning technologies, group learning, learning communities, service learning, and simulations.

A culture of innovation is deeply ingrained in the community college movement, which itself is an innovation in higher education. Community colleges, for example, were among the first institutions to embrace the use of technology to increase access to learning, offering a wide variety of courses first by television and now through the Internet. The League for Innovation in the Community College, founded in 1968, provides forums through its publications and conferences to spread innovative practices to colleges in the United States and internationally. *Innovation Abstracts,* a publication of the National Institute for Staff and Organizational Development (NISOD) at the University of Texas Community College Leadership Program, focuses on the dissemination of innovations in teaching and learning in community colleges. A current example of innovation is The Community College Open Textbook Project at California's Foothill-DeAnza Community College. The project, funded by the William and Flora Hewlett Foundation, is an effort to cut the high costs of textbooks for students through the creation of high quality free or low cost textbooks that would be available online.

FUNDING, GOVERNANCE, AND ACCOUNTABILITY

Community colleges receive most of their funding from federal, state, and local taxes, with most of the support coming from local and state sources (Vaughan, 2006). Although funding policies vary widely from one state to another and even from one community college to another, public community colleges are the segment of higher education most reliant on taxpayer funding. Nationally, community colleges receive 37% of their funds from state taxes, 21% from local taxes, 17% from student tuition and fees, 16% from federal funds, and 9% from other sources (Knapp, Kelly-Reid, Ginder, & Miller, 2008). Community college leaders have become more entrepreneurial in response to recent state budget cuts. Contract education provided to local businesses often generates revenue for community colleges. Community college leaders are also supplementing revenues by strengthening local fundraising efforts through the work of college foundations.

The community college CEO usually has the title of president, chancellor, or superintendent/president. The CEO of public community colleges most commonly reports to an appointed or elected board of trustees, depending upon the policies of the state. Some states have a state board that oversees community colleges, sometimes in combination with local boards. The boards have the responsibility to approve policies, to secure adequate funding for the institution, and to see to it that the institution is administered properly. Boards also have the obligation to protect the interests of the community and to plan to accommodate the needs of future generations of students.

Boards of trustees also serve an important accountability function, helping to ensure that resources are wisely spent and in alignment with the institution's mission.

Public community colleges are held accountable at several other levels as well. The colleges submit data to state agencies, accreditation agencies, and to the federal government. Information most commonly submitted to the states includes graduation rates, transfer rates, passing scores on licensure examinations, student satisfaction, and job placement rates.

Community colleges are accredited by regional accreditation agencies that ask the colleges to perform an extensive self-study every 7 to 10 years, at which point a team of visiting professionals evaluates the campus, with interim reports made to ensure that accreditation status is maintained. Regional accreditation is necessary for colleges to be able to provide their students with access to national sources of financial aid, which helps students pay for their classes.

Current Challenges Facing U.S. Community Colleges

Despite their widely recognized value, community colleges in the United States are facing unprecedented challenges. In the early years of the new millennium, enrollments have increased dramatically, and college leaders have struggled to meet demand in the face of steep state budget cuts, limited facilities, faculty turnover, the high cost of updating technology, and increasing numbers of students who need remedial work before they can take college-level classes. Community colleges in areas with factory closures, such as North Carolina, South Carolina, Pennsylvania, Mississippi, Colorado, Maryland, Ohio, New Jersey, Washington, and Kansas, reported significant enrollment increases as workers who are laid off have sought retraining at their local community colleges. While several states and individual community colleges have been successful in winning voter approval of bond issues (a mechanism to borrow money that is repaid by increased taxes during the duration of the bond) to renovate or build new facilities, operational budgets, as a result of deteriorating state economies, have experienced several years of decline.

Enrollment pressures are driven by multiple factors. Historically, community college enrollments have increased during economic downturns as the unemployed and underemployed turned to the colleges as the path to a better future. Now, U.S. higher education is beginning to experience the leading edge of a bulge in the population of traditional-aged college students (18- to 24-year-olds)—the children of baby boomers and new immigrants. Furthermore, the percentage of high school graduates who attend college has increased from 50% in 1980 to more than 66% by 2007 (Snyder, Dillow, & Hoffman, 2008). The U.S. Department of Education projects that by 2010, nearly 75% of high school seniors will probably attend college (Snyder et al., 2008) Students and their families understand that education beyond high school is more necessary than ever to be successful in today's world.

Enrollment increases are also being sparked by the enrollment of students who already have college degrees. Twenty-eight percent of noncredit community colleges' students have a bachelor's degree or higher, and nearly half of these noncredit students have some form of postsecondary credential, including bachelor's, master's and doctoral degrees. More than 25% of part-time community college students enrolled for credit have some form of postsecondary credential (Knapp et al., 2008). In order to stay competitive in today's volatile economy, people are using community colleges to gain practical, marketable employment skills, recognizing lifelong learning as an economic necessity for staying employed or becoming reemployed.

Spikes in U.S. community college enrollments also have been fueled by significant tuition and fee increases in universities. Many students and their families turn to nearby community colleges to complete lower-division course work before transferring to a university, resulting in significant cost savings. Completing lower-division course work at a community college is also much less expensive for the state. This fact led to a proposal in California to divert some freshmen from the University of California to the state's community colleges for the freshman and sophomore years, with a guarantee of transfer to the university.

At the same time that community colleges were faced with historic enrollment demands, they were struggling with severe budget cuts. Data from the Grapevine project at Illinois State University indicate that state funding for public community colleges dropped by nearly $584.8 million between 2002–2003 and 2003–2004, with 22 states (44%) reporting decreased funding (Palmer & Franklin, 2006). Community college leaders struggled to meet the accelerating demand with declining public resources. Many colleges and systems responded by increasing tuition costs for students. After several years of relatively stable tuition levels, tuition increased by more than 27% in community colleges from 2002 to 2005. Tuition costs vary by state and even by institution within a state. The average cost of tuition and fees at public community colleges in 2007–2008 was $2,361, compared to $6,185 at public colleges and universities (College Board, 2007).

Although community college leaders and governing boards have been forced to increase tuition costs for students, they sought to limit the burden on students by implementing a variety of cost-cutting actions. At some colleges, faculty and staff expenses were cut either through early retirement incentives or reductions in force. The employment of part-time or adjunct faculty has steadily increased in community colleges as a way of offering classes at lower cost. Hiring freezes and employee travel restrictions also have been a common reaction.

Even in good economic times, the percentage of state funds going to higher education in the United States has been shrinking for more than a decade. Faced with competing needs for public funding to accommodate increased enrollments in K–12 and increased costs for Medicaid and corrections, state policymakers have cited the well-publicized benefits to the individual of having a college degree. They have thus argued that students and their families should pay more of the cost of higher education. There have been proposals in some states to privatize public higher education, with some institutions seemingly willing to give up their remaining public support in order to free themselves of state regulation and achieve fiscal stability. This would be very difficult for community colleges, however, because of their greater reliance on government funds and the fact that they cannot turn to federal research grants or alumni fundraising to the extent that many universities can.

Although current financial problems will probably dominate the agendas of state and federal policymakers for the next few years, the National Center for Public Policy and Higher Education stresses the need for a longer-range perspective. Higher education in the United States has not yet made a strong enough case for policymakers to understand the societal benefit of higher education. This public benefit can be most clearly demonstrated by community colleges as the institutions that prepare students to enter or reenter the workforce, integrate new citizens into U.S. society by providing language and citizenship courses, and open avenues to higher education for low-income and first-generation students—populations projected to supply increased numbers of the future workers essential to the nation's well-being. As has been noted, over the long term, states and the nation will face great challenges from intensifying international competitiveness, the need to ensure educational opportunity to growing and increasingly diverse high school graduating classes, and the demand for college-educated employees to replace large numbers of retiring baby boomers. Community college leaders assert that nothing less than the nation's economic future rides on the broad and unfettered access their institutions provide and the highly diverse student population they serve.

Higher education in the United States is clearly at a crossroads. A tidal wave of new students is seeking admission to the nation's colleges and universities at a time when greater levels of education are increasingly important to the country's well-being. Policymakers will have to decide whether to provide the funding to public higher education, including community colleges, that is necessary to meet current and future needs.

Local business and industry are more and more stepping up support to community colleges. One clear example is the support that community colleges with well-established health-care programs now receive from local hospitals and the health-care industry to expand facilities, increase clinical space, and support faculty salaries to increase the capacity of nursing and other allied health programs. Microsoft and SBC Communications (now AT&T) have provided grants to community colleges to build capacity in information technology (IT) programs and to keep IT faculty up to date. Looking to the future and emerging career fields, the National Science Foundation has provided significant support for community colleges, most notably to fund Advanced Technological Education programs and centers to enable the colleges to prepare the technologists needed for growing and high-demand industries such as environmental and geospatial technologies.

We are now living in an increasingly global society and economy. Most of the products purchased in this country have either been manufactured in other countries or have components that were made or assembled abroad. In fact, many U.S. companies have foreign subsidiaries. It is more important than ever for the citizenry of the United States to understand people from other cultures, and it is important for people who live in other countries to have an accurate understanding of U.S. culture. Community colleges are playing an important role by globalizing their curricula, promoting study-abroad programs, and recruiting international students. Community colleges constantly are reaching out to welcome students and faculty from around the world. More than 86,000 international students attend U.S. community colleges to obtain their first 2 years of a university education (Institute of International Education, 2008). And to ensure that U.S. students and faculty are becoming more globally competent, community colleges have internationalized their curricula, expanded their study abroad programs, enhanced faculty professional development opportunities, and increased international exchange programs for students and faculty.

The United States still has equity gaps to close as well. Minorities do not have the same levels of higher education access or success. Only 11% of Hispanics held baccalaureates in 2002, compared with 17% of Blacks and 28% of Whites (Phillippe & González Sullivan, 2005). Because community colleges offer lower costs and have the most diverse student bodies, they are the most likely solution for closing these equity gaps.

In the coming years, there will be a shift away from placing value solely on access to education and training to whether students are successful once they gain access. This trend started in the early 1990s with the principles of the "learning college" movement. This trend continues as accreditation commissions have asked institutions to measure student-learning outcomes. The need to improve success rates for students, especially those who are first-generation college students, minorities, or students from low-income families, has attracted the support of major foundations in the United States. The Community College Survey of Student Engagement, based at the University of Texas at Austin, is also focused on helping community colleges improve the success rates for students by increasing their engagement with the college and its services.

Another significant community college initiative to improve student learning and success is Achieving the Dream: Community Colleges Count, funded initially by the Lumina Foundation for Education and now by 19 different foundations. The initiative, now involving 83 colleges in 15 states, is assisting the colleges to develop data systems to track student success and strategies to improve success rates, especially for first generation and minority college students. Each college is provided with a data facilitator and a coach to assist the college faculty and leadership. Annual Strategy Institutes provide faculty and leadership of the colleges an opportunity to share experiences and best practices. Initial results show that some of the strategies have proved to be successful in increasing student learning and success rates among the most at-risk student populations.

Legislation in some states to allow selected community colleges to offer bachelor's degrees is the topic of considerable debate. This movement is fueled primarily by the shortage of teachers and the need for more baccalaureates in applied areas. Proponents of the community college baccalaureate argue that the movement is compatible with the community college value of providing access to needed educational programs. Opponents label this trend "mission creep" and argue that it will detract from the egalitarian and open-access mission of community colleges.

Another significant challenge that U.S. community colleges are just now beginning to face is the need to replace significant numbers of faculty and leaders. As noted earlier, many community colleges were established in the 1960s and 1970s. Many of the faculty and administrators who were hired at these developing institutions are now reaching retirement age. This large turnover of faculty and leaders is both a challenge and an opportunity. It is a challenge to adequately prepare and recruit the faculty and leaders of the future. But it is also an opportunity to bring greater diversity and new energy and enthusiasm into the community college world.

Conclusion

Because of the success of community colleges in providing educational opportunity and in the economic development of the United States, they have influenced how other countries provide education beyond the secondary level. In fact, a growing number of policymakers in other countries are beginning to develop institutions patterned after the model established in the United States. Community colleges in Vietnam, Thailand, and the Republic of Georgia were established with the assistance of U.S. educators and policymakers. Most recently, community colleges have been established in Saudi Arabia. Government officials from India, China, Ukraine, Egypt, and South Africa are currently examining the potential for developing community colleges.

A significant advantage of the community college model is that public 2-year colleges are considered to be a part of higher education in the United States, approved by the same agencies that accredit 4-year universities. Countries that have established further education (FE) or technical and further education (TAFE) institutions, which are both somewhat similar to U.S. community colleges, focus on vocational and technical programs and do not typically afford students the opportunity to transfer to a 4-year university to complete a bachelor's degree. FE and TAFE colleges are generally separate from higher education in the countries that have use those models. However, the Council for Industry and Higher Education (CIHE) in the United Kingdom recently completed a study of U.S. community colleges and British FE colleges that are part of the Mixed Economy Group, a group that represents the 29 FE colleges in England. These Mixed Economy Group colleges do offer higher education as well as FE courses and are more like community colleges, especially those that have begun to offer bachelor's degrees (see King, Widdowson, & Brown, 2008).

National associations for community college–like institutions often attract attendees from other countries to their annual conferences. International organizations such as the World Federation of Colleges and Polytechnics (WFCP) and the International Association of Colleges (IAOC) provide forums for community colleges and FE colleges to share information and best practices. Through the efforts of these organizations, practitioners in community colleges and the institutions around the world that share the same values can learn from one another and work to advance opportunities for higher education and workforce training.

References

American Association of Community Colleges. (2007). *State-by-state profile of community colleges: Trends and statistics* (7th ed.). Washington, DC: Author.

American Association of Community Colleges. (2008). *Facts 2008* [Brochure]. Washington, DC: Author.

Boggs, G. R., & Cater, J. J. (1994). The historical development of academic programs in community colleges. In G. Baker III, J. Dudziak, & P. Tyler (Eds.), *A handbook on the community college in America: Its history, mission, and management* (p. 218). Westport, CT: Greenwood Press.

Brint, S., & Karabel, J. (1989). *The diverted dream: Community colleges and the promise of opportunity in America, 1900–1985.* New York: Oxford University Press.

College Board. (2007). *Trends in college pricing.* Washington, DC: Author.

Institute of International Education. (2008). *Open Doors 2007: Report on international educational exchange.* Retrieved September 15, 2008, from http://opendoors. iienetwork.org/?p=113133

King, M., Widdowson, J., & Brown, R. (2008). *Higher education and colleges: A comparison between England and the USA.* London: The Council for Industry and Higher Education. Retrieved September 26, 2008, from http://www.aacc.nche.edu/ Content/ContentGroups/Headline_News/June_2008/cihe_report.pdf

Knapp, L. G., Kelly-Reid, J. E., Ginder, S. A., & Miller, E. S. (2008, June). *Enrollment in postsecondary institutions, fall 2006; graduation rates, 2003 & 2003 cohorts; and financial statistics, fiscal year 2006* (NCES 2008-173). Washington, DC: U. S. Department of Education, Institute of Education Sciences, National Center for Education Statistics.

McPhee, S. (2004). *Hot programs at community colleges* (Research Brief AACC-RB-04-1). Washington, DC: American Association of Community Colleges.

Palinchak, R. S. (1973). *The evolution of the community college.* Lanham, MD: Scarecrow Press.

Palmer, J. C., & Franklin, D. (Eds.). (2006, October). *Grapevine summary of state higher education tax appropriations for fiscal year 2006.* Normal, IL: Illinois State University, Center for the Study of Education Policy. Retrieved September 15, 2008, from http://www.grapevine.ilstu.edu/historical/Appropriations%202005-06.pdf

Phillippe, K. A., & González Sullivan, L. (2005). *National profile of community colleges: Trends and statistics* (4th ed.). Washington, DC: Community College Press.

President's Commission on Higher Education. (1947). *Higher education for democracy: A report of the President's Commission on Higher Education.* (Vols. 1–6). New York: Harper.

Snyder, T. D., Dillow, S. A., & Hoffman, C. M. (2008, March). *Digest of education statistics 2007* (NCES 2008-022). Washington, DC: U. S. Department of Education, Institute of Education Sciences, National Center for Education Statistics.

U.S. Census Bureau. (2003, October). *Language use and English-speaking ability: 2000.* Retrieved September 15, 2008, from http://www.census.gov/prod/2003pubs/c2kbr-29.pdf

U.S. Census Bureau. (2005). *Race and Hispanic origin in 2005.* Retrieved September 15, 2008, from http://www.census.gov/population/www/pop-profile/files/dynamic/RACEHO.pdf

Vaughan, G. B. (2006). *The community college story* (3rd ed.). Washington, DC: Community College Press.

Zeiss, T., and Associates. (1997). *Developing the world's best workforce: An agenda for America's community colleges.* Washington, DC: Community College Press.

ASIA

7

Vocational and Continuing Higher Education in China

Gerard A. Postiglione, Liangjuan Wang, and Don Watkins

We begin this chapter with a historical overview of higher education in China and a description of community-oriented junior colleges (postsecondary vocational education) and adult higher education (lifelong learning). We discuss China's interest in the U.S. community college model and describe some of the characteristics of the community-oriented colleges in Beijing. We conclude with a discussion of China's burgeoning postsecondary vocational education sector and its challenge to meet the rising demand for higher education, relevant work skills, and improved global competitiveness.

DEVELOPMENT OF HIGHER EDUCATION IN CHINA

Not surprisingly, China's higher education history is long and impressive. The government ran colleges as far back as the Zhou Dynasty (1046–256 BC), and it was during the Eastern Zhou Dynasty (770–256 BC) that Confucius established an education tradition that lasted for centuries and captured the imagination of the world. A higher education in the Confucian classics was required for the imperial examination system that began in the Sui Dynasty (581–618) and lasted until 1905, by which time China's examination system for the civil service had already exerted an influence on European practices (Hayhoe & Liu, in press). By the Song Dynasty (960–1270), several learned academies were established that emphasized the integration of teaching and research, collegiality among students and teachers in academic pursuits, and creative approaches to learning (Lee, 1985).

We express our appreciation to John Frankenstein for his comments.

Although scientific research was part of higher learning, the emphasis remained on learning the classics until Western natural sciences made their way to China via missionaries in the 18th century (Elman & Woodside, 1994). The humiliations of the Opium Wars before the mid–19th century led scholars to advocate for Western technology, thereby kicking off a longstanding debate about the balance between the essence of Chinese traditional knowledge and the usefulness of Western technological know-how. Metropolitan University, later to become Peking University, was established in 1898 and was transformed by its president, Cai Yuanpei (1916–1940), into a modern university that still continues to set the pace in China for higher education. After the nationalist government replaced China's last imperial dynasty, universities came to be modeled on those in Europe and the United States. Before the new government came to power, the communist colleges emphasized theory and practice, study, and application (Pepper, 1996). When the People's Republic of China was established in 1949, the country had more than 200 universities, including about 80 private institutions, with a total enrollment of only about 150,000.

Since then, higher education moved both forward and backward. Mao Zedong nationalized China's universities during a period of socialist transformation that was influenced by the Soviet Union. Universities were separated from research institutes, teaching emphasized a close link between education and labor, and student fees were abolished. College and university graduates were allocated to work according to a centralized plan. Many colleges were administered by their respective ministries (agriculture, railroad, textiles, forestry, etc.).

When relations with the Soviet Union broke off in the late 1950s, the structure of higher education remained intact. The number of higher education institutions increased from 205 to 227, and enrollments grew from 166,504 to 403,176. The Hundred Flowers Campaign, inviting intellectuals to air their views, was followed by an anti-rightist crackdown the following year. The pace of higher-education expansion quickened during the Great Leap Forward period (1958–1962), and by 1966 the number of colleges and universities reached 434 with 680,000 students. Chairman Mao launched the Cultural Revolution in May 1966, which crippled higher education for a generation. As the Cultural Revolution ended, enrollments rapidly shot up from 273,000 in 1977 to 401,000 in 1978. However, a lack of facilities and qualified teachers caused plans to be scaled down to 275,000 in 1979, 281,000 in 1980, 279,000 in 1981, and 315,000 for 1982. As Deng Xiaoping came to power, higher education gradually recovered in line with China's economic reforms and opening to the outside world. The shift from a centrally planned to a market economy brought unprecedented change, and overseas study tilted toward the West. Since then, over a million students left for overseas study. By 1985, colleges and universities numbered 1,016, although most enrolled only a few thousand students. (See Hayhoe, 1989, 1996; Pepper, 1996.)

Reforms in 1985 gave autonomy to higher education institutions over curriculum, academic staff, and student recruitment (Min, 1997). Gross enrollment (of those 18–22 years old) was about 2% in 1980 and 3% in 1990. Tuition fees for most students became standard by 1995, paralleled by new arrangements for student loans. Colleges and universities expanded to reach economies of scale, while the national enrollment rate rose past 4%. Further expansion occurred in the late 1990s, by which time the government discontinued the system of job allocation for graduates. As more and more aspects of higher education became affected by market forces, colleges began to generate more of their own revenue, cooperate with industry, run enterprises, borrow funds for capital construction, raise student fees, admit fee-paying adult learners into various programs of study, and consolidate their programs with other institutions.

The ministry of education maintained direct control over a small number of elite colleges and universities. Four hundred colleges and universities formerly under other central ministries were transferred to provincial or local authorities. By 2000, enrollments ballooned after 612 colleges and universities were consolidated into 250 (Postiglione, 2002). In 1994, 4.5% (5.28 million) enrolled in higher education, and, by 2007, enrollment reached 23% (27 million). Enrollment rates rose from 4% (18–22 years old) in 1995 to 20% in 2005. In 2000, two million new students were admitted to regular institutions of higher education, and adults (over 25 years old) also began to enter regular institutions of higher education in modest numbers. Just before the turn of the century, 4.36 million students were enrolled in regular higher education, and 3.05 million in adult education institutes. The regular and adult sectors remained intact, though the boundaries between them became slightly blurred.

The decision to expand higher education at that time also acted to delay entry into the work force during the East Asian economic crisis. In 2003, China set out a human resource blueprint that would increase enrollments to over 20% by 2010 (attained in 2007), 40% by 2020, and 50% by 2050. Government began to provide strong encouragement to private (or what is known as *minban*, or popularly run) higher education. While the private sector remained weak, it did provide many more opportunities for those who aspired to higher education. The Private Education Promotion Law in 2002 was followed by the Regulations on Sino-Foreign Cooperative Education in 2003.

This unprecedented expansion presented a major challenge to China's capacity for high-quality and relevant higher education. Moreover, inequities continued to grow, and disparities across regions became larger. Longstanding problems such as corruption in academic practices remained, and new ones such as high rates of unemployment among graduates continued to challenge forward progress in higher education.

COMMUNITY-ORIENTED JUNIOR COLLEGES AND CONTINUING EDUCATION

In general, Chinese higher education has continued its unprecedented metamorphosis within the nation's transition from a planned to a market economy. Both administration and finance have become more decentralized to make higher education responsive to the diversified communities it serves. There has also been a concerted effort to increase the efficiency of colleges and universities and the larger system within the limitations imposed by government. However, it is postsecondary vocational education that China has identified as a key area of education reform and as the core sector responsible for sustaining rapid economic development into the 21st century. China's minister of education stated, "Judging from its socio-economic developmental level, the country needs a large number of people with scientific knowledge and expertise in various fields of endeavor. Such people should be produced mainly through postsecondary vocational education" (Zhou, 2006, p. 29).

There is a consensus that although the country needs a system of world-class universities, it is critical that postsecondary education follow the needs of the workplace and stay aligned with social progress and economic restructuring. That means raising the standard of the labor force for global competitiveness. For this, China has turned to its postsecondary vocational education (community-oriented junior colleges) and adult continuing higher education (for lifelong learning) within the larger system of Chinese higher education. However, China found itself with many postsecondary junior colleges and adult universities that were still academically oriented and relatively low-standard. Taking these institutions and building their capacity to deliver relevant vocationally oriented postsecondary education for a changing economy was a major challenge. China's leaders, including Vice Premier Li Lanqing, expressed reservations about the extent to which those colleges and universities could be persuaded to support such a conversion.

> I have suggested that where conditions permit, each university run a vocational and technical college, and that junior colleges and adult universities be gradually restructured into postsecondary vocational colleges. Yet, I fear that universities might simply alter their status to "vocational and technical college" in name only, and retain the same low standards of regular junior colleges. (Li, 2004, p. 419)

China's Higher Education Law, enacted in 1998, specifies that higher education consists of junior college education, regular higher education, and graduate education, delivered in full-time and part-time mode, provided by a wide variety of institutions, all permitted to offer continuing education in response to social demands and confer formal and nonformal credentials. Enrollment of students in higher education has surpassed that of the largest providers in the world, including the United States, India, Russia, and Japan (Shen, 2003; Xing, 2003).

Higher education in China can be viewed as consisting of regular and adult sectors, with the total number of students almost equally divided between them. Regular higher education is provided at universities and vocational–technical colleges. Adult higher education is provided in a wide variety of formats and has moved from being a remedial form of schooling to a driving force that figures prominently into national development planning. China's major effort is focused on making vocational postsecondary education and adult higher education into the mainstay of a lifelong system of continuing higher education, and to closely integrate what it calls community higher education– postsecondary education focused on local needs, with the development of human resources for national growth.

The regular sector, still largely consisting of public universities, provides programs for 4- or 5-year bachelor's degrees, 2- or 3-year master's degrees, and 3- or 4-year doctoral degrees. A number of public universities have been identified by government as having the potential to become world-class universities, and a considerable national-level investment, associated with two major initiatives (i.e., the 211 and 895 plans) underlies this aim (see Min, 2004; Postiglione, 2005).

Vocational–technical colleges, also largely public institutions, provide a 2- or 3-year degree similar to an associate degree from a junior college. Some vocational–technical colleges cooperate with universities by making it possible for selected students to earn a bachelor's degree. Those who wish to enroll in universities or vocational–technical colleges must first pass the national college and university entrance examination, which is held every July. *(Note.* We use the term *associate degree* here only for the convenience of the reader. The only place in China where associate degrees are institutionalized is in community colleges of the Hong Kong Special Administrative Region of China, some of which also confer associate degrees in mainland China through partnerships with colleges there.)

In order that postsecondary vocational education remains synchronized with community-level economic development, the authority to approve postsecondary vocational–technical colleges has been decentralized from the central to provincial level. This includes authority over the establishment, scale, and curriculum of the colleges. Moreover, vocational–technical colleges have expanded at breakneck pace. The survival of these job-oriented institutions depends on their adaptability to a rapidly changing marketplace. Their customized training programs serve industries and enterprises, and they employ a credit-unit system that leads to conferral of both a diploma and vocational certificate. This double certificate system has become familiar to those in the manufacturing and service industries, as well as in areas as diverse as software development and agriculture.

The adult higher education sector, where most of the part-time students are enrolled, is composed of a broad array of institutions, and most of the credentials awarded are not degrees but rather diplomas or other specialized certificates. This sector includes radio and television universities (RTVUs), distance education, cadre management colleges in different industrial and service sectors (i.e., mining and banking), communist party cadre colleges, women's union colleges, ethnic minority colleges, and worker colleges. It also includes the self-study examination system.

China's RTVUs belong to the adult higher education sector but rank first in size among the world's top ten mega-universities. RTVU students earn credits per course for academic diplomas or technical certificates, as well as junior college or regular college degrees. RTVUs also provide on-the-job training courses and enroll senior secondary school graduates, senior secondary vocational school graduates, and those with equivalent qualifications. RTVUs practice open enrollment in the sense that is not mandatory to take entrance examinations, although students must excel to earn course credits, which remain effective for 8 years.

Another path for students to earn a junior college or bachelor's degree is through the self-study examination system. Examinations cover over 500 subjects; therefore, self-study students can major in a wide variety of areas. They generally spend more than 4 years to pass the different subject examinations for their major course area. There is a great deal of interaction and overlap between self-study examinations and other sectors of higher education. The examinations are administered by hundreds of regular universities. Students generally enter into public or, increasingly, the private (*minban*) colleges and universities to prepare for self-study examinations, but the credential is issued by the ministry of education.

Private colleges and universities in China have come to take on an increasingly larger role in Chinese higher education, including in both the regular and adult higher education sectors. Their main job has been to help students to prepare for the self-study examination or help those who fail the annual national college and university entrance examination and want to prepare again. As the quality of private colleges and universities improves, however, an increasing number of private colleges are also being permitted to offer approved degree programs.

A competitive variant of private colleges are the so-called independent colleges, part of the nongovernmental sector but run by regular public universities with private resources. These are basically state-owned, privately run, second-tier colleges. Private colleges have contended that the independent colleges have an unfair competitive advantage by capitalizing on the already established reputations and resources of their parent public university.

Exploring the U.S. Community College Model

Beginning in the 1980s, China's interest in U.S. community colleges, as an innovative form of postsecondary vocational education, grew rapidly. Few Chinese junior colleges actually use the name *community college,* and those that do are as much multipurpose institutions as others that are not formally called community colleges.

Among those that use the name are Chaoyang Community College and Xicheng Community College, both in the city of Beijing. Although they differ in many ways from most U.S. community colleges, especially in their historical evolution as worker colleges in the days of the socialist planned economy, like U.S. community colleges, they have become colleges oriented toward the human resource needs of their local communities.

The U.S. community college model has provided China's colleges with a useful perspective as they search for ways to address the growing diversity of needs in urban districts and western rural regions, including the need to build skilled labor capacity, retrain workers laid off by shrinking state-owned enterprises, and prepare skilled migrants for township and county enterprises. It is worth quoting the vice premier on this point:

> In organizing vocational and technical colleges, we have also drawn on the experience of some foreign countries. In the United States, postsecondary vocational education emerged after World War II, when the country was flooded by masses of demobilized soldiers. "Vocational education centers" were set up in communities to provide education and vocational skill training as a way to solve their employment problem. The results were very good, so the centers became permanent establishments. Some evolved over time into a type of "community college" providing three interconnected types of education: vocational education, general freshman and sophomore courses, and short-term training programs. Some community colleges became so successful that even presidents of some large corporations attended their training programs. Some working staff with doctorates came at intervals for knowledge renewal. A significant number of high school graduates chose to first do two years in a community college in pursuit of a sub-bachelor's degree or sophomore equivalent before continuing their studies in a general college, transferring the credits earned at a community college. Our vocational and technical colleges should also build such a linkage and articulation arrangements so that postsecondary vocational graduates can transfer their credits and enroll for further study at a regular university. (Li, 2004, pp. 421–422)

It became apparent that China had a good understanding of U.S. community colleges. It is also clear that China's regular university graduates were not able to meet the multiple demands of a market economy. Moreover, market forces led to a situation in which middle-aged laid-off workers with a low level of education needed new skills and a better idea of how to survive in the new economy. An estimated 140 million rural workers were migrating to cities to find work, many of whom might have a junior or senior secondary school education but few relevant vocational and technical marketable skills.

The director of vocational–technical education in China's ministry of education, Liu Junyi, emphasized China's need for community-oriented colleges for regional economic development, lifelong learning opportunities, and an urbanizing rural sector. He cited these characteristics:

- Openness. Community colleges must break out of the traditional walled-in education model.

- Diversity. Community colleges should offer a diverse range of credential-granting and noncredential-granting educational opportunities.

- Flexibility. Community colleges should be dynamic and adaptable to changing needs.

- Resource sharing. Community colleges will have to rely on local and existing resources.

One might say that China's interest in community colleges began in the 1980s during the early phase of reform and opening to the outside world, when foreign innovations were being assessed for their potential contribution to China's modernization. Among the international agencies aiding China's efforts to learn about and experiment with community college models were the World Bank and the Ford Foundation. The World Bank supported study overseas visits, and the Ford Foundation supported capacity-building in particular colleges, as well as research related to the training of migrants.

Through hundreds of visits and two-way international exchanges, Chinese educators and officials explored a variety of education models to determine the most effective ways to produce skilled labor and advanced professionals to meet China's needs. In addition to North American community colleges, China has considered Germany's technical and dual-system vocational colleges; Australia's technical and further education system; and similar institutions in France, South Korea, and Japan. With the support and encouragement of the American Association of Community Colleges (AACC), more than 80 U.S. community colleges have developed affiliations and exchanges with their Chinese counterparts. These colleges include Maricopa Community College (Arizona), LaGuardia Community College–City University of New York, San Francisco City College (California), and Lorain County Community College (Ohio).

One organization that was closely involved in capacity-building in China's junior college sector was the U.S.–China Education Foundation (USCEF). As early as 1984, it collaborated with Sichuan Province to establish the Heihutan Village School of Agriculture, a 2-year college designed to help modernize rural areas. USCEF provided support for a U.S. agriculture specialist to advise the college on farm mechanization and for an Oregon State University professor to lecture at the college and advise it on curriculum. This initiative incorporated some of the features of U.S. community colleges: open access for secondary school graduates, general education as part of the requirement leading to a diploma, and short-cycle and part-time courses open to village adults and farmers.

By 1988, the Heihutan College was recognized in Sichuan and neighboring provinces as an effective institution that applied community college concepts. By 1990, the college became self-sustaining and still provides several thousand rural residents with full-time or short-cycle education. Its success and close relationship other such partnerships (i.e., China's Shanxi Province and City University of New York) led to further partnerships and community college modeling for China.

USCEF also awarded grants to Chinese junior colleges that incorporated community college features for capacity-building. The grant projects included career counseling centers, paraprofessional social work training, community outreach programs, and training for district enterprises. Each of six Chinese junior colleges sent two professors for 6-week internships at U.S. community colleges: Mesa Community College and PIMA Community College (Arizona), Pikes Peak Community College (Colorado), Middlesex Community College (Massachusetts), and Howard Community College (Maryland). With the coordination of the National Committee on U.S.–China Relations, a Chinese leadership delegation visited community colleges in New York, Iowa, Texas, and Arizona and participated in AACC's centennial meeting in Chicago.

Case Studies

In 2003, USCEF conducted brief case studies of several community-oriented multipurpose junior colleges in Beijing. Their investigation included interviews with junior college heads and surveys of community college practices. In 2001, these vocational colleges accepted students directly from secondary schools who took the national college and university entrance examination but did not score high enough to enter other regular universities. They also admitted adult learners. These colleges constitute a broad array of multipurpose institutions that serve a variety of community needs. Although most of the credentials they award are not bachelor's degrees, their diplomas and other specializes certificates can lead to job opportunities in the labor market. They are also linked to RTVUs, distance education, and cadre management colleges in different industrial and service sectors. In the following sections, we summarize some of the characteristics of the colleges, which emerged from USCEF's investigation.

Finance

Shijinshan Community College received 22%–50% of its funding from the government and raised about 45% from student tuition fees. The rest was raised from the community, although college heads cited difficulty in raising sufficient funds. They often relied on short-term training programs to generate income, which could amount to as much as CNY 7 million each year. Government funding was about CNY 4 million and was earmarked for employees and retired persons. The government also appropriated special funds for capital construction, CNY 1.4 million in 2003.

Zhongguancun College had various sources of finance that totaled CNY 9 million each year. The government appropriated 45.6% of the total, and the college could earn 54.4% from tuition fees or other training programs. Chaoyang Community College received 40% of its funding from government and raised about 47% from tuition fees. Xicheng College received CNY 7 million from government (22% of its total budget) and about CNY 20 million (78%) from the community through training programs and other sources. About half of all the funding went to teachers' salaries and 20% to administration. The student tuition fee was about CNY 2,000–3,000 per year, compared with about 4,000 to 6,000 at regular public universities. Generally, tuition fees were collected according to the number of course credits taken, the cost of one credit being about CNY 105. For a major specialty area of study, a student might pay CNY 2,000. Some majors (such as art) cost more—about CNY 2,500–3,000 each year. The average fee for a student at Chaoyang Community College was about CNY 2,600 per year.

Enrollments

In 2003, the number of part-time students in community-oriented vocational junior colleges exceeded the number enrolled in full-time study. One college had 10,000 part-time students and only 3,000 full-time students. Xuanwu College was a part-time institution with about 2,400 part-time students in credential-granting programs and 3,500 students in noncredential programs. Zhongguancun College had 4,400 students, but 3,000 students were enrolled as nondegree students, accounting for 73% of the total.

Chaoyang Community College had 3,266 full-time students; 1,500 of them were in credential-granting programs and 1,500 in RTUV courses to improve their ability to pass national self-study examinations. In addition, Chaoyang Community College ran cooperative study programs with other universities in Beijing, including the Foreign Economic and Trade University (700 students) and Beijing Industrial University (300). As many as 15,000 were part-time, nondegree students, and 200 were in a training classes for the self-study examinations. About one third (2,000–3,000) wanted to pursue degrees, compared with two thirds (5,000–8,000) who did not.

There were many training programs for the jobless, made free with government support. There were also training courses for rural migrant workers in many community oriented junior colleges, some funded by government. Course offerings were broad and included civil servant training, Olympic knowledge seminars, training for the elderly, and English for adults.

Structure

Community-oriented junior colleges in China are often amalgamated units. Different branches of adult education and other institutions are incorporated together in a manner in which the label community college makes perfect sense. For example, Xicheng Community College was an amalgamation of Xicheng Economic and Scientific University (established in 1986); Xicheng Employee University; a branch of the Beijing RTVU (with about 2,000 students, 800 working toward a bachelor's degree); and Xicheng Financial and Trade Middle Level Specialized College. There were more than 10,000 students in the Xicheng Community College in 2003, with 3,500 of them reading for the higher-level specialized diplomas.

Xuanwu Community College was an amalgamation of Xuanwu Part-Time University, Xuanwu RTVU, Xuanwu Elder People's University, and Xuanwu Communist Party School. Chongwen Community College included Chongwen Workers University, Xuanwu RTVU, Finance College, and Beijing Zhengyi Vocational College. Chongwen Community College also had several branches in the Qianmen and Yonwai districts of Beijing.

Credentials

There were three kinds of credentials granted by Beijing community colleges:

1. Adult education specialized diplomas (similar to associate degrees).
2. RTVU diplomas and degrees. (The RTVU program at Shijingshan Community College grants adult specialized diplomas and bachelor's degrees).
3. Cooperative college diplomas. (Community-oriented junior colleges may cooperate with regular universities, whereby the students earn both a diploma and university degree. For example, Xuanwu Part-Time University cooperates with Beijing University of Science and Technology).

CHINA'S HUMAN RESOURCE BLUEPRINT

The most important document concerning China's future competitiveness within the context of its rapid economic globalization is *Strategic Concepts for the Development of Chinese Education and Human Resources for the Next Fifty Years* (hereafter referred to as the Blueprint; see Sharpe, 2005). Published in 2003, this document marked the first time that China organized scholars, experts, research institutions, and government organizations from education, economics, population control, laws, finance, and agriculture to compose a large research report on education. The Blueprint called for a 99% enrollment rate for 9-year compulsory education (primary education of 6 years plus 3 years of junior secondary education) by 2020, when 100% of junior secondary school students will enter senior secondary education. The current 54% enrollment rate in senior secondary education will grow to 73% by 2010, 85% by 2020, and 100% by 2050, when more than half of secondary school graduates will enter college or university

101

and the percentage of gross domestic product invested in education will increase from its current 4% to 7.8%.

With respect to postsecondary vocational education, the Blueprint indicated a clear intention to move ahead rapidly.

- The proportion of employees receiving a junior college education or above should increase from 4.66% in 2000 to more than 10% by 2010.

- By 2020, 13,000 out of every 100,000 people should be receiving a junior college education or above.

- By 2020, workers in the commercial and service sectors should receive an average of 11 years of schooling, and 20% should receive a junior college education or above.

- By 2050, 31,000 out of every 100,000 people should have received a junior college education or above; about 30,000 should be at senior college level. The amount of education workers receive should be 14 years; the average years of education for workers in the commercial and service sectors should be 13.5, and, of these workers, 40% should have had an education of junior college or above, matching the level achieved by developed countries at the beginning of the 21st century.

The Blueprint makes clear the central role of postsecondary vocational colleges and continuing adult education for China's drive to become a fully developed and highly competitive global economy. However, at present, postsecondary vocational education and training must still help solve the emergent problems of a massively diverse labor market serving an economy that is constantly upgrading the sophistication of its productive.

Conclusion

China's community-oriented postsecondary sector of vocational colleges and adult continuing education are hard pressed to adapt and adjust to the rapidly changing economic, social, and educational environments in which they now operate. Like China's regular colleges and universities, the postsecondary vocational sector will have to rely more on transnational collaboration to address new challenges. The changing nature of collaboration has been beneficial to China's universities and placed them on more equal footing with universities in other countries. The same patterns can spur developments in the postsecondary vocational sector.

With respect to China's postsecondary education and its human resource needs, national borders will continue to become less relevant. Global telecommunications, the international flow of funds, and even some Internet-based vocational education programs now operate more independently than ever before. Although government may control the flow of people, there is a transnational flow of commerce, communications, and ideas that operate beyond the reach of governments. There is acceptance of the view that cross-border collaboration, if done well, can offer mutually beneficial advantages on multiple levels. There is a new recognition that the intensified international sharing of ideas, strategies of learning, and students is not only of enormous value to postsecondary vocational education systems and institutions but also essential to their long-term survival. To this end, motivations, goals, mechanisms, outcomes, and challenges associated with Sino-foreign collaborations are worthy of closer examination in the coming years.

Economic globalization has made it more urgent that China consider how the long-term success of vocational higher education will become dependent upon its ability to reconstitute itself as part of an integrated multinational system of vocational higher education across East Asia. It may be some time before East Asia becomes a free trade zone with a common currency and convertible educational credentials across colleges and universities. However, it already has begun to acknowledge its shared cultural traditions, historical affinities, and developmental experiences. There are salient themes, such as harmony, moral cultivation, social networks, paternal leadership, and political authoritarianism, that are shared across China's borders in neighboring countries, and these can form the basis for partnerships in postsecondary vocational education that can lead to mutually beneficial outcomes for economic development and social progress across the East Asian region into the second half of the 21st century.

China's system of vocational higher education will continue to move from the periphery of world attention to center stage. It will continue to refine how it negotiates the balance between cross-border collaboration and international competition. At the same time, there is a concern that cross-border collaboration may increase homogeneity across vocational higher education at a time when there is an urgent need to seek unique solutions to the new challenges based on Chinese cultural heritage and the long historical evolution of higher education in China.

References

Elman, B., & Woodside, A. (Eds.). (1994). *Education and society in late imperial China 1600–1900.* Berkeley: University of California Press.

Hayhoe, R. (Ed.). (1989). *China's universities and the open door.* Armonk, NY: M. E. Sharpe.

Hayhoe, R. (1996). *China's universities, 1895–1995: A century of cultural conflict.* New York: Garland.

Hayhoe, R., & Liu, J. (in press). China's universities, cross-border education and dialogue among civilizations. In D. Chapman, W. Cummings, & G. Postiglione (Eds.), *Border crossing in East Asian higher education.* Hong Kong: Comparative Education Research Center.

Lee, T. H. C. (1985). *Government education and examinations in Sung China.* Hong Kong: Chinese University of Hong Kong.

Li, L. (2004). *Jiaoyu fangtanlu* [Interviews on education]. Beijing: People's Education Press.

Min, W. (1997). China. In G. A. Postiglione & G. C. L. Mak (Eds.), *Asian higher education: An international handbook and reference guide* (pp. 37–55). Westport, CT: Greenwood.

Min, W. (2004). Chinese higher education: The legacy of the past and the context of the future. In P. Altbach & T. Umakoshi (Eds.), *Asian universities: historical perspectives and contemporary challenges* (pp. 53–84). Baltimore, MD: Johns Hopkins University Press.

Pepper, S. (1996). *Radicalism and education reform in 20th-century education: The search for an ideal development model.* New York: Cambridge University Press.

Postiglione, G. A. (2002). Chinese higher education at the turn of the century: Expansion, consolidation, and the globalization. In D. Chapman & A. Austin, *Higher education in the developing world: Changing contexts and institutional responses* (pp. 149–166). Westport, CT: Greenwood.

Postiglione, G. A. (2005). Higher education in China: Perils and promises for a new century. *Harvard China Review, 5*(2), 138–143.

Sharpe, M. E., Inc. (Trans.). (2005, July/August). Strategic concepts for the development of Chinese education and human resources for the next fifty years. *Chinese Education and Society, 38(*4*), 61–69. (Original work published 2003)

Shen, Z. (2003, February 17). *Shanghai jiang shuaixian shixian gaodeng jiaoyu puji hua: 2002 nian gaodeng jiaoyu maoruxuelu yida 51%, 5 nianhou jiangda 60% yishang* [Shanghai will take the lead in the massification of higher education: Gross enrolment rate reaches 51 % in 2002 and set to move beyond 60% in five years). *China Education Daily.* Retrieved December 23, 2007, from http://www.jyb.com.cn/ gb/2003/02/17/zy/jryw/1.htm

Xing, D. (2003, June 24). *Zhongguo gaodeng jiaoyu guimo shouci chaoguo meiguo yueju shijie diyi* [The scale of higher education in China surpasses the United States for the first time, leaping to first position in the world]. *Eastday News.* Retrieved December 23, 2007, from http://news.eastday.com/epublish/gb/paper148/20030624/ class014800014/hwz968718.htm

Zhou, J. (2006). *Higher education in China.* Singapore: Thompson Publishers.

The Emergence of the Community College Associate Degree in Hong Kong

Gerard A. Postiglione and Steven Sai Kit Kwok

As the chapters in this book show, the U.S. community college model has been applied with increasing frequency in recent years in many parts of the world. The application of that model, however, may not have been more rapidly and successfully implemented than in the Hong Kong Special Administrative Region (hereafter referred to as Hong Kong) of the People's Republic of China (hereafter referred to as China, mainland China, or the mainland). At the turn of the 21st century, and while in economic decline, Hong Kong decided to rely singularly on community colleges to double the number of students enrolled in postsecondary education within 10 years, a goal it achieved 5 years ahead of schedule, by 2005. Moreover, it achieved this goal even though the cost of a year in an associate degree program at a community college exceeded the cost of attending a university.

HISTORICAL AND ECONOMIC CONTEXT

Hong Kong has long been a vibrant regional center driven by urban metropolitan development. Its development has been driven, foremost, by a rich Chinese cultural heritage that anchors its value system, a thriving internationalism that shapes its political system and economic competitiveness, and a highly mobile society of migrants that contributes to a high turnover of human resources. The education system is viewed as central to Hong Kong's historic role as a bridge between China and the world, and Hong Kong's new vision to become Asia's world educational hub, a position strengthened by its geographical position, world-class communication and transport infrastructure, bilingual capacity, rule of law, and academic freedom.

The authors wish to acknowledge the University of Hong Kong Research Grants Committee for its support.

In 1997, Hong Kong was handed back to the China under a one-country, two-system formula that granted Hong Kong a high degree of autonomy in all matters including education after two decades of rapid economic growth (see Chan & Postiglione, 1996; Postiglione & Tang, 1997). Free speech and movement are highly cherished characteristics in Hong Kong society, but a lack of representative democracy, a legacy of the colonial era, remains a highly emotive issue. Among the more positive aspects of the colonial legacy has been the safeguarding of the rule of law and freedom of the press and a no tolerance policy toward corruption, which has helped Hong Kong fortify its position as a global financial center and the second-largest banking center in East Asia, as well as one of the most open and free media centers in Asia.

A capitalist ideology is robust in Hong Kong's economic sphere, despite the fact that most schools and universities are government-funded, something that may begin to change with privatization. Capitalism in Hong Kong has led to a high degree of inequality. Income distribution, as measured by the Gini coefficient, is one of the highest in Asia at 53.3 in 2007 (Central Intelligence Agency, 2008). This inequality is reflected in the fact that, despite its riches, in 2005 Hong Kong ranked 21 out of 177 on the United Nations' Human Development Index (UN Development Programme, 2008). Although the percentage of the population living in poverty has increased, poverty has gained the attention of government and private sector initiatives, and a recent upturn of the economy has slightly eased pressure on this issue. Cheaply priced goods from China, including clothing, food stuffs, and household goods (along with government-subsidized housing, nearly half of all housing), have helped ease the plight of the working classes in Hong Kong.

After more than two decades of rapid economic growth, the 1997 Asian economic crisis derailed Hong Kong's economy for several years. The SARS epidemic of 2003 further crippled development prospects. Deflation lasted 68 months. However, Hong Kong's gross domestic product grew by 8.1% in 2004 (slightly faster than the 3.1% figure for the previous year), making it the second best performance since 1987 (Hong Kong SAR Government, 2008a). The economy doubled in size over the past two decades at an average of 4.8% in real terms (compared with the world economy growth rate of 3.5%). The inflation rate was -0.4%. Despite its small size, Hong Kong is the world's 11th-largest trading entity. Its container port is the busiest in the world, and its airport is also one of the busiest. Moreover, it is the world's 6th-largest foreign exchange market and 14th-largest banking center.

Hong Kong has expanded its service economy in line with the global demands pushing it toward a knowledge economy. There is virtually no primary production (agriculture, fisheries, mining, etc.). Secondary production (manufacturing, construction, electricity, gas, and water) experienced a significant decline in its share of overall production, shrinking from 23% in 1983 to 11% in 1993 to 3% in 2003, as most manufacturing operations moved across the border into China where labor costs were lower. The tertiary sector consisting largely of services often based on small-scale firms, many with family roots, expanded from 67% in 1983 to 89% in 2003. Wholesale, retail, import and export trades, restaurants, and hotels have expanded their share of the tertiary sector from 23% (1984) to 32% (2004). Finance, real estate, and business services have grown from 5% to 15%, trade, storage and communications from 8% to 11% and community, social and personal services from 17% to 27%. Visible trade expanded annually by an average rate of 22% in value terms. That dropped to 8% from 1994–2004 due to direct shipping through enhancement of port facilities and simplification of customs (Hong Kong SAR Government, 2008a).

The economic links between Hong Kong and the mainland have been the most important factor in economic growth. Mainland China is Hong Kong's largest trading partner, accounting for 44% of all trade value, and 91% of Hong Kong's reexport trade was related to the mainland. Hong Kong was the mainland's third-largest trading partner (after the United States and Japan), accounting for 10% of mainland's total trade value (Postiglione & Tang, 1997).

There has been a sharp increase in the flow of people and services between Hong Kong and the mainland, and Hong Kong is a principal gateway to the mainland for business and tourism. Hong Kong is a principal source of direct investment into China, accounting for 43% of the total inward direct investment in the mainland. The most important partner area is the Pearl River Delta; estimates are that 11 million Chinese workers (10 million in Guangdong) were employed directly or indirectly by Hong Kong ventures (Hong Kong SAR Government, 2008a).

The mainland-initiated Center for European Policy Analysis trade agreement has granted Hong Kong a special status in trade (no tariffs), and this has recently been extended to the trade in educational services. Much of the business expertise that transformed it from a fishing village to center of trade and commerce came from the mainland, and its manufacturing sector took off with the migration of Shanghai region entrepreneurs after 1949. Its manufacturing base of textiles and garments has gradually shifted over the border into China, leaving Hong Kong to rely almost solely on its service sector for its economic growth. This includes an increased emphasis on tourism and the film industry. Nevertheless, Hong Kong faces increased competition from neighboring cities on the Chinese mainland, including from Shanghai and Guangzhou, as well as other regional centers such as Seoul and Singapore. Much of this competition is human resource related, and the mainland government's initiative to establish a number of world-class universities has had an enormous effect on higher education planning in Hong Kong.

The total employment figure for Hong Kong in 2004 was 3.6 million: Approximately 32% were employed in wholesale, retail, import and export trades, restaurants, and hotels; 27% were employed in community, personal, and social services; 15% were employed in financing, insurance, real estate, and business services; 11% were employed in transport, storage, and communications; and only 5% were employed in manufacturing. In December 2004, the average monthly wage was HKD 11,549 per month (approximately USD 1,480) for workers in supervisory, technical, and clerical positions and in the wholesale, retail, and import–export trades and restaurant and hotel sectors. The unemployment rate in 2004 was about 3.1%, still higher than the rates in the 1980s and 1990s, which hovered between 1% and 2%. The 2005 figure for unemployment dropped to about 2.5% (Hong Kong SAR Government, 2008a, 2008b).

Since 1997, however, Hong Kong has experienced a series of crises that have left it with a stagnant economy and a polity frustrated by government incompetence (see So & Chan, 2002). Meanwhile, cities like Beijing, Shanghai, and Guangzhou challenge Hong Kong's vaunted position as China's economic powerhouse. In this new equation, the director general of the World Trade Organization identified the pressing role of educational reform in Hong Kong.

The rise of an increasingly skilled Chinese workforce, as well as direct transportation links with Taiwan, means that Hong Kong will have to fight to keep its privileged place. If recently launched educational reforms have the intended effect of producing a more flexible, creative, and skilled workforce, Hong Kong will have a fighting chance to keep its vaunted position as China's international window over a longer time period (see Panitchpakdi & Clifford, 2002). It is within this context that the Hong Kong imported the community college associate degree model from the United States and situated it within a new postcolonial society that did not have the funds to greatly expand university education due to an economic decline that began in 1997 and continued until 2005.

Higher Education in Hong Kong

Hong Kong's higher education policies are made independently of mainland China's education policies. However, with increased economic integration, there is an unavoidable recognition that educational policy decisions need to take mainland developments into consideration. In terms of size, Hong Kong has 12 degree-granting institutions, 8 of which are publicly funded. The 2000 policy address by the chief executive of Hong Kong set a target of having 60% of the 17–20 age cohorts in higher education by 2010, a goal that would double that figure (Chief Executive, 2000; see also HKU SPACE, 2008). Due to economic crises, achieving this target was planned through offering slots in wholly self-financing community colleges. Although student fees for the community college slots leading to 2-year associate degrees are higher than for university bachelor's degree slots, the demand for higher education was so great that the 60% target was achieved in half the time expected. In terms of the shape of the system, a major policy shift will convert the traditional British 5+2+3 education system to a 3+3+4 structure (3 years of junior and senior secondary education with 4 years in the university system). Although competition among the seven publicly funded universities is intense for the best students and the most research funds, new incentives have been introduced to speed cross-institutional collaboration as a way of cutting costs and strengthening areas of teaching and research. The minister of education has also proposed merging two of the top three universities, a measure that has thus far been successfully resisted.

The Hong Kong higher education system is heavily influenced by its colonial heritage. It has followed the British model for most of its history. It has been small in scale and fully government funded, but with a high degree of autonomy from government. By mid-century, Hong Kong had only one university, the University of Hong Kong, established in 1911. Steeped in Western academic traditions, with English as the medium of instruction, its graduates became the backbone of the civil service and the teaching profession.

The Chinese University of Hong Kong, established in 1964, provided higher education to the growing number of graduates from secondary schools in which instruction was conducted in Chinese. The scale of higher education remained modest until a 1989 decision made by the governor of Hong Kong to nearly double the number of students admitted to universities. The proportion of the relevant age group (17–20) in first-degree slots climbed from about 2.2% in 1981 to nearly 18% in 2000–2001, amounting to 14,500 slots (Sutherland, 2002, p. 1). Between 1990 and 1998, the number of universities grew from two to seven. Eight institutions are publicly funded through the University Grants Committee (UGC; Hong Kong SAR Government, 2008c). There are three other degree-awarding tertiary institutions that are not funded by UGC, the publicly funded Hong Kong Academy for Performing Arts, the self-financing Open University of Hong Kong, and the Hong Kong Shue Yan University.

There has been an unprecedented expansion of both self-financing associate degree programs and nonprofit community colleges in Hong Kong since autumn 2000. As was stated earlier, in 2000, the chief executive of Hong Kong announced the government's initiative to support the progressive increase in postsecondary education opportunities (Chief Executive, 2000; see also HKU SPACE, 2008). The government's planning target was that, by 2010, 60% of senior school leavers would have access to postsecondary education, a target that was met by 2005. The target was achieved ahead of time because the government introduced a series of support measures for both students and providers of postsecondary programs, which are described in detail later in this chapter. In light of these measures, one could observe that given that Hong Kong had never had community colleges or associate degree programs, the government took a bold initiative to press ahead with the associate degree movement. It was reported that Hong Kong had an accumulative total of about 14,324 associate degree graduates between 2002, the first graduation year, and 2006 (Information Portal for Accredited Self-financing Postsecondary Programmes [iPASS], 2008).

The Associate Degree in Hong Kong

According to the Education Bureau's policy announcement, *Expansion in Post-secondary Education Opportunities,* the key features of associate degree programs in Hong Kong are to "provide an enriched education at post-secondary level that prepares students for work, further study, leisure and active citizenship. It should also cultivate a spirit of lifelong learning and develop the students' ability to learn how to learn" (Education Bureau, 2007). In terms of learning outcomes, these programs "should equip students with generic skills as well as specialised knowledge/skills that are sufficient to enable them to perform effectively at para-professional level, to further their studies in universities or to pursue professional studies" (Education Bureau, 2007). The generic skills cited were languages, information technology, interpersonal, communication, quantitative, and analytical and the ability to learn how to learn.

Most associate degree programs take 2 years, normally admitting students who have passed one A-level subject or two AS-level subjects, plus five HKCEE (Hong Kong Certificate of Education Examination) subjects. Associate degree programs are also open to mature students and generally adopt the principle of "lenient entry, stringent exit." The basic difference between associate degree and higher diploma programs is that associate degree programs put more emphasis on general education, while higher diploma and professional diploma courses are more vocationally oriented.

The government, education providers, and students all are concerned about the quality assurance mechanism for this new category of qualifications. The self-accrediting associate degree programs are required to undergo their own internal quality assurance mechanism for their regular degree programs. Others must be validated by a recognized quality assurance agency, such as the Hong Kong Council for Academic Accreditation.

Regarding the value of the associate degree qualifications, the credential is a standalone exit qualification for employment at the para-professional level. Graduates can pursue further studies or professional development (full or part time) or enter the job market. "As an exit qualification for further studies, an AD award is normally equivalent to 50% of a 4-year university degree (North American model) or one-third of a 3-year university degree (British model). In other words, AD graduates can articulate to Year 3 of a 4-year university degree (North American model) or Year 2 of a 3-year university degree (British model). As an exit qualification for employment purpose, AD should generally be considered as equivalent to that of a Higher Diploma" (Education Bureau, 2007). The government has also taken the lead in announcing the acceptance of the qualifications of associate degree as one of the entry requirements for appointment to 13 civil service grades. However, when asked by the Legislative Council, the government failed to provide any statistics on the government's recruitment of associate degree graduates since 2005 (Legislative Council, 2008).

In the 2004–2005 academic year, there were 20 institutions offering full-time accredited self-financing subdegree programs. The major institutions included the

University of Hong Kong, the Chinese University of Hong Kong, the Hong Kong Baptist University, the Open University of Hong Kong, the Hong Kong Polytechnic University, the City University of Hong Kong, the Hong Kong Institute of Education, Vocational Training Council, and Lingnan University. There were also a number of new education providers that were undergoing academic accreditation. Associate degree programs cover a variety of disciplines, including arts and social sciences, science and technology, information technology, business and administration, design, and architecture.

Tuition fees for self-financing associate degree programs offered by the 20 local institutions ranged from HKD 30,000 to HKD 50,000. To improve further education opportunities for those lacking means, the government provides a package of financial assistance schemes to eligible students, including means-tested grants, low-interest loans (the ceiling of grants or loans for 2004–2005 was HKD 55,890), non-means-tested loans, and travel subsidies. Details of the schemes can be obtained from the Student Financial Assistance Agency (2008). Students in self-financing programs paid as much as HKD 1,000 (USD 120) more per year than did their counterparts in publicly funded bachelor's degree programs at one of the eight mainstream institutions.

By 2005, despite the rapid expansion of associate degree programs, there was no indication that this self-financing form of education had reached a saturation point. A new Chinese University-Tung Wah Group Hospital Community College would accept its first intake of students in September, 2005. HKU SPACE (School of Professional and Continuing Education) and Po Leung Kuk opened a joint community college in 2007.

The Hong Kong Success Formula: Government Support

In contrast to U.S. public, comprehensive community colleges, Hong Kong-style 2-year universities are independent, self-financing, and market-oriented. For regions and countries that no longer enjoy economic prosperity but would like to expand postsecondary education opportunities for their youngsters, Hong Kong's experience with nonprofit 2-year universities and self-financing associate degree programs could provide some positive lessons.

Support for Institutions

From the start, the Hong Kong government has deeply engaged itself in Hong Kong's associate degree movement. It has provided an array of financial support for postsecondary education institutions and subdegree students. For the postsecondary providers that are nonprofit and provide full-time accredited postsecondary programs, the government has provided assistance and support in the following ways.

Interest-free start-up loans. In the first stage, short-term loans are offered to enable postsecondary providers to rent premises for 2 years and to cover the costs of basic refurbishment and equipment. In the second stage, medium-term loans are offered to providers with good track records established during the short-term loan to purchase or build permanent college premises and to cover the costs of refurbishment and equipment. Medium-term loans cover only requirements additional to those already financed by the short-term loan.

Land grants at a nominal premium. Reserved sites are granted to successful applicants by private treaty at a nominal premium for an initial term of 10 years, with the possibility of renewal. Lessees are required to pay the government rent at 3% of the prevailing value of the land from the date of the land grant. Other basic terms and conditions of the land grant will be determined by the director of lands. Lessees are required to enter into a 10-year service agreement with the government and are required to submit a development plan that sets standards, quantity, and quality targets for the education programs offered. The 10-year period was proposed for two reasons: (1) to give postsecondary program providers sufficient time to construct the premises and build up the student population and (2) to coincide with the maximum 10-year repayment period of the interest-free start-up loans. As one example, the government granted the Hong Kong Polytechnic University/Hong Kong Community College a site of 4,400 square meters, not far away from the university, and a medium-term loan of HKD 424 million.

Accreditation grants. The government set aside $30 million for introducing a time-limited scheme to provide one-off accreditation grants to postsecondary education providers, to help them offset the high cost of accreditation: It can cost private institutions around HKD 1 million to accredit two new courses. These high costs partly resulted in the bankruptcy and closure of Hong Kong Learning Community College in May 2005, the first closure in Hong Kong community college history.

Financial Assistance for Students

For students of all self-financing subdegree programs, the government provides the Financial Assistance Scheme for Post-secondary Students (FASP). To be eligible, applicants are required to be aged 25 or below and be registered full time in locally accredited self-financing postsecondary programs that lead to a qualification at the subdegree level or above. The ultimate aim of FASP is "to assist needy students in paying tuition fees, academic expenses and living expenses so that no eligible students are denied access to post-secondary education because of lack of means" (Student Financial Assistance Agency, 2008). Financial assistance is provided in the form of grants and loans.

Support for Program Quality

In 2005, the Education Bureau (2007) announced several strategies for ensuring program quality:

- Self-accrediting institutions should subject their self-financing postsecondary programs to the same quality assurance mechanisms used for their regular programs.

- Non–self-accrediting institutions must undergo an institutional review by the Hong Kong Council for Academic Accreditation and submit their courses for external validation.

- Institutions should use the common descriptors for associate degree programs, developed by the Education Bureau.

Also in 2005, the Joint Quality Review Committee (JQRC) was established to take stock of quality assurance processes primarily for self-financing subdegree programs under universities. JQRC adopted a two-stage review consisting of a preview and an institutional review. The preview focuses on the quality assurance processes in preparation for the full institutional review, which has the additional purpose of endorsing self-financing subdegree programs for placement in the Qualifications Framework, which had been proposed in 2004 and was formally launched May 2008 (see www.hkqf.gov.hk/txte/home.asp). (For more information about JQRC, see www.jqrc.edu.hk.)

CONCLUSION

Among the factors responsible for the rapid implementation of the community college associate degree program in Hong Kong are the following:

- The Federation for Continuing Education in Tertiary Institutions plays a dominant role in the community college movement. Of the 20 education institutions offering full-time accredited self-financing subdegree programs, 11 are members of the federation.

- Hong Kong's higher education has long been undersupplied both under British colonial rule and under the post-1997 Hong Kong government. Since the higher education supply was allowed to increase through a 2-year community college structure, most associate degree programs have been extensively oversubscribed.

- University community college self-accreditation has improved the status of programs. Most community colleges that provide associate degree programs are extensions of their parent universities or their continuing education institutions.

- In addition to general and liberal arts education, 2-year associate degree programs offer essential skills training in English and Chinese languages, information technology, reasoning and logics, and research methods—in high demand in the increasingly global economy.

- Associate degree graduates have transfer possibilities to complete a bachelor's degree. In contrast, 3-year higher diploma programs are more vocational and generally are terminal qualifications.

- In 1997–2004, Hong Kong suffered an economic downturn that rendered the employment prospects of school leavers dimmer than ever. The community college associate degree provided a new pathway to employment for students who otherwise could not pursue further education.

- The accreditation mechanisms for associate degree programs are rigorous. Hong Kong's accredited postsecondary programs have been recognized by universities in 10 countries or territories: Australia, Canada, mainland China, France, Macao, the Netherlands, New Zealand, Switzerland, the United Kingdom, and the United States. Furthermore, the associate degree is recognized as one of the entry requirements for appointment to 11 civil service grades in Hong Kong (iPASS, 2008).

REFERENCES

Central Intelligence Agency. (2008). *The 2008 world factbook.* Washington, DC: Author. Available from https://www.cia.gov/library/publications/the-world-factbook

Chan, M. K., & Postiglione, G. A. (Eds.). (1996). *The Hong Kong Reader: Passage to Chinese Sovereignty.* Armonk, NY: M. E. Sharpe.

Chief Executive of Hong Kong. (2000). *Chief executive's policy address 2000.* Retrieved July 29, 2008, from http://www.policyaddress.gov.hk/pa00/eindex.htm

Education Bureau. (2007). *Policy highlights: Expansion in post-secondary education opportunities.* Retrieved July 29, 2008, from http://www.edb.gov.hk/index.aspx?lang no=1&nodeid=1355

HKU SPACE, Centre for Research in Continuing Education and Lifelong Learning. (2008). *Chronicle list of events and policies related to continuing education and lifelong learning in Hong Kong.* Retrieved July 29, 2008, from http://research.hkuspace.hku. hk/eng/chronicle.html

Hong Kong SAR Government, Information Services Department. (2008a). *Labour market situation* [Hong Kong 2004 archive]. Retrieved September 7, 2008, from http://www.yearbook.gov.hk/2004/en/06_02.htm

Hong Kong SAR Government, Information Services Department. (2008b). *Labour market situation* [Hong Kong 2005 archive]. Retrieved September 7, 2008, from http://www.yearbook.gov.hk/2005/en/06_02.htm

Hong Kong SAR Government, Information Services Department. (2008c). *Overall education landscape* [Hong Kong 2003 archive]. Retrieved September 7, 2008, from http://www.yearbook.gov.hk/2003/english/chapter07/07_04.html

Information Portal for Accredited Self-financing Post-secondary Programmes (iPASS). (2008). *No. of graduates of full-time accredited self-financing post-secondary programmes, 2002-2006.* Retrieved August 10, 2008, from http://www.ipass.gov. hk/eng/stat_gd_index.aspx

Legislative Council. (2008, May 14). *LCQ3: Recognition of associate degree qualification for civil service appointment* [Press release]. Retrieved September 7, 2008, from http://www.info.gov.hk/gia/general/200805/14/P200805140139.htm

Panitchpakdi, S., & Clifford, M. L. (2002). *China and the WTO: Changing China, changing world trade.* New York: Wiley.

Postiglione, G. A., & Tang, J. T. H. (1997). *Hong Kong's reunion with China: The global dimensions.* Armonk, NY: M. E. Sharpe.

So, A., & Chan, M. K. (Eds.). (2002). *Crisis and transformation in China's Hong Kong.* New York: M. E. Sharpe.

Student Financial Assistance Agency. (2008). *Financial assistance schemes.* Retrieved July 24, 2008, from www.sfaa.gov.hk/eng/schemes/index.htm

Sutherland, S. R. (2002, March). *Higher education in Hong Kong: Report of the University Grants Committee commissioned by the secretary for education and manpower.* Wanchai, Hong Kong: University Grants Committee. Retrieved July 28, 2008, from http://www.ugc.edu.hk/eng/ugc/publication/report/her/her.htm

United Nations Development Programme. (2008). *Human development report.* New York: United Nations. Retrieved July 31, 2008, from http://hdr.undp.org/en/statistics

Institutions in Transition:
Japan's "Community Colleges"

Joyce S. Tsunoda and Yasuko Iida

Japan does not use the term *community college,* but it has three kinds of postsecondary institutions that are comparable to U.S. community colleges: junior colleges, professional training colleges, and colleges of technology. Junior colleges are 2-year colleges that offer 2- or 3-year programs in fields such as humanities, social sciences, education, home economics, which lead to associate degrees. The majority of the students in these colleges are women. The junior colleges were established in 1950 on a provisional basis, but were granted permanent status in 1964. Professional training colleges (also called specialized training colleges) accept high school graduates and those who have earned high school equivalency certification. Their programs typically last 2 or 3 years, but in certain fields, they may last 4 or more years. Japan has almost 3,000 professional training colleges. Colleges of technology enroll students directly from middle school and provide 5 years of technology training in engineering-related fields. Japan has 63 colleges of technology.

Japan's postsecondary institutions are named differently, according to the sources and manner of their funding. In addition to support from private sources, private institutions receive some funding from the central government, distributed through an agency called Promotion and Mutual Aid Corporation for Private Schools of Japan. Publicly funded institutions are classified as either *nationals*, which receive funding directly from the central government, or *publics*, which receive both national and local funding distributed by their local governments. According to the ministry of education (2003), 47.3% of high school graduates apply to universities, and 8.3% apply to junior colleges. Universities accept 41.3% of applicants, and junior colleges accept 7.7%.

Almost 23% of high school graduates enter professional training colleges; .8% enter colleges of technology.

Development of Japan's Education System

Japan's current national education system was shaped just after World War II. Two laws enacted in 1947, the Fundamental Law of Education and the School Education Law, established the 6–3–3–4 system (6 years of elementary education, 3 years of middle school, 3 years of high school, and 4 years of college) and promoted the principle of "all people's right to receive an equal education correspondent to their abilities" (Dower, 1990, p. 392). Upper secondary schools were established in 1948 and a new higher education system, referred to as the university system, was established in 1949. Existing vocational schools became part of the new university system, resulting in a national network of 18 public colleges and universities, 87 private colleges and universities, and 69 national universities. When many of the vocational schools failed to meet the academic standards of the university system, the government authorized the creation of a new category of institutions, junior colleges, as a provisional measure. In 1950, 17 public and 132 private junior colleges were launched. A 1964 amendment to the School Education Law gave junior colleges permanent status and recognized them as an official part of the higher education system. Having permanent status enabled junior colleges to receive government subsidies for programs and research.

Junior Colleges

The number of junior colleges grew rapidly in the 1960s and 1970s, as did enrollment in them. Some of the new colleges were freestanding, while others operated as 2-year institutions within universities. In 1960, 10% of high school graduates advanced to either a junior college or a university. In the 1970s, nearly 25% did. By 1980, 37.4% of high school graduates advanced. The percentage of female high school graduates who advanced increased remarkably, from 17.7% in the 1970s to 33.3% in 1980 (Association of Private Junior Colleges of Japan, 2000). Thus, junior colleges contributed to increased female participation in higher education. Attending junior colleges, dubbed "bridal preparatory schools," became socially appropriate for young girls who were expected to ultimately assume the traditional role of wife and mother.

By the late 1980s, a faltering economy combined with a downward trend in Japan's birthrate led to a decline in junior college enrollment. Other factors, too, affected junior colleges enrollment and program offerings. With increasing numbers of girls going directly from high school to 4-year institutions, the colleges gradually lost their bridal preparatory image. To combat this reduction in the number of female applicants, junior colleges began to offer more vocational programs that prepared graduates for employment in fields open to women, such as early childhood education, dietetics, nursing, and allied health. Junior colleges also expanded programs in information and management sciences, human services, and foreign language skills to meet changing employment opportunities.

Efforts to internationalize the junior college environment led to establishment of study abroad and other cooperative relationships with foreign institutions, including formal relationships with the American Association of Community Colleges and various U.S. community colleges. During the late 1980s to mid-1990s, when student exchanges and visits between U.S. community colleges and Japan's junior colleges were at their peak, there were nearly 500 junior colleges throughout Japan. Approximately 50 were public junior colleges, approximately 10 were affiliated with national universities, and the remaining were private junior colleges. Two national associations, the Japan Association of Public Junior Colleges and the Association of Private Junior Colleges of Japan, were formed in 1951 and continue to serve their memberships today.

In most cases, public junior colleges are relatively small, with fewer than 500 students, and offer specialized programs, such as in nursing or commerce. Private junior colleges tend to be larger and to offer more comprehensive programs. Both private and public junior colleges require entrance examinations, and the traditional roles of faculty in research appear to remain the valued norm. The concept of "open door" is not part of the lexicon of Japanese junior colleges.

Colleges of Technology and Professional Training Colleges

In the 1960s, a movement to include another category of institutions as part of the higher education system was well under way. These were specialized technical schools to educate and train engineers and other technologically skilled personnel for Japan's growing industrial economy. In 1962, the 5-year technical school system was launched to provide training in specialized fields including engineering construction and maritime technologies. These colleges of technology, established within nearly every prefecture, were expected to play an important part in revitalizing local communities. These accept students who complete lower secondary schools, the equivalent of intermediate or middle schools, and offer intensive programs of vocational–technical education.

By the mid-1970s, the industrial structure of Japan was transforming from heavy industry to high technology, and increasing demand for a high-technology workforce outstripped the capacities of the existing universities and colleges to produce them. Therefore, in 1975, the School Education Law of was once again amended to set and clarify standards for establishing and maintaining college-level specialized training institutions as part of the higher education system.

Under the revised legislation, professional or specialized training colleges were authorized. These are defined as colleges that provide 800 hours or more of technical education a year to high school graduates in the fields of industrial science, agriculture, medical care, health maintenance, education and social welfare, and practical business. Depending on the field, training programs at these colleges last either 2 or 3 years.

Students who have graduated from these programs since 1996 and who have completed 1,700 hours of training may be granted specialist degrees that are deemed equivalent to the associate degrees earned by junior college graduates. Beginning in April 1999, graduates of professional training colleges have been allowed to apply for admission to universities provided that two specific conditions are met: (1) their program of training is at least 2 years in length or a total of 1,700 hours longs and (2) transfer is approved by the minister of education. Also, in very limited situations, professional training colleges have been authorized to award bachelor's degrees to students who fulfill requirements specified through the National Institution for Academic Degrees and University Evaluation.

EDUCATION REFORMS IN RESPONSE TO CHANGE

Sixty years after the end of the world war that changed Japan, the country is once again facing major changes in all aspects of its national life. The people who experienced the war, Japan's defeat, and the war's aftermath are passing away. The robust economy that was built out of the ashes of war now seems to be tired and worn out. The traditionally apolitical citizenry is confronting fundamental issues such as Japan's national identity, its place in the global society, constitutional revision, and the revamping of the massive government bureaucracies. Japan's demographics pose further concerns. Currently estimated at 1.22%, Japan's fertility rate is predicted to fall below 1% by 2010 (U.S. Central Intelligence Agency, 2008). The proportion of the population that is 65 and older continues to grow, while the proportion of those 14 and under continues to decrease, prompting questions about the country's capacity to support itself in the future.

Economic changes have forced changes in traditionally valued business practices such as lifelong employment. There are also significant changes in attitudes of young people toward education and work. Even though there are greater opportunities and more options for higher education than ever before, many young people are choosing not to follow the expected rites of entering higher education and then settling into a job. "Freeters" (those who by choice are living on part-time and frequently-changing jobs) and "NEETs" (not in employment or education) confound and frustrate parents and the country as a whole.

Within this unsettling environment, educational reform is moving at a pace set by the Ministry of Education, Culture, Sports, Science, and Technology. The privatization of national universities and the strengthening of graduate education are high on the ministry's agenda. Although junior colleges are facing great pressures, their survival is not a prominent part of the national agenda.

Higher education in Japan has always been managed at the national level. Very prescriptive rules have governed the establishment of both public and private institutions of all types, as well as subsequent changes in academic programs and curricula.

Operational matters such as enrollment targets and faculty numbers and qualifications have also required the approval of the central ministry. For example, a junior college that wanted to meet local needs or increase its enrollment would have to undergo a time-consuming approval process before it could alter the scope and nature of its programs.

There are some indications that the central government is relaxing its tight hold over universities and colleges and promoting greater local responsibility. Privatization legislation implemented in July 2003 (the National University Corporation Law) delegated greater power and responsibility to the CEOs of colleges and universities and increased the numbers of outside members on university executive committees. The legislation also introduced the concepts of competition, institutional accountability, and self-improvement through third-party evaluation (accreditation) and made faculty and administrative staff members employees of the universities rather than of the government.

The higher education community views the move toward less government control with both hope and apprehension. Although educators often complain about centralized control, they seem to accept, and even depend on, this paternalism, regarding it as a kind of security blanket. Although the privatization legislation applies to universities, the principle of local autonomy and responsibility is expected to trickle down to Japan's junior colleges and publicly funded professional training colleges.

Credit for implementing the legislative provision for third-party accreditation must be given to the leaders of the Japan Private Junior College Association. Working with U.S. accreditation associations, they formulated a comprehensive system that includes institutional self-study and third-party visitations. This accreditation system was implemented in the fall of 2005.

The Tale of Three Institutions

In this section, we provide case studies of three institutions to illustrate what is happening to so-called community colleges in present-day Japan. One of the institutions capitalized and expanded on its vocational education mission, the second chose to discontinue its original identity and role as a junior college, and the third became an integral component of a consolidated mega-university system. (Quotes from professionals at these institutions came from personal interviews with them.)

The Jikei Group

In response to the increasing demand for a highly trained and solidly educated technical workforce, as was mentioned earlier, a 1975 amendment to the School Education Law formally authorized and set standards for professional training colleges, also referred to as specialized training colleges, as part of the higher education system of Japan. The Jikei Group is a thriving example of this category of colleges. The group is a private system of professional training colleges comprised of 35 separate colleges enrolling more than 25,000 students throughout Japan. It is an educational enterprise that fully capitalizes on its core mission of vocational education, and adds to it the vital elements of humanistic and global education. Its founder, chairman, and CEO, Kunihiko Ukifune, described the group as follows:

> Our Group has three basic educational policies. The first is practical education aimed at acquiring the knowledge and techniques necessary to be competitive and successful in the business world. The second is humanistic education aimed at developing our students' character so that they can have interpersonal communication skills and teamwork skills both of which are indispensable for the workplace. The third is global education aimed at raising our students' understanding and access to various values, and at the same time building their identities as Japanese. We put these policies into action in our schools. We have had active partnerships with institutions worldwide including the United States, Canada, China, Australia and some European countries with student and faculty exchanges. For example, the "Semester in Japan" program with the University of West Florida has been taking place every summer since 1991.

The Jikei Group began in 1976 with the establishment of the Shin-Osaka Dental Technician Academy, which was subsequently renamed Shin-Osaka Dental Technician College. This was rapidly followed by the opening in 1978 of two more colleges, the Osaka College of Medical Technology and the Tokyo College of Medico-Pharmaco Technology for training of paramedical technicians in the two greater metropolitan regions of eastern and western Japan. The growth and development of Jikei colleges and programs, strategically located throughout Japan, continue to this day. The following are but a few of the many program offerings: biotechnology, with specialties ranging from fermentation (for rice wine, miso, and soy sauce production) to DNA protein analysis; clinical engineering (to operate and service life-support equipment); paramedics; speech, language, and hearing therapy; acupuncture and moxibustion; animal care; animation and multimedia art; performing and broadcasting arts; and music. The most recently opened colleges in include a film school and a college of patisserie. (See the Jikei Group Web site at www.jikeigroup.net for the names and locations of all of the Jikei Group institutions.)

The Jikei Group is supported by the Jikei Company Ltd. and other associated company groups within the system whose main functions are to provide operational, technical, and service support to the colleges and to the students. For example, Jikei Space, Inc., provides management and maintenance support services for all the college buildings, including dormitories. Brain Staff Consultants is in charge of the computer systems of the entire group.

A board of directors headed by Ukifune governs the organization. The colleges are headed by executive directors who are the chief operating officers of the organization. The colleges' administrators and faculty are selected on the basis of their professional expertise and accomplishments and are given wide latitude of responsibility in the academic and training operations of the respective colleges. Ukifune is a sharp and pragmatic businessman whose credentials include an honorary doctorate in international education from the University of West Florida. When asked about the uniqueness of the Jikei Group, he replied,

> First of all, we have a cooperative system with business and industry. Students tackle tasks from real companies, and users evaluate their work. We also have another system called the "major educational system," which allows students to find out for themselves which course of study is most suitable for them. We are committed to structuring curriculum for each individual rather than having exactly the same for everyone. Each college makes an effort to let students know about the real conditions and practices in each field of specialization, while at the same time nurturing students' hopes and dreams and helping them to become professionals in their chosen fields.

> The group operates with the aim to realize the four trusts: trust from the students and their guardians, trust from the high schools, trust from the business world, and trust from the local community. We repeatedly emphasize the importance of vocation-focused education, the preparation of syllabi and curricula to suit the objectives, and collaborative work with the business world into which students will enter. In the area of design or music, for example, the given business or enterprise gives a specific theme for which the students endeavor to create a "product" such as a car design or a musical piece. The student's creation is then evaluated by the teacher and the industry. Individualized counseling is provided for each student to acquire skills necessary on the work site. In a selected area, the curriculum is customized for each student. At the same time, we provide humanistic education that is indispensable to work as specialists in the business world.

Where government certification is a requisite for employment, all possible efforts are made to achieve 100% success rate in licensure examinations. A career center assists students in fully applying what they have learned in their work environment. The group is highly valued by employers, and all students find jobs in their desired fields. An investment in state-of-the-art facilities and equipment, as well as continuous programs of professional development for faculty and staff, form the cornerstones of the Jikei Group.

The quality of the teaching is reexamined and improved through the support of the Jikei Education Science Center.

When asked what type of education is required to survive in the 21st century, Ukifune responded,

> English education and information technology education. The ability to use both English and information technology as communication tools is becoming indispensable. These skills are being incorporated into our curricula. Students are encouraged and supported in planning and arranging for study and internships abroad.

On plans for the future, he said,

> The higher education system is undergoing reforms toward diversification of certification. Graduates of professional colleges can now receive "senmonn shi," equivalent to associate degrees, and "koutou senmon shi," equivalent to a baccalaureate. Master's programs are to be opened to graduates of professional colleges. Regulations are being relaxed for establishing professional training colleges. Therefore, courses of study will be widely available to meet all levels of personnel that the business world needs. Night schools will be simultaneously opened, and e-learning and distance education will be widely available. Types of students are now varied and include the traditional students directly from high-schools, college or university graduates, and many foreign students.

Maintaining and building on its relevancy and responsiveness, the future for proactively positioned professional training colleges looks bright indeed.

Hakuoh University Women's Junior College

Hakuoh University and Hakuoh Women's Junior College is a private institution located in the city of Oyama in the prefecture of Tochigi, which lies north of Tokyo and may be considered the entrance to the Tohoku (northeastern) provinces of Japan. The northeastern provinces still remain largely rural and relatively unsophisticated in many ways. However, the charm of "old Japan," where human relationships matter and family values still influence the young, can still be found even among the freeways, gas stops, and ubiquitous shopping malls and convenience stores. The world famous Nikko region with its historical shrines dedicated to Tokugawa Ieyasu, founder of the Tokugawa Shogunate that ruled Japan for 250 years until the arrival of Perry's Black Ships, is located in the picturesque mountains of Tochigi. Expanded bullet train services from Tokyo Station to the Tohoku region can reach Oyama City in less than half an hour. At Oyama Station, passengers can see in the skyline the towering building of Hakuoh University's east campus, which houses its newly opened Graduate School of Law.

Hakuoh University's roots are in the historical Ashikaga City, which thrived as a feudal strongpoint during the Muromachi Period of Japan (14th century). Hakuoh University began as the Ashikaga Textile Women's School in 1915, which was incorporated into a high school in 1927, bringing needed educational opportunities to the rural region. The Hakuoh Educational Foundation was incorporated in 1951, followed by the establishment of the junior high school in 1961 and the Women's Junior College in 1974.

The founder, the late Kazuyoshi Kamioka, a lifelong educator, wanted to make a difference for ordinary students through higher education. An idealist inspired by the spirit of Jonathan Livingston Seagull, he chose the words *plus ultra* (more beyond) as the motto of his educational institution. The name *Hakuoh* means white seagull. Kamioka's dream was to open an institution that effectively bridged the gap between theoretical and practical education and to enable students to acquire skills for working and living in an increasingly global and technological society. He was particularly interested in Eigo-ka, English teaching and learning, and wanted to strengthen the skills of Japanese teachers who taught English in local schools.

When Hakuoh Women's Junior College opened its doors in 1974, it was authorized by the national ministry of education to enroll 100 students in early childhood education to become teachers for preschools and kindergartens, 50 students in Eigo-ka for preparation as English teachers in the middle schools of the region, and 100 students in business communication and clerical skills. All of these fields enabled local young women to prepare for employment. But that was not all. Along with the practical skills, students were given opportunities to enroll in arts and cultural studies, with a special focus on music, including the rare handbell orchestra that has won several national and international awards.

In 1986, an application was submitted to the ministry of education to add a 4-year university to its enterprise in order to offer fields of study that could not be authorized under the junior college structure. When the application was finally approved in 1991, the Faculty of Business Management was established, followed by the Faculty of Law, and in 1999, graduate programs were added in both business management and law.

The institution officially became Hakouh University and Junior College. With 4,000 plus students coming from the wider Kanto-Tohoku (northeastern) region, Hakuoh University is a major contributor to the economic base of Oyama City and the neighboring localities of southern Tochigi prefecture. The college was truly a community's college in the fullest sense of the term.

Given its historical roots and remaining true to the founder's vision, the decision to discontinue the separate function and identity of the Hakuoh Junior College was not an easy one to make. This decision in 2003 was an inevitable one, necessitated by the pressure to remain competitive in the highly volatile and competitive educational market. As mentioned elsewhere in this chapter, the decline in college-age population, as well as the changing ambitions of young women, made the operation of a traditional junior college economically untenable, especially for a private college located in a relatively rural region.

Other factors contributed to the demise of this junior college. One was the nationally centralized educational policies that prescribed and limited program offerings at the junior colleges. The other factor was the lack of articulated academic transfer pathway for graduates of junior colleges to enter the universities. For Hakuoh Junior College students in the 2-year education program for preschool and kindergarten teachers, a natural and often desirable career option was to be certified to teach at the elementary school level. Such certification, however, could only be obtained through a 4-year university program. But there was no articulated transfer pathway into a university for these students. Likewise, the expansion of a successful program for training English teachers for middle schools to also train high school English teachers was not permitted under the centralized policy that limited high school teacher training to a 4-year university.

Articulation with universities and credit transfer remain a major challenge for Japan's junior colleges and contribute to the continuing decline in junior college enrollment. While there have been successful attempts at systematic credit transfer, such as that at the University Consortium Kyoto, which involved public and private universities and junior colleges largely in Kyoto, which is known as a university town, such efforts appear not yet to be common in other parts of Japan.

Given such circumstances, there was very little option for the leaders of Hakuoh other than to take the step to absorb the existing junior college programs under the university umbrella. This decision resulted in the creation of a new 4-year program of educational development that incorporated the junior college's early childhood education program and the move of the junior college's business education into the university's business management program as a subprogram. In spring 2006, Hakuoh Junior College graduated its last class, and the name "Hakuoh Junior College" became history.

Tokyo Metropolitan University

As of April 2005, there was no public junior college in Tokyo. In order to understand this situation, a look at the history of the publicly funded higher education in metropolitan Tokyo is necessary. The Tokyo metropolitan government funds the operations of publicly funded higher educational institutions, excluding the national universities and colleges that are funded directly by the national government.

When the recent national university reform movements began, the Tokyo metropolitan government also decided to proceed with its own efforts to consolidate and streamline the operations of the various colleges and universities directly under its jurisdiction. Therefore, in April 2005, after several years of discussions and arguments, a single unified university corporation was forged out of the merging of three metropolitan universities and one metropolitan junior college.

This unified metropolitan university is named Tokyo Metropolitan University (Shuto-Daigaku Tokyo) and is under the jurisdiction of a public university corporation. This mega-university claims all of Tokyo as its university campus and promotes collaboration among not only its member institutions but also with all other educational institutions within Tokyo as well as industries and government. Efforts toward academic articulation are being made with the introduction of the credit bank system. Administrative functions such as personnel management are being streamlined.

It is important to note that each of the four metropolitan institutions that were consolidated can look back with pride to their respective histories as productive professional training schools or junior colleges in the late 1940s and 1950s. These four institutions were

- Tokyo Metropolitan University, by far the largest university in the Tokyo metropolitan system, formed in 1949 out of the merger of six professional training school precursors.

- Tokyo Metropolitan University of Technology, established in 1986, originally as a college of technology providing critical technical training in engineering and industrial technology, including aeronautics, during the hearty economic growth periods of the 1950s and 1960s.

- Tokyo Metropolitan University of Health Sciences, which was originally the Tokyo Metropolitan College of Allied Medical Sciences, a 3-year junior college, which became a baccalaureate-granting university in 1998. We focus on this particular junior college later in this section.

- Tokyo Metropolitan Junior College, the last metropolitan junior college remaining in Tokyo prior to April 2005, was originally two separate junior colleges that were merged in 1996.

The rise and fall of the metropolitan junior colleges in Tokyo may be a sign of the changing times. The first junior colleges in Tokyo, the Tokyo Metropolitan College of Commerce and the Tokyo Metropolitan College of Technology, were among oldest of the public junior college in Japan. These two junior colleges founded in 1954 offered day and night courses for Tokyo's working students who eagerly sought education, training, and retraining during Japan's economic growth period of the 1950s through the1970s. Yet, today, these junior colleges have disappeared into the mega-university system.

On the other hand, it is also a reflection of changing Japanese society that enabled the Tokyo Metropolitan College of Allied Medical Sciences to keep its basic mission essentially intact as it transformed from a junior college into a 4-year university, and subsequently integrated into the consolidated mega-university system as the Faculty of Health Sciences. As an important component of the newly unified Tokyo Metropolitan

University, the Faculty of Health Sciences currently offers four schools of study: nursing, physical therapy, occupational therapy, and radiological technology. Located at the center of the greater Tokyo metropolitan area with more than 12 million residents, the former junior college continues to provide relevant education and training opportunities for nearly 900 students. Masahiro Shigeta, the current dean, proudly stated, "We intend through education and research to prepare students to be excellent health professionals to serve the metropolitan residents to fulfill longevity in good health and sense of well-being and fulfillment."

Reflecting on the history of the College of Allied Medical Sciences, one cannot avoid seeing the intertwining threads of political ambitions and economic realities. Nursing education in Japan languished for a long period as vocational training for women with relatively lower-level academic backgrounds. But as the society's needs for highly competent "co-medical" professionals with strong scientific background, reasoning skills, and leadership potential became apparent, political attention began to shift in this direction.

Thus, in the early 1970s, an ambitious proposal for a Tokyo Health Sciences University as the most advanced education and research center in nursing and rehabilitation in Japan was raised by the metropolitan political leadership. But as political leadership changed, so did the plans, and a more realistic plan of establishing a junior college was put into place. Thus the 3-year junior college was established in 1986, offering programs in four allied health areas and nursing, with a total enrollment of 600 students. This junior college replaced three metropolitan vocational schools that had been offering programs in nursing, rehabilitation, and radiological technology. The 3-year junior college was subsequently authorized to offer 1-year advanced courses in midwifery and in public health nursing, thus setting the stage for the transformation into a 4-year institution in 1998, under a different Tokyo metropolitan administration.

The ultimate unification of all of the Tokyo metropolitan colleges and universities, as mentioned earlier, took place under the current administration guided by the strong hands of Governor Shintaro Ishihara. The total unification plan was not met with unanimous support of the personnel of the affected colleges and universities. Nevertheless, the consolidation became a reality in April 2005. While it is still too early to tell, there are hopeful signs that the new directions may be infusing new energy and boosting the far-flung Tokyo metropolitan higher educational community with a sense of renewal and revitalization. As Dean Shigeta said,

> The mission of the new unified university is to seek the ideal image of human society within the greater metropolis environment. The education and research are to proceed on the basis of promoting the key principles of metropolitan environment improvement, enhancing academic quality within a dynamic industrial society, and to realize the potential of an energetic society of people with longevity.

That, indeed, is a noble ambition, made possible by the achievement of the unsung heroes, the metropolitan junior colleges and professional schools that led the way.

CONCLUSION

The "community colleges" of Japan as identified in this chapter are the junior colleges, the professional or specialized training colleges, and colleges of technology. Each category of institution has its assigned role and place within the educational hierarchy. Each was established and developed under the carefully laid-out rules and guidelines of the central government ministry. And each will most likely live or die as separate and discrete entities. That seems to be the Japanese way.

Among these institutions, the junior colleges appear to be most susceptible to the winds of change that blow around them. The case studies of two junior colleges, one private and the other public, may typify the fate of other Japanese junior colleges. There are unofficial speculations that within the next 5 years, possibly 20 or so junior colleges may close their doors. There appears to be no public outcry or campaign to stop this direction. Instead, the potential junior college students are heading for the 4-year institutions that have become more open with admission. Others students are attracted to the pragmatic vocational institutions represented in this chapter by the Jikei Group.

In Japan, the concept of "education as a business" does not raise eyebrows as much as it does in the United States. The nonprofit and for profit line in Japanese education appears blurred. Many colleges and universities, not just the more recently established professional training colleges, have been started by business-minded founders with the blessing of the government ministry. While higher education is valued in Japan, issues such as access, diversity, and equity do not yet appear to be burning issues on the public agenda. Current top issues in higher education appear to be national university governance, graduate school reforms, and something referred to in the government literature as "enhancements to undergraduate education."

A careful reading of the *FY 2003 White Paper on Education, Culture, Sports, Science and Technology* unveiled the following statement:

> ...under the new framework to guarantee quality and more competitive environment, each higher education institution is to develop its own future vision ... in taking the view that society as a whole benefits from higher education, it is necessary to strengthen cooperation with society greatly with respect to both education and research. When doing so, it is necessary to reconsider the respective positioning of universities, graduate schools, junior colleges, colleges of technology and professional training colleges, while taking into account wide-ranging educational opportunities after secondary education. It has been suggested that the essential social missions and development directions of each of these

types of higher education have become unclear. (Ministry of Education, Culture, Sports, Science and Technology, 2003, chap. 3, sect. 1)

This statement could indeed serve as the *michi shirube* or "guideposts" for the Japanese higher education community to be used in develop its own future. It seems to be saying: "Take responsibility to plan and develop your own future. And, in so doing, look at the whole forest, instead of the individual trees."

REFERENCES

Association of Private Junior Colleges of Japan. (2000, October 25). *Nippon Shiritsu Tanki Daigaku 50-nen shi [The Association of Private Junior Colleges of Japan, 50th anniversary]*. Tokyo: Author.

Dower, J. W. (1990). *Embracing defeat: Japan in the wake of World War II*. New York: Norton.

Ministry of Education, Culture, Sports, Science and Technology (MEXT). (2003). *FY 2003 white paper on education, culture, sports, science and technology: Higher education to support a knowledge-based society full of creative vitality. New developments in higher education reform*. Tokyo: Author.

U.S. Central Intelligence Agency. (2008). *The 2008 world factbook*. Washington, DC: Author. Available from the CIA Web site: https://www.cia.gov/library/publications/the-world-factbook

10

The Community College System of Thailand

Allen Cissell and Tanom Inkhamnert

Thailand's community college system, which began with 10 colleges in 2002, is by any measure a success. Just 3½ years after they opened, the colleges awarded associate degrees to 1,736 students. By 2008, the system has expanded to 19 colleges that enroll more than 16,000 regular associate degree students and 35,000 part-time students. Its annual budget has increased from 50 million baht (USD 1.25 million) in 2003 to 441 million baht in 2008, an amazing increase in 5 years (S. Songthong, personal communication, July 2008). Because the colleges were deliberately located in rural areas, they have brought higher education to many who never had access to it before. And, in a true departure from Thailand's tradition of central ministry control, the colleges are promoting local control and governance. For these reasons and more, the community colleges are popular and a source of pride in the communities where they are located. In only a few years, they have made truly impressive gains for Thailand's 61 million people.

HISTORY

Establishing a community college system in Thailand was first considered in the early 1970s. Beginning in 1961, the Thai government has followed a series of 5-year national economic and social development plans. The third of these plans, for 1972–1977 (National Economic and Social Development Board [NESDB, 1973]), recommended the creation of community colleges, and preliminary plans were made to establish a community college in Phuket province, in the south of Thailand. Unfortunately, nothing was done beyond the preliminary planning.

The fourth economic and social development plan, for 1977–1981 (NESDB, 1977), strongly urged a policy that would "lay the groundwork for setting up community colleges in various regions in accordance with economic and social needs." During that period, Prince of Songkla University in Phuket created a community college, but several factors led to a lack of support for this experiment, among them that there was no articulation agreement between the college and the university, and no provision for transferring credits. As support waned, the community college was phased out.

Another experiment in community college development took place in 1982–1986. The government concluded that Thailand was producing too many teachers and proposed converting four teacher's colleges to community colleges. Before the conversion could begin, however, the decision was reversed by the Thai parliament. Although no community colleges were created, the teacher's colleges were for the first time allowed to offer curricula beyond teacher training.

Under the sixth economic and social development plan for 1987–1991(NESDB, 1987), some specialized colleges that taught single subjects, including physical education, drama, art, and agriculture, were called community colleges, but by traditional criteria, they were not community colleges at all. They offered only single subjects, were controlled by the central government, and had very limited enrollment. Few jobs were available for those who did graduate. Many of these schools eventually closed because of low enrollment.

Throughout the years from 1972 to 2000, when Thailand saw numerous ups and downs in community college development, foresighted Thai educators, many of whom had been educated in the United States, kept alive the idea that community colleges would benefit the country. The U.S. government also promoted the idea of community colleges in Thailand. In 1994, the U.S. Agency for International Development (USAID) proposed to establish a U.S.–style community college in each of Thailand's four regions. However, before this idea could be implemented, the United States declared Thailand to be a fully developed country and withdrew USAID funding for this and other developmental activities.

The 1997–1998 crash of Southeast Asia's economy convinced many in Thailand that the country was falling behind its global competitors in human resource development, that its growing population did not have access to meaningful higher education, and that its economy would continue to falter unless its workforce was better educated. These convictions gave new momentum to Thailand's community college movement. One result was the passage of the 1999 National Education Act. This legislation obligated the government to provide 9 years of compulsory education (it had been 6), with an additional 3 years available free to those who wanted it, for a total of 12 years of free education. With greater access to primary and secondary education, it was projected, the number of high school graduates from 2000 to 2006 would increase to 800,000 a year, or by 50%. In 2000, only 25% of high school graduates were enrolled as first-year students in public or private colleges and universities, but this number was projected to increase, making it clear that Thailand would need to improve access to higher education.

In a February 2001 speech to the national assembly, the new prime minister promoted community colleges as a way to bring higher education to the rural areas, offer lifelong learning to all, and educate those who had previously missed their chance for higher education. He announced that community colleges would be founded in provinces where higher education had not been available. Within a short time, an office of community college administration was created within the ministry of education. The minister and deputy minister of education and two others became responsible for creating community colleges in Thailand. All four of these key administrators had earned advanced degrees in the United States, where they had become familiar with the concept of the comprehensive community college.

Three key sources—the Institute for International Education (IIE), the Kenan Foundation in Asia, and the U.S. embassy in Thailand—encouraged Thailand's community college development by providing advice, consultants, and minor funding. These three, along with the Thai ministry of education, the U.S. Department of Education, a private donor, and the community colleges of Hawaii, funded a March 2001 conference on community college development, held at the East-West Center in Hawaii. During the 3-day conference, Thai community college leaders met with representatives of U.S. community colleges, IIE, and other organizations. The meetings focused on community college philosophy, organizational issues, workforce development activities, governance, and management issues. Participants also visited Hawaii's community colleges. At the end of the conference, participants created an informal group, named the East–West Community College Partnership, to work on the development of Thai community colleges.

Since its formation, the partnership has received funding from the U.S. Department of State, USAID, and other sources outside Thailand, as well as from the Thai government and the Kenan Foundation in Asia. To support the creation of Thailand's community college system, the partnership has worked with individual college directors, trained teachers and trustees, and provided curriculum needs analysis. The ministry of education has also sent delegations of Thai educators to the United States to visit community colleges, observe college programs, and receive training.

Start-Up

In 2002, just 15 months after the office of community college administration was created, 10 community colleges opened in rural Thailand. Each offered four kinds of programs:

- Remedial programs, to prepare both students and adult learners with the skills needed to enter other programs.

- Short-term intensive programs (similar to continuing education or adult education courses in the United States) in languages (Cambodian, to support border trade, and English, to support tourism), community health, agriculture (recovery of deforested land), winemaking, and other subjects.

- Vocational programs for those already in careers, such as photography, electronics, and Thai classical music and dance.

- Associate degree programs in early childhood development, auto mechanics, accounting, tourism, agriculture, electricity technology, community development, and other areas.

The 10 community colleges opened with borrowed faculty and in borrowed facilities, including secondary schools, temples, government offices, vocational schools, and community centers. Tuition was (and still is) low, equivalent to about USD .15 per hour for short courses and USD .75 per credit hour for a full class.

CURRENT PROGRAMS, STAFFNG, AND GOVERNANCE

Each of Thailand's community colleges is allocated 16 tenured faculty positions and 4 nontenured positions. Nontenured faculty members are on 5-year contracts, with a review at the end of each year. Full-time salaries are low, rarely exceeding USD 150 per month.

Each college is governed by an unpaid 19-member board of trustees that represents the interests and needs of the community. Some of the trustees are ex-officio; these might include a representative from the local chamber of commerce, one from a university, and a provincial government administrator. Others are selected by a search committee of the director and the ex-officio members. Community members apply to serve on the board and are approved or rejected by the search committee.

Today, the short-term intensive courses include computer use for small businesses, jewelry making, local tourism, batik and silk production, and other programs of local interest. The colleges are developing new associate degree programs in emergency medical services, pharmacy technology, gerontology, and teacher improvement and development.

Notable Programs

Each of the Thai community colleges has unique characteristics and programs. Two programs are of particular note. The director of Pijit Community College wanted to introduce computers and the Internet to truly rural areas where they had not been available at all. To create a mobile computer lab, the college's automotive staff rebuilt the engine and body of an old school bus, outfitting the interior with enough work stations so that at least 10 people can work at one time. The bus is driven to the many small villages and towns in the region, where residents can learn about computers and the Internet. In addition to being a valuable instructional tool in itself, this mobile computer lab has become a significant way to recruit students for the college's other off-campus programs.

Sakow Community College created a program to serve the needs of the organic food market, with asparagus as the chosen food. The college and private growers formed a cooperative that sells asparagus exclusively to Japan. This kind of partnership is rare in the rural areas where the Thai community colleges are located. It provides a good model for other colleges and businesses to follow.

CURRENT CHALLENGES

Thailand's community colleges continue to face a number of start-up difficulties, including the lack of dedicated facilities, high turnover among college leaders, lack of strong support from industry, and government bureaucracy. Classes are still taught in borrowed facilities, and the government officials who are in charge of community college funding are strongly opposed to allocating funds for the colleges to construct or acquire their own buildings. Despite this opposition, the colleges' growth and popularity, combined with local pride and a need for identity, make it likely that they will eventually have their own buildings and campuses, perhaps as a result of merging with vocational colleges.

Almost all of the first 10 community colleges had more than one director in their first 4 years, and staff turnover has been high. Leadership of community college development at the ministry of education has remained relatively constant, but at the individual colleges, personnel changes have been a significant distraction from developing the colleges and their curricula.

Thailand's community colleges are in rural areas, away from the country's economic growth centers. As a result, they do not have a strong industry base to work from, or many businesses available to partner with. This lack inevitably limits the programs that the colleges offer, and therefore the extent to which they can train students for jobs in the country's growing economy.

Perhaps the biggest obstacle to community college development is Thailand's long history of centralization and bureaucracy. In a study of the Thai government and economy, business guru Michael Porter noted that Thailand is "world class in bureaucracy and fragmentation of business associations, which do not talk to one another" (Sasin News, 2003). Thailand's bureaucracy seems to have considerably slowed the initial plans to rapidly expand the community college system and to develop its curricula in innovative and creative ways.

CONCLUSION: LOOKING TOWARD THE FUTURE

These problems aside, Thailand's community colleges have continued to grow, and the long-term outlook is positive. By 2008, the system had 19 colleges, all in rural areas. Significant progress has been made in teacher development and in developing curricula to meet local and national needs. There are plans to create a community college in Bangkok, with 10 locations, and the government's long-term goal is to have one community college in each of the country's 72 subprovincial areas.

The Thai legislature and the ministry of education have drafted and debated new legislation that it is hoped will settle questions of community college control, budgets, and articulation and credit transfer. If the community colleges are able to become independent of central government control, develop and retain creative and innovative leaders at the individual colleges, and create solid credit-transfer agreements with other colleges and universities, they will realize the design originally envisioned for them and make a huge contribution to Thailand's continuing development. The clear successes that the colleges have had thus far speak well for such future achievement.

REFERENCES

National Economic and Social Development Board. (1973). *Third national economic and social development plan, 1972–1976.* Bangkok, Thailand: Author. Retrieved May 1, 2008, from http://www.unescap.org/esid/psis/population/database/poplaws/law_thai/th_018.htm

National Economic and Social Development Board. (1977). *Fourth national economic and social development plan, 1977–1981.* Bangkok, Thailand: Author.

National Economic and Social Development Board. (1987). *Sixth national economic and social development plan, 1987–1991.* Bangkok, Thailand: Author.

Sasin News. (2003, May 5). *The Ireland of Asia: It's now or never.* Bangkok, Thailand: Chulalongkorn University. Retrieved May 1, 2008 from www.sasin.edu/news/article/121

11

The Vocational and Technical Schools of Higher Education in Turkey

Ahmet Aypay

Turkey's higher education system consists of 4-year universities and 2-year Vocational Schools of Higher Education (VSHE). The majority of VSHEs operate within university structures. A national council of higher education (CHE in English or YÖK in Turkish) oversees the entire higher education system. As of 2007, Turkey had 628 VSHEs, 599 of which have been associated with public universities, 24 with foundation universities, and 5 with independent foundations. These schools enrolled a total of 614,586 students—384,456 in technical, business and economics, and health and marine programs, and 213,130 in open education associate degree programs. VSHE students constituted 28.4% of Turkey's higher education students, close to the 30% average for industrialized countries (YÖK, 2005a, 2007). A few VSHEs offer programs based on academic disciplines, while most programs are based on interdisciplinary studies and general education (such as behavioral sciences, human sciences, and social and natural sciences). Some VSHEs are limited to one specific program area, such as health, technical sciences, social sciences, divinity, or judicial services.

HISTORY

Turkey's VSHEs can be traced to 1911, when the ministry of public works opened a vocational school to train civil servants in applied sciences. After an engineering department was added, the school became known as a technician school, and its administration was transferred to the ministry of education (Kavak, 1992). By 1969, Turkey had 23 two-year technician schools. These schools were housed in vocational high schools, which had convenient facilities and workshops. In order to improve the quality of their students, the schools began to require that graduates of vocational high school–level craft and construction programs take an entrance exam (Kavak, 1992).

In 1952, to meet the country's industrialization goals, the technician school system was expanded. Three-year technician schools were established to serve people who worked full time (Baskan, 1999). In 1965, two schools of another type were created, one in Istanbul and one in Ankara. Both operated in the buildings of vocational and technical high schools. These were higher-level schools that provided 3 years of training and were intended to help students transfer to 4-year institutions. Both were later closed (Karasar, 1981), for reasons including a lack of their own buildings and a lack of transfer opportunities (Karhan, 1983).

By 1972, Turkey had established 6 higher technician schools in addition to 23 technician schools (Kavak, 1992). While university 2-year schools might have been more concerned with transfer, transfer was not a goal for both the university and the ministry schools, because they aimed to establish closer links with industry. However, the ministry 2-year schools were less successful in achieving their goals (Karhan, 1983). With the demand for higher education increasing rapidly, universities began to establish their own 2-year vocational schools in the mid-1970s. In a parallel development, the ministry of education established 24 two-year schools. The goal was to train people in the skills that the economy needed. Law 1750, which was enacted in 1973, established many goals for the 2-year schools:

- Improve the academic skills of students who were not properly prepared to go to 4-year institutions.
- Prepare students for a vocation.
- Educate students who left 4-year programs after the freshman year because their academic achievement was low.
- Train students for the workforce.
- Improve the quality of undergraduate education by making the 2-year colleges a step for mass education (see Ataünal, 1998; Aypay, 2003; Kaya, 1984).

The universities' 2-year schools were full-time, formal education programs. In the ministry's schools, the first year was taught through distance education and the second year was taught through classroom attendance. The programs, which included technical subjects, social sciences, and life sciences, were directed toward preparing people for midlevel jobs, not for transfer to 4-year institutions. However, by about 1979, many graduates were unable to find employment, so enrollment dropped. The 2-year schools, both university and ministry, stopped admitting students in 1979 (Nazik, 2003).

Signifcant Decisions in Higher Education

In 1971, one of Turkey's state universities sued private colleges, arguing that they were a threat to equality of education opportunity. The supreme court ordered that 41 four-year private colleges be shut down. With Law 1472, the government made these private colleges public and annexed them to existing state universities in the 1971–1972 academic year.

In 1973, Law 1750 introduced reforms to the university system and led to the creation of a higher education council. Higher Education Law 2547, passed in 1981, led to a systems approach for the creation of new universities. A nationwide student selection and placement office was created in order to administer merit-based selection exams for university admission.

Before 1981, the majority of VSHEs were under the ministry of education, and the rest were either part of university systems or under other ministries. Under Higher Education Law 2547, all public 2-year colleges were annexed to universities (Kavak, 1992). Recently, however, private foundations have been able to create independent 2-year colleges without first establishing a university. The legislation offered new definitions for 2-year colleges, their degree programs, and their administration. A 2-year college is "a higher education institution that emphasizes teacher-training of a certain vocation" and "an institution with four semesters to train mid-level manpower in certain vocations." An associate degree program is "based on secondary education that lasts at least for four semesters and aims at training mid-level workforce in the first phase of higher education." The law defined the director, the 2-year college board, and an administrative board as the administrative units of 2-year colleges (YÖK, 2004). The last expansion of the higher education system was in 1992, when 23 state universities and institutes of technology were established.

Access to Higher Education

Turkey has historically had two types of high schools: general, which offer an academic education, and vocational and technical. After graduating from high school, a student who passed an entrance exam could enroll in either a 4-year university program or a 2-year VSHE program. In 1999, the council of higher education changed the requirements for access to higher education. The intent was to prevent students who had graduated from religious vocational high schools from entering 4-year higher education programs. But the Turkish constitution mandates equality before the law, so the council could not legally single out graduates of religious schools. Instead, it instituted two ways of channeling all vocational high school graduates away from 4-year programs.

First, it instituted a nationwide competitive exam that graduates of all high schools, academic or vocational, must pass in order to be admitted to a 4-year program. Then it established an open-door policy under which vocational high school graduates can enroll in VSHEs without taking an examination. Admission is based on high school grade point average. The better the GPA, the higher the quality of the VSHE a student will be admitted to (Aypay, 2003). Graduates of academic highs schools are still required to pass a national selection exam in order to be admitted to a VSHE.

With fewer students being admitted to 4-year programs, the demand for VSHEs increased. To keep up with demand, VSHEs had to borrow resources, physical facilities, equipment, and teaching personnel from existing vocational high schools. This solution had some problems. VSHE students did not like finding themselves in their old high school buildings, sometimes taught by their former high school teachers. Faculty members and administrators at VSHEs complained that the open-door policy lowered the quality of their students. Fewer graduates of general academic high schools chose VSHEs, so the balance between vocational high school graduates and academic high school graduates changed. In 2005, about 70% of VSHE students were graduates of vocational high schools (YÖK, 2005b).

Faced with complaints from students and educators, the government made a public promise to return to the old system of access to 4-year higher education, with all high school graduates competing equally by taking an entrance exam. Although it has had support from VHSEs and vocational and technical high schools, the government's attempts to restore examination-based access have thus far been unsuccessful.

Program Types

Open education (distance education) has been a growing trend in 2-year postsecondary schools of higher education recently. The interest in open education has traditionally been for 4-year institutions. Currently, there is growth in associate degree programs as well: 213,130 students enrolled in open education programs in the 2004–2005 academic year (YÖK, 2005a).

Anadolu University's open education faculty offers associate degree programs in a wide variety of fields, including banking and insurance, online information systems, office management and secretarial training, international trade, home economics, public relations, divinity, veterinary services, sales, health institution administration, social sciences, agriculture, hotel and tourism, and local government administration. Programs that prepare students to teach the English language or preschool lead to transfer to 4-year schools. The university's open education faculty also offers special in-service training and associated degree programs to the army, the police, and other institutions (for more information, see the university's Web site at www.anadolu.edu.tr).

As of 2003, Turkey had only two Internet-based VSHEs, run by Mersin University and Sakarya University. Demand for distance education programs is expected to grow, and Internet-based VSHEs need attention (YÖK, 2005a).

Motivating Factors for Development

As has been the case around the world, the establishment of VSHEs in Turkey is closely related to industrialization and the need to train a workforce with mid-level skills. The programmatic functions of these 2-year colleges have been transfer to 4-year institutions, vocational and technical education, adult education, and service to society.

VSHE graduates who want to transfer to a 4-year institution face a number of hurdles. First, they must pass a student selection examination administered by the Student Selection and Placement Center. However, universities are not legally required to enroll specific numbers of VSHE graduates, so not all who pass the exam are given a university place. In many cases, less than 10% of a university's students are VSHE graduates. VSHE graduates who do get admitted to universities are required to take an additional year of course work before beginning the standard 4-year program. Moreover, VSHE graduates claim that they have not been warmly welcomed at some universities. The number of programs offered by VSHEs expanded greatly since 1992. In 2002, the total number of programs was 230. Of those, 139 of were technical, 52 were in business and economics, 24 in health, and 15 programs in open education (Aypay, 2003; ÖSYM, 2002).

Adult Education, Continuing Education, and Workforce Training

Partly as a result of the open access policy that has been in effect since 2001, adult education is an increasingly important function of Turkey's VSHEs. In some other countries, 2-year vocational and technical schools can be classified as multipurpose colleges. In Turkey, they are typically either specialized colleges or binary program colleges. VSHEs train students who do not have a strong academic background, including graduates of vocational high schools. They offer associate degree programs in technical fields, business and economics, health sciences, social services, and marine sciences (Kavak, 1992).

As Cohen and Brawer (1996) stated, various economic, social, and political factors influenced the establishment of 2-year vocational school systems around the world, while economic reasons were the main driver for the expansion of these systems. In Turkey, which began following an export-oriented economic growth model in 1980, increased need for midlevel skilled technicians became the most important reason for expanding the VSHE system. Increased demand for higher education, equality of education opportunity, and mass education, as well as a change in society's view that longer periods of education are necessary, were other contributing factors (Baskan, 1999; Kavak, 1992).

Access was one of the motivating factors, but it was not emphasized. The Higher Education Law 1750 in 1973 allowed greater opportunities to transfer to 4-year institutions. However, Higher Education Law 2547, in effect since 1982, restricted that transfer function. This law increased the authority and control of the council of higher education to manage the planning function and coordination of the higher education system. The council has played a dominant role in higher education, and its approach to universities has drawn criticism from some academics (Aypay, 2003).

The Future of and Challenges for VSHEs

VSHEs have a big part in plans to expand Turkey's higher education system and the country's economic and technological competitiveness. According to the council of higher education's key policy documents, "the natural growth in the Turkish Higher Education System will be in 2-year Vocational and Technical Schools" and "In order to train the necessary manpower the economy needs, VSHEs will be emphasized" (Devlet Planlama Teşkilatı [DPT], 1999). The council of higher education would like to increase enrollment in VSHEs to 30% of all students enrolled in college, which is the average in the industrialized world. As of 2005, VSHE enrollment reached 30% of all students enrolled in college (YÖK, 2005a, 2007).

Turkey has three types of VSHEs. Those in the first group, which are considered top-tier schools, have their own physical facilities, are well equipped, and have adequate numbers of high-quality faculty members. In the past, 31 of these institutions have been supported through World Bank projects, with 969 of their faculty members being sent abroad for training. The second group, which consists of approximately 60 VSHEs, is close in quality to the first group. With a little assistance, they could join the top tier.

The third group of VSHEs requires massive development and new funding. They are usually located in small, remote areas and have very low enrollment. Their main problems are poor-quality physical facilities, inadequate numbers of faculty members, low faculty quality, and low-quality programs. The curricula of many programs need to be revised and improved. Other persistent problems are lack of financing; administrative issues; and inadequate articulation among vocational and technical high schools, VSHEs, and universities.

A survey of 40 VSHEs showed that 72% did not have their own physical facilities. When asked whether their tools and equipment were sufficient, only 10% said they were; 45% said partly sufficient; and 20% said insufficient. Asked whether they had enough faculty members, 15% said that they did; 38% said partly sufficient, and 23% said insufficient (Aypay, 2003).

Problems Associated With Open Access

Enrollment in 2-year colleges has increased from 70,801 in 1991 to 400,000 in 2005 (YÖK, 2007). Reasons for this increase include a growing population, an increase in the number of years of compulsory basic education, and the demand from local authorities and political parties that 2-year colleges be established in their hometowns.

Turkey's goal is to bring its statistics for VSHE enrollment and faculty numbers in line with those of the industrialized world. In 2005, Turkey's 2-year colleges had approximately 7,000 full-time instructors, a ratio of 1 instructor to 59 students (YÖK, 2007). In the same year, the worldwide faculty-to-student ratio was 1 to 12 (OECD, 1997). Since the implementation of the law of 4702, almost all VSHE students come from the vocational and technical high schools (MEB & YÖK, 2002).

According to a 2002 study (ÖSYM, 2002), based on 286,000 student responses, it was concluded that VSHEs serve Turkish students of lower socioeconomic status. Among the findings were that 90% of VSHE students' mothers had a high school or lower level of education and that only 4% of the students' fathers had university degrees. Almost 80% of the students reported a mean household annual income below USD 400. VSHE students reported different reasons for attending a 2-year college. Eighty percent enrolled to develop skills in their existing vocation; 30%, to develop a vocation; 20%, to increase their knowledge in their vocation; 20%, to earn a stable income; and 8%, to earn a diploma and thus gain social respect.

Student Quality

The rapid growth of the 2-year vocational and technical schools in Turkey has brought problems, including inadequate faculty numbers, low faculty quality, and the need to revise VSHE programs. Issues that remain unsolved are related to financial flexibility, administrative and governance issues, lack of staff, articulation with the secondary vocational and technical schools and universities, and the mismatch in skills between VSHE programs and the needs of industry.

Student enrollment in Turkey's VSHEs is on average quite low, preventing the system from realizing economies of scale. Dundar and Lewis (1995) found that, in some cases, the average instructional costs for a VSHE were higher than for the 4-year university that the VSHE was part of. They said that "as institutions get larger, both average and marginal costs decline up to a point, and then as institutions get even larger both types of costs increase but marginal costs increase at much higher rates." Costs increased significantly as a result of falling student-to-teacher ratios and increased student participation in programs that required VSHEs to purchase instructional equipment.

Dundar and Lewis (1995) recommended that Turkey concentrate on expanding VSHE enrollment and establish enrollment boundaries that reflect student demand. "The mission and rationale for vocational training should be market driven and the system should work toward facilitating this mission both in its expansion and in its contraction for most efficient public policy" (Dundar & Lewis, 1995). Balcı and Kavak (1996) concluded that VSHEs in towns with populations below 5,000, with fewer than 500 students, and with only a small number of programs were inefficient. They suggested that these small VSHEs, usually located at the subprovincial level, be amalgamated based on local population numbers as well as student numbers. VSHEs should be at the provincial level but should offer programs at the subprovincial level.

Organization and Administration

Turkey's VSHEs are located within university structures. Typically, a VSHE will be in a rural subprovincial area while the university it is part of is in a more populated provincial area. VSHE directors are appointed by university rectors, and they choose their own assistant directors. There are no legal criteria for what qualifications a person must have to be a VSHE director or assistant director. As a result, different universities follow different practices for appointing directors. One study showed that 75% of VSHE directors had a primary appointment elsewhere. Many directors do not commit full time to a VSHE because they are spending time at the other institution (Aypay, 2003). For a director who is pursuing an academic career, it is considered more prestigious to be at a 4-year institution.

Four-year and 2-year institutions typically compete for resources and staff, and VSHEs do not always get their fair share. Staff problems also arise when VSHE faculty members who have doctorates work for directors who do not. Academic career is more valued than experience in universities. Law requires department chairs to have doctorates; if there is no faculty member with a doctorate who could be named chair, a temporary appointment is made.

Organizational adaptation to environment is more difficult when VSHEs are located in university structures. Universities usually resist changes to protect the academic tradition that took centuries to form. However, one of the powerful aspects of VSHEs is their skill in adapting to their environment and to changes in society and technology. As with community colleges throughout the world, it is size, rather than organizational form, that differentiates VHSEs from other higher education institutions in Turkey (Balcı & Kavak, 1996; Demir & Işıksoylu, 1996).

Centralized administrative structures at universities have certain advantages, one of which is providing standardization in a variety of areas: purchasing, information processing, planning of physical facilities, staffing, financing, equal allocation of resources, and promotions. Competition among universities also contributes to standardization in coordination, service to society, and human resources development for all 2-year colleges. The centralized structure is useful if the competing institutions are similar. However, 2-year colleges and 4-year colleges are not similar in many ways. Therefore, 4-year colleges have a clear advantage over 2-year colleges within university structures.

Until recently, only universities had the authority to establish programs, but the council of higher education now has the final authority. Universities can propose starting, ending, or merging programs, but the council makes the final decision. The private sector has begun to assist VSHEs. In the past, if a foundation wanted to establish a VSHE, it had to establish a university first, then open a VSHE within the university. By law, a foundation can now open a VSHE directly, without creating a university first. This recent development is likely to have important consequences for VSHEs, helping them be more flexible in adapting to changing environments.

National Priorities in Vocational and Technical Education

Turkey has made full membership in the European Union (EU) a priority. Although membership may not be awarded until 2015 or later, Turkey has taken steps to integrate its economy with the EU's. VSHEs are part of this effort: The programs most commonly offered by VSHEs are technical, with an emphasis on technical skills and knowledge needed around the world.

As of 2005, Turkey had a total of 258 VSHEs. Of the programs offered, 60% were in technical areas, 23% in administrative areas, and 7% in health sciences. Ten percent of programs were open education. From 1994 to 2005, technical programs increased by 10%, while business and economics programs decreased by 14%. Nontechnical programs increased, too, from 243 in 1994 to 1,100 in 2005. The focus is typically 60%–65% on theoretical knowledge and 30%–35% on applied skills (YÖK, 2005a).

The Second Industrial Training Project of 1989–1997included a revision of 15 programs that accounted for 70% of all student enrollments. The principles taken into account while revising the programs were proficiency, validity, consistency, variety, flexibility, accreditation, use of information and communications technology, compatibility with modular programs, and training in real settings (MEB & YÖK, 2002).

Overview of a VSHE

This section briefly describes Çanakkale VSHE, which is in the Aegean coastal city of Çanakkale in western Turkey. The city, historically known as Troy, has a population of 75,000. Çanakkale VSHE was established in 1976 by the ministry of education and later became part of Trakya University, a state university established in 1982 that is some 2.5 hours' drive from the city of Çanakkale. When Çanakkale Onsekiz Mart University was established in the city in 1992, the VSHE naturally became part of this new university. It is the only VSHE in the city of Çanakkale and one of 15 VSHEs in the province of Çanakkale.

In 2006, the school's total enrollment was 2,284 (ÇOMU MYO, 2006). Technical programs included graphics (46 day students), photography (75 day), computer technology and programming (108 day, 105 evening), construction (301 day, 83 evening), mechanics (215 evening), electrical (325 evening), furniture and decoration (86 evening), textiles (94 evening), and child development (92 evening). Economics and administrative programs included accounting (155 day, 108 evening), business (178 day, 108 evening), and office management and secretarial training (103 day, 94 evening).

Çanakkale is considered to be one of Turkey's top-tier VHSEs. Its programs attract students, and enrollment has not declined since 1992. The school's programs emphasize vocational investigation, problem-solving skills, and evaluation and decision-making skills.

Its facilities include two computer labs, one technical drawing studio, a photography studio and dark room, a concrete and tool lab, a film recording studio, a geological laboratory, an asphalt laboratory, and a secretarial office. It also has two professional workshops, one at each of the two vocational high schools in the city. The school has adequate numbers of qualified faculty members and sufficient laboratory space to serve its programs. However, with enrollment continuing to increase as a result of the national open access policy, its physical space is starting to be insufficient.

The curriculum was revised recently with collaboration between the ministry of education and the higher education council. Faculty members from many VSHEs participated, as did a large group of other education experts. In addition to the new curriculum, Çanakkale VSHE offers electives based on the region's economy and technological development.

Çanakkale VSHE's three main problems are related to student quality, lack of physical facilities, and issues related to newly established programs. As in other VSHEs, Çanakkale's faculty and administrators would like to end open access and enroll better-qualified students. They claim that vocational and technical high school graduates, who are now the majority of the school's students, are not ready for higher-level training.

Under pressure from the council of higher education, Çanakkale VSHE established some programs corresponding to those already offered in the vocational and technical high schools, with articulation agreements between the institutions. Because the programs opened without all necessary preparations being completed, there were initially some problems. The main goal was to put existing high school facilities (and some instructors) to use during the evening, which has indeed happened. However, some VSHE students were demoralized by having to return to the high schools they had graduated from.

The strengths of Çanakkale VSHE are that it has a 30-year history, a limited number of problems in terms of training and teaching, and enough high-quality faculty members. Also, because Çanakkale VSHE was an older institution when Çanakkale Onsekiz Mart University was established, its reputation and relationship with the university are better than those of the other VSHEs attached to the university. Its weaknesses are as follows:

- Çanakkale VSHE has more programs than the administration planned. It is common for Turkish VSHEs to separate programs into two institutions, with social and administrative programs in one and technical programs in the other. The administrators of Çanakkale VSHE are willing to take this approach. However, dividing programs this way can lead to the inefficient use of VSHE resources.

- Çanakkale is not an industrial city, so job opportunities are limited. Work-study is mandatory for Çanakkale VSHE students but does not guarantee that they will find jobs. The school must make work-study more effective by becoming better integrated with the needs of the local economy, where agriculture is the mainstay.

- The contribution that Çanakkale VSHE can make to its immediate environment is limited by the city's lack of a large industrial base. The school does provide laboratory courses in concrete and asphalt testing, as well as seminars and training programs when there is a demand from the public.

THE FUTURE OF THE VSHE SYSTEM

Because the open access policy is not likely to change, VSHEs can expect to enroll ever greater numbers of high school graduates who are not academically well prepared. VSHEs may need to begin providing preparatory courses to these students. Turkey has a large and growing school-age population, and the demand for higher education is increasing. Only 20% of the 2 million students who compete for university places each year get accepted (YÖK, 2005a). Turkey wants to expand its VSHE system to meet the growing need for higher education.

Although there has been a sharp increase in enrollments, the number of students in private universities is quite low. Twenty-five private foundation universities train only 2% of all students in higher education. Recent developments in these institutions are expected to increase the numbers of students in private universities.

Turkey leads in its development of vocational education, technical education, and 2-year technical schools and colleges. It has a strong history of trying to match its postsecondary technical training with the needs of an increasingly global economy. With further effort and dedication, Turkey's citizens will have world-class technical and postsecondary training.

REFERENCES

Ataünal, A. (1998). *Cumhuriyetin 75. yılında yükseköğretim* [Higher education in the republic's 75th anniversary]. Ankara, Turkey: Ministry of Education.

Aypay, A. (2003). *Türkiye'de meslek yüksek okullar.* [Vocational schools of higher education in Turkey]. Unpublished research report, Çanakkale Onsekiz Mart University, Turkey.

Balcı, S., & Kavak, Ş. (1996, May). *Meslek yüksekokullarının mevcut durumu ve yeniden yapılanması üzerine bir model önerisi* [Status of two-year colleges and a model concerning their restructuring]. Paper presented at the "Restructuring Two-Year Colleges in 21st Century" symposium, Üniversitesi Basımevi, Ankara, Turkey.

Baskan, G. A. (1999). *YÖK/Dünya Bankası endüstriyel eğitim orojesi uygulamalarının değerlendirilmesi* [Evaluation of YÖK/World Bank industrial training project]. *Dumlupınar University Journal of Social Sciences, 1,* 65–110.

Cohen, A. M., & Brawer, F. B. (1996). *The American community college* (3rd ed.). San Francisco: Jossey-Bass.

ÇOMU MYO. (2006). *Çanakkale meslekyüksek okulu* [Çanakkale VSHE]. Retrieved March 4, 2006, from www.comu.edu.tr/akademik/myokullar.php

Demir, M., & Işıksoylu, M. A. (1996, May). *Meslek yüksekokullarının yükseköğretim yasasından kaynaklanan sorunları* [The problems of two-year colleges concerning higher education law]. Paper presented at the "Restructuring Two-Year Colleges in 21st Century" symposium, Üniversitesi Basımevi, Ankara, Turkey.

Devlet Planlama Teşkilatı (DPT). (1999). *Kalkınma planı: Sekizinci beş yıl* (2001–2005) [8th development plan: 2001–2005.]. Ankara, Turkey: DPT Yayınları.

Dundar, H., & Lewis, D. R. (1995). Costs and economies of scale in Turkey's postsecondary vocational schools. *Higher Education, 30,* 369–387.

Karasar, N. (1981). *Ön lisans eğitimi ve teknik eğitimde uygulanabilirliği* [Associate degree training and its feasibility in technical training]. Ankara, Turkey: Ankara Üniversitesi Eğitim Bilimleri Fakültesi Yayınları.

Karhan, K. (1983). *Ara insan gücü* [Mid-level manpower]. Unpublished manuscript, Ankara, Turkey.

Kavak, Y. (1992). *Meslek yüksekokulları: Değişim ve iş hayatıyla ilişkileri* [Vocational schools of higher education: Change and relations with worklife]. Ankara, Turkey: Evren Ofset.

Kaya, Y. K. (1984). *İnsan yetiştirme düzenimiz: Politika, eğitim, kalkınma* [Our training system] (4th ed.). Ankara, Turkey: Bilim Yayınları.

MEB & YÖK. (2002). *MYO program geliştirme projesi* [VSHE curriculum development project]. Ankara, Turkey: YÖK.

Nazik, A. (2003). *MYO'ların Türkiye'de ve yükseköğretim içindeki durumu, gereklilikleri ve temel görevleri* [The status, needs, and necessity of VSHEs in higher education]. Paper presented at Çukurova University, Adana, Turkey.

Organisation for Economic Co-operation and Development (OECD). (1997). *Education at a glance: OECD indicators.* Paris: Author.

ÖSYM. (2002). *ÖSS kılavuzu* [Handbook of higher education programs]. Ankara, Turkey: ÖSYM Yayınları.

YÖK. (2004). *I. ulusal meslek yüksek okulları müdürler toplantısı* [First national VSHE directors' meeting]. Ankara, Turkey: Detay Yayıncılık.

YÖK. (2005a). *Türk yükseköğretiminin bugünkü durumu* [Status of Turkish higher education]. Ankara, Turkey: Ankara Üniversitesi Basımevi.

YÖK. (2005b). *Yükseköğretimin durumu* [Status of higher education]. Ankara, Turkey: Author.

YÖK. (2007). *Türkiye'nin yükseköğretim stratejisi* [Higher education strategy of Turkey]. Ankara, Turkey: YÖK Yayınları.

12

Higher Colleges of Technology in the United Arab Emirates

Paul A. Elsner and James Horton

The United Arab Emirates (UAE) flourishes among the Middle Eastern nations as a premier, modern, technologically advanced alliance of seven emirates governed by a federation, with specific powers stipulated to a central federal government, as well as some authority ordained for member emirates. The seven states merged to become the UAE, independent from United Kingdom colonization, in 1971. The *2006 World Fact Book* of the U.S. Central Intelligence Agency (CIA) highlights the nation's remarkable success as a Western-modeled economy:

> The UAE has an open economy with a high per cent capita income and a sizable annual trade surplus. Its wealth is based on oil and gas output (about 30% of GDP), and the fortunes of the economy fluctuate with the prices of those commodities. Since the discovery of oil in the UAE more than 30 years ago, the UAE has undergone a profound transformation from an impoverished region of small desert principalities to a modern state with a high standard of living. At present levels of production, oil and gas reserves should last for more than 100 years. The government has increased spending on job creation and infrastructure expansion and is opening up its utilities to greater private sector involvement. Higher oil revenue, strong liquidity, and cheap credit in 2005 led to a surge in asset prices (shares and real estate) and consumer inflation. (U.S. CIA, 2006)

In late 2003, a delegation of consultants visited the UAE, conducting interviews at 11 colleges in the UAE's Higher Colleges of Technology (HCT) system. The following excerpt from the final report submitted to HCT after that visit provides some insights into the cultural and socioeconomic context for higher education in the UAE:

> The astonishing transformation of the United Arab Emirates (UAE) since the establishment of the State just 30 or so years ago is a testament to inspired and visionary leadership. This is a country that knows where it is going. The vision is clear: the UAE will be an open, sophisticated "cutting edge" economy, driven by western values, but at the same time, remain consistent with and faithful to traditional Gulf and Islamic values. The UAE is determined to prove that the two cultural prerogatives can be reconciled.
>
> It is quite appropriate that the UAE government has as a policy the increasing emiratization of the economy, i.e., an increasing participation of Nationals in the workforce, and an increasing number of Nationals holding positions of authority and leadership. The implications of this policy are profound and far-reaching. It will result in a significant increase in the participation by women in the workforce and a greater participation by both genders in the private sector. . . .
>
> The United Arab Emirates (UAE) is a federation with seven rulers, each presiding over geographies that are very different from one another in population, economic resources, size and economic development goals and potential. The UAE is governmentally a Muslim nation, but it permits other religions to operate in the country. Only 20% of the 2.8 million population are nationals. Nationals, modern day descendants of the original Bedouin tribes, are mostly employed in government service where the salaries are initially higher, hours fewer and predictable, and where greater job security exists. However, government employment opportunities are becoming saturated.
>
> Nationals constitute only 2% of employees in private business and industry even though firms entering the Emirates to do business must be at least 51% locally owned. In order to generate greater employment of nationals in private industry a program of emiratization has begun by requiring the banking industry to have Nationals as 20% of their employees, rising to 40% by 2010. The insurance industry has also recently come under this government mandate. . . .
>
> *Invest Dubai,* Vol. I, Issue I, Summer 2003, a publication created for the World Bank/IMF meeting, reports in an interview with Dubai Crown Prince, Sheikh Mohammed bin Rashid Al Maktoum that economic development targets are in finance, business, tourism, aviation, information technology, media, services, trade and industry. The focus is to attract multinational corporations and the best-

qualified professionals in those fields. Essentially Nationals are not yet competitive for these positions.

The long-range implications of miniscule participation of Nationals in the economy of the country while outside investment and ownership is courted could result in Nationals having less and less influence in the direction of the country and a decreasing opportunity to own and participate in the development of wealth.

Within this scenario, the Higher Colleges of Technology, a system of public colleges in the Emirates, have the primary mission to prepare Nationals for gainful employment. While the enrollments have grown from a few hundred 15 years ago to nearly 15,000 in 2003, the financial structure of the colleges and other considerations have been such that the colleges are turning qualified students away.

The HCTs are also complicated by a desire to provide an American/Western style of education that looks somewhat like community colleges, but the HTC is constrained by the more European model that restricts admission based on past educational performance and results of national examinations. (Paul Elsner and Associates, 2003)

The wisdom of the HCT system reflects the balance and vision of His Highness Sheikh Nahayan Mabarak Al Nahayan, an expansive thinker and decisive ruler who oversees HCT as the UAE's minister of higher education. In addition, he serves as president of the newer Zayed University and de facto as a principal emissary for cultural and scientific affairs, as well as for the nation's broader educational policy. Tayeb Kamali, a native Arab who operationally oversees the entire HCT system, serves as his vice chancellor. Kamali's background includes doctoral credentials from Western universities, as well as an astute perception of emirate culture and public nuances. Kamali's tenure follows a succession of expatriate, Western-directed vice chancellors.

Thomas Bailey, director of the Community College Research Center at Columbia University and one of the participants in the 2003 visit to HCT, offered the following perspective from notes he took during the visit:

HCT activities must be understood in the context of ongoing development plans for the UAE, particularly in its efforts to wean itself off an oil-dominated economy. The policy of "emeritization" is a crucial component of this strategy. Nationals are already well-represented in the public sector, but the next important step of the policy is to bring them into the international sectors of the economy in greater numbers. These are the fastest growing and most dynamic economic sectors, which are now almost completely dominated by an expatriate labor force. While reliance on expatriates appears to be working now, over the long term, it will result in a distorted, unbalanced economy. In effect, the national population will be confined to the public sector and less able to benefit directly from the modern growth of the economy. This will place greater burdens on the public sector to provide resources to the population either through oil revenues or through other business-related government revenue streams. A much healthier, sustainable strategy would be to have the national population benefit directly from employment and entrepreneurship in international sectors rather than indirectly through government resources. One goal of our work is to help determine how HCT can contribute to that crucial objective.

HCT History

In 1988, the first four HCT campuses opened in Abu Dhabi and Dubai with 239 students. Today there are 18 campuses, located in Abu Dhabi, Dubai, Al Ain, Fujairah, Ras al Khaimah, Sharja, and Madinet Zayed, with an enrollment of more than 19,000 students. Each city location has a separate campus for men and women. Madinet Zayed, the newest location in the remote western area of the emirates, serves a small disparate population and uses one facility with common library and dining facilities scheduled separately for men and women.

The Centre for Research and Training (CERT) is now a separately incorporated entity that specializes in customized programs for industry and government. CERT has acquired significant private funding and, for all practical purposes, serves as a separate business. It now has the capability to provide venture capital funding for business development and expansion. The location of the IBM's Blue Gene at CERT is a significant addition that positions the emirates as a major provider of supercomputing services throughout the Middle East and North African nations.

Only emirate nationals can attend HCT. Currently, 60% of the students are women, and all students are high school graduates who achieve a combination of a national test score and class placement to be eligible to attend an HCT college. English is the primary language of instruction and its proficiency is required.

While the colleges remain separate, there are no restrictions for male faculty teaching within women's colleges. Young men coming out of high school have many opportunities for lucrative careers within the police or the military. Young women do not have these opportunities and are therefore very eager and dedicated students. Students are challenged by faculty members from more than 40 countries who speak English in every conceivable dialect.

Structure and Management

A governing council has a lateral relationship with Sheikh Nahayan, chancellor of HCT. The council, comprised of government and business leaders, is required by statute to approve HCT policies. The council meets once a year to consider policy revisions, review the college system's performance, past year expenditures, and budget requests for the subsequent year. However, the council cannot approve the budget since this remains the sole responsibility of the federal government. Sheikh Nayahan forwards requests for funding beyond the level recommended for the federal budget office to the Federal National Council for consideration. While the vice chancellor is given a great deal of latitude by Sheikh Nahayan, it remains imperative that he be continually involved in the decision-making process. However, the conduct of business poses a very different situation for Western administrators.

As mentioned earlier, Sheikh Nahayan is not only the minister of higher education and president of the University of the UAE and Zayed University, but also he manages a number of major business interests that require a great deal of his time. The primary method for meeting with the chancellor involves attendance at an evening or weekend *majlis*. (The word means "a reception room" where guest are received, but it is now generally used as a term for a time when a sheikh or ruler receives guests and business associates.)

Sheikh Nahayan holds a majlis reception virtually every day of the week, which is open to anyone who would like to show respect or seek his assistance in business or personal matters. The normal course of business for the vice chancellor is to attend majlis in the evening, participate in the formalities, and wait to have a private meeting with Sheikh Nayahan. Since an enormously full schedule warrants little time for extensive background briefings, decisions are often made very quickly. Therefore, the vice chancellor must be well prepared to present issues relevant to a decision in a very succinct manner.

Each college or major central office functional area is headed by a director, a position very similar to campus deans or presidents in Western multicampus systems. The policy council meets once a month to work through operational issues and create policy recommendations for ultimate approval by the chancellor and the policy council.

In the early years, Sheikh Nahayan maintained very strong central control of all HCT programs and activities, believing this would ensure optimal quality development as new colleges were established. All budget decisions hinged on central office determination of program, staffing, and facilities needs. Curriculum was created and tightly controlled from the central office, which also shouldered responsibility for central quality control through a variety of mechanisms, including centralized testing and site visits.

Anyone familiar with multicampus systems can predict the pressure for change as HCT campuses matured and developed their own individual character. Directors increasingly identified with their individual campuses and developed strong ties with the rulers and governments of the individual emirates. Campuses have generally desired more autonomy and have begun independent experimentation with curriculum and delivery methodologies.

Funding

HCT funding is technically the sole responsibility of the federal government. How revenue flows into the federal budget from the UAE's resources remains unclear. Only a portion of this total income is designated for federal government expenditures.

The emirate of Abu Dhabi contains virtually all of the country's oil and provides the majority of revenue for the federal budget. Dubai, on the other hand, wins all of the international attention, yet it yields virtually no oil. Consequently, it has positioned itself as the business and trading capital of the entire region. The fact that individual emirates may decide to provide separate support for the campus located within their own jurisdiction further complicates the challenge of creating an equitable budgeting system.

For example, the municipality of Dubai provided all of the capital funding for Dubai women's and men's colleges. Consequently, these colleges have splendid facilities that would rival anything in the United States. An individual emirate ruler or government may also provide specialized scholarship or equipment funding. A combination of Sheikh Nayahan's influence and the ability of individual campus directors to develop relationships with influential members of their respective emirates results in access to these funds. Colleges located in the more rural and less affluent emirates have reduced potential for this additional assistance and must depend almost exclusively on funds allocated from the federal system.

HCT has traditionally been well funded. In recent years, operational resources ranged around AED 37,000, or about USD 10,000 per student. Generally, the colleges offer favorable student-to-faculty ratios (16:1) and leading-edge instructional technologies. A laptop computer purchase represents the only expense requirement for students who enjoy a tuition-free education.

Operational costs of HCT run inherently high because of the separate campuses for men and women. Despite some attempt to combine the management structure, many duplicated expenses still exist. Complicating this fact is the increasing pressure to admit all qualified secondary school graduates. Since Sheikh Nayahan remains adamant about ensuring HCT's ongoing academic quality, he therefore supports a policy of limiting enrollment to preserve ideal faculty–student ratios and leading-edge instructional technology. In recent years, as many as 1,500 students have been unable to enroll because of this matriculation cap.

Like other multicampus systems worldwide, HCT struggles to find the balance between centralized control and campus autonomy. A rational, formula-driven process, based on enrollment and program cost, increasingly determines budgets. Campuses continue to follow a centralized learning-outcomes model but have more latitude to develop creative approaches to the academic process. Dubai Women's College has initiated a creative instructional methodology that requires students to be involved in the development of their own learning activities and record specific examples as to how these activities are helping the student achieve the college's learning outcomes. As colleges become more responsive to the educational needs of their communities, the need to control costs and ensure high-quality education throughout the country will require continual refinement of the balance between central control and the freedom for innovation at the campus level.

The Learning Environment

It is important to understand Sheikh Nahayan's tremendous influence on the learning environment. A truly visionary leader, he remains highly respected throughout the country and region. From the beginning, he envisioned a college system that would rank among the best in the world. His requirement for any benchmark consisted of identifying educational programs with an outstanding international reputation.

For example, the University of Melbourne served as the benchmark chosen for the HCT educational program. The relationship progressed to the point where Melbourne faculty would travel to the UAE to evaluate the program and independently grade student work. Sheikh Nayahan quickly adopted learning outcomes appropriate for each awarded qualification. Every student was therefore expected to demonstrate qualification-appropriate competence in the following "graduate outcomes":

1. Communications and information literacy
2. Critical and creative thinking
3. Global awareness and citizenship
4. Technological literacy
5. Self-management and independent learning
6. Teamwork and leadership
7. Vocational competencies
8. Mathematical literacy (HCT, 2006, pp. 6–7)

In addition, his desire to achieve U.S. regional accreditation resulted from an extension of this adoption of learning outcomes and the concept of institutional effectiveness. HCT is currently pursuing accreditation through the Southern Association of Colleges and Universities.

Western faculty and staff often struggle with the implementation of the sanctions Sheikh Nayahan imposed for academic dishonesty. Just one offense denies the student admission to any federally funded institution of higher education for life. Influential families often appeal directly to Sheikh Nahayan to overturn staff decisions, but he does not waver. Instead, he offers the rationale that academic dishonesty, while common in the secondary schools, has no place in higher education. He also emphasizes that students must embrace the importance of the legitimacy of HCT student credentials, along with honesty and integrity, in the world of international business.

Sheikh Nayahan's expectation for women is particularly interesting. He encourages them to be successful and able to assume their position within the professional ranks of business and government. For example, when meeting female students, he often uses the opportunity to challenge the accepted practice of avoiding shaking hands with a woman unless she offered. Instead, he always initiates the handshake as a way of letting the women know it represents standard etiquette within the international business community, regardless of gender.

HCT offers diplomas, higher diplomas, and bachelor's degrees in engineering, information technology, business, health care, media/communication technology, and education, with a number of options under each of these major categories. Each program area must include advisory groups that represent employers who will ultimately hire the graduates. While constantly adjusted to meet the demands of specific occupations or the needs of business and government, the curriculum is also designed to be sensitive to Arab customs and Islamic beliefs—one reason HCT publishes most of its own texts. The colleges respect the need to present high-standard technical information at a level appropriate for non-native English-speaking learners. Many of these texts have been adopted by institutions of higher education in other Arab countries.

HCT offered certificates for several years but dropped them in 2004 because employers did not distinguish between graduates with certificates and those with diplomas or higher diplomas. Since HCT has developed an excellent reputation for preparing competent, ready-to-work graduates, certificate students lacked the preparation to meet this expectation.

Nearly all students must complete the foundation year, which is similar to remedial programs in other countries, before proceeding into any of the diploma, higher diploma, or baccalaureate programs. English represents the biggest hurdle for most of these students. While they study English in high school, their proficiency typically falls short of the college level, even though they have met the minimal entry requirements. Students achieve greater success when the foundation year courses, particularly in mathematics, bear some relevancy to their choice of discipline. For example, an applied medical math course taught to students entering the health-care field met with the greatest success.

EMPLOYABILITY AND EMERITIZATION

Students must integrate a work experience as part of their curriculum at HCT to gain practical experience and an acquaintance with potential employers. The experience is complicated in many organizations, particularly those under government pressure to hire nationals, because the mentors assigned to the students often feel threatened by the prospect of losing their job to an HCT graduate. Companies are also threatened by the economic reality that they can hire highly educated and experienced workers from the subcontinent at wages far below what is expected by Westerners or emirate nationals.

The companies with the best record for mentoring and hiring HCT students are those that offer a combination of government and private ownership. Examples include Etisilatt, a giant telecommunications company, and Abu Dhabi National Oil Company. There are other examples of foreign-based, private-sector firms that are committed to the national goals of emeritization and are very supportive of HCT.

Obtaining and tracking accurate employment data poses a challenge. Many graduates continue to have their names appear on the unemployment register in hopes of gaining better positions even though they are currently employed. Women often do not take their names off of the unemployment register because they are actually hoping for a government position that offers a culture and time commitment that is much more in sync with the demands and customs of family life.

Many HCT graduates have achieved distinguished positions in all types of businesses throughout the country. Undoubtedly, these business leaders will influence their companies to hire more HCT graduates. HCT's marketing and public relations personnel face the challenge of making these success stories more public. The system publishes *Al Rawi,* a newspaper that primarily highlights the success of graduates and HCT's strong ties with the corporate sector.

The English and Arabic press have also been responsive to news releases. Again, major news organizations now employ a number of HCT graduates and have therefore become more receptive. Despite this positive trend, however, the employment of graduates will not progress to level needed in the UAE unless the government continues to place pressure on private-sector companies to meet government quotas for employing nationals.

Perhaps the greatest potential for graduates lies in starting their own businesses. The ruler of Dubai has dedicated a significant amount of resources to fund start-up entrepreneurial efforts. The colleges now place an increasing emphasis on entrepreneurial pursuits and often host student-run businesses on campus. Many of these new ventures have become successful enterprises after the students graduate.

STAFFNG

HCT currently employs approximately 950 faculty and more than 800 staff members representing 40 countries. Obviously the human resources staff operates in a constant mode of recruiting and hiring—an enormous and very expensive process. The human resources managers have developed a system for tracking this process that would be of interest to other international institutions of higher education.

The process involves ongoing screening by relevant faculty and staff across the system. Discipline-specific teams continually review and rate candidates' applications and curriculum vita through an Internet system. The result is a very efficient process for reviewing the thousands of applications received each year. The English fluency requirement draws a concentration of Westerners from the United States, Canada,

United Kingdom, Australia, and New Zealand. Only potential campus or central office directors are invited to visit the UAE.

Most faculty and staff base their decisions on discussions with recruiters, as well as their own research about working and living in the UAE. The living accommodations and travel allowances also appeal to a large group of people willing to experience an expatriate lifestyle and are motivated to join an institution helping to build a nation. Candidates often have acquaintances already employed in the UAE, so they are comfortable with the prospects of living in this country and experiencing its unique culture. Western women quickly discover that there are no restrictions on their dress, driving, or typical activities. Naturally, everyone is expected to honor the local customs, especially during Ramadan and other holy days.

The cities offer excellent shopping, and Westerners can find almost anything they want. Staff members who work in the rural areas do not have as much accessibility, but it does not take long to reach Dubai or Abu Dhabi due to the country's small size. Undeniably, HCT's diverse expatriate community members are interesting, dedicated to their students, and generally enjoy living in the UAE as well as working for an exceptional academic institution. HCT issues 3-year contracts, and the average tenure spans at least two contracts.

Students and Academic Life

Any experienced college-level instructor will recognize the students: They possess a similar diversity of ability and commitment to their studies as well as many of the same challenges of balancing family, social, work, and school life. Female students, in particular, take the program very seriously. Attending HCT offers a stimulating and welcome change from the typical confinement and restrictions of the home. Their eagerness to learn and excel always impresses new faculty who teach at the women's colleges.

One mistaken assumption is that all students are affluent. While some do hail from prosperous families—a fact substantiated by the cars parked at the men's colleges—many students, much like their counterparts in any country, have modest means. Others live in very rural areas that require at least a 2-hour ride on the bus to reach a campus.

In loco parentis is alive and well, especially at the women's colleges. Female students are either bused to the campus or transported by an approved relative. Women cannot leave the campus without specific permission and approval by an authorized relative. More than one women's college student council has petitioned for more lenient regulations. Things are slowly changing, particularly in the urban areas.

Directors and faculty at the women's colleges have become very creative in providing interesting activities for their students, ranging from art to campus-based businesses. While both the men's and women's campuses enjoy intramural athletics, men cannot to participate in women's sports for reasons of modesty. Furthermore, local custom prohibits them from touching an Arab woman, even if she faints or is injured.

THE FUTURE OF HCT

HCT's success plays a vital role in the ongoing development of the UAE. Since the country remains tax-free, the continued funding of HCT at a level necessary to maintain its high standards still poses a challenge. Every week at least two private institutions apply for accreditation within the country. Sheikh Nayahan has established a ministry of higher education with a number of responsibilities, including decisions regarding the recognition of colleges and universities that can operate within the country.

Perhaps one unique irony of the UAE is that many government officials also have a personal or financial interest in these private institutions. The percentage of HCT graduates employed by the private sector must increase. This may happen as more nationals attain high-level managerial and leadership positions and as government pressure intensifies. However, government pressure can also become a negative incentive to companies considering a location in the UAE. Dubai's success as a business center has been the result of no taxes and a very friendly business climate without many of the regulatory controls found in many countries.

Anyone who visits HCT is impressed by the students, faculty, facilities, and technology of this young college system. Anyone who has worked for HCT leaves with a sense of pride in having the opportunity to be a part of an organization that is making a significant difference in the development of this amazing country.

REFERENCES

Higher Colleges of Technology. (2006). *The HCT learning model: 2006*. Retrieved June 12, 2008, from www.admc.hct.ac.ae/hd1/documents/Revised%20Learning%20Mo del_2006.pdf

Paul Elsner and Associates. (2003, October). *Report of a visit to Higher Colleges of Technology: United Arab Emirates*. Unpublished report, Paul Elsner and Associates, Phoenix, AZ.

U.S. Central Intelligence Agency. (2006). *2006 world fact book*. Washington, DC: Author.

Case Study: The Higher Colleges of Technology in the UAE

Tayeb Kamali

In the 1960s, the discovery and exploitation of oil and gas reserves in the Arabian Gulf countries of Saudi Arabia, Qatar, Kuwait, Bahrain, Oman, and what is now the United Arab Emirates (UAE) had a significant impact on those countries in a very short time. The sudden influx of oil and gas revenues into what were thinly populated and undeveloped regions presented the rulers with an unprecedented opportunity to develop physical infrastructure at a dramatic pace. Within two decades, the Arabian Gulf countries achieved amazing results in construction and infrastructure development projects.

From the mid-1960s to the mid-1980s, help from multinational companies and a great influx of expatriate labor, supported by technical and professional advisors, made it possible for the countries to create housing, roads, schools, hospitals, and telecommunications networks that met the standards of the developed world. Particular emphasis was placed on building a large network of K–12 schools to ensure that every child would have free and easy access to basic education. The governments of the Arabian Gulf countries gave incentives to increase family size in order to meet the ever-expanding human resource needs of their increasingly affluent economies. Traditional universities were established to educate the administrative and managerial leaders needed to assume key government and public sector positions. These positions were initially held by expatriates who assisted in this massive undertaking.

Economic growth meant that workforce needs continued to outstrip the supply of trained nationals. The incentives to increase the national population began to show results during the 1980s. The first public government-funded school was established in Sharjah in 1953 with 230 students. In 2003–2004, approximately 306,752 students were enrolled in 780 public schools and 234,250 in 426 private schools (Abu-Samaha & Shishakly, 2008).

Gulf Cooperation Council (GCC) country planners began to focus on the increasing numbers of school leavers and the type of occupations that would be available to them in the coming decades. Many statistical indicators pointed the planners toward conclusions similar to the findings of Hamad Al-Sulayti (2003), one of the region's leading researchers:

> [Employers] complain that our schools are incapable of producing an adequate supply of trained and technically qualified workers. The acute shortage of indigenous workers is both quantitative and qualitative. GCC Countries have to strike a balance between the need to prepare professionals such as engineers, doctors and lawyers, and the need for middle-level workers such as technicians and semi-skilled workers. The acute shortage of local technicians and skilled workers should drive GCC governments to shift their emphasis from Universities to lower-cost training colleges and polytechnics in order to enhance their capabilities of providing better quality training for larger numbers. (p. 275)

The Mandate, the Vision, and the Mission

In the words of the founding president of the UAE, Sheikh Zayed bin Sultan Al Nahyan, "Education is like a lantern which lights your way in a dark alley" (see Abed & Hellyer, 2001, p. 219). Sheikh Zayed led the nation during an era that saw the UAE transform itself from a small cluster of emirates to one of the most modern countries in the world. A visionary, he saw his dream of a unified nation materialize in his lifetime. Throughout his presidency, the country witnessed dramatic changes, undergoing a metamorphosis from the pre-oil days to unparalleled development. Sheikh Zayed not only led the country into the 21st century, he also put the UAE on the world map.

In 1987, Sheikh Zayed gave a clear mandate to the chancellor of UAE University, Sheikh Nahayan Mabarak Al Nahayan, to establish a system of technical institutions to train and develop young UAE nationals in technical specializations. Sheikh Nahayan set the vision for a world-class higher education institution that would be the leading provider of tertiary education in the UAE, would meet the country's need for a large and skilled workforce, and would become the best-in-class institution in the Gulf region. The new, federally funded system was named the Higher Colleges of Technology (HCT). Its mission statement, crafted in 1988 by Sheikh Nahayan, addressed both the president's mandate and the chancellor's vision. It has stood the test of time during the rapid development of HCT and the UAE:

> The Higher Colleges of Technology are dedicated to the delivery of technical and professional programs of the highest quality to the

students, within the context of sincere respect for all beliefs and values. Graduates of the colleges will have the linguistic ability to function effectively in an international environment; the technical skills to operate in an increasingly complex technological world; the intellectual capacity to adapt to constant change; and the leadership potential to make the fullest possible contribution to the development of the community for the good of all its people. (HCT, 2008a)

Sheikh Nahayan's visionary leadership, dedication, and untiring efforts have been the cornerstones in translating this vision into measurable outcomes and success. From the outset, he asserted that the strong foundation of a world-class institution would be uncompromising attention to quality, integrity, and continual improvement of the teaching–learning process. He has insisted that HCT graduates be prepared to work effectively in an international environment, emphasizing the importance of international accreditation and the benchmarking of programs and processes.

The president's plan to establish HCT demanded an ambitious time line. Implementation had to precede the government decrees and processes necessary to formally set up this federal institution with its own budget and award-granting status. Sheikh Nahayan initiated a fast-track implementation to convert the president's vision into the practical reality of state-of-the-art campuses offering career-oriented programs. A select number of technical programs, curriculum details, and infrastructure were expeditiously put in place with the assistance of international experts. In interpreting its mission, HCT embarked on technical education that would

- Be relevant to the needs of local government, business, and industry.
- Prepare graduates for a globally competitive marketplace, with English as the language of instruction in programs that were benchmarked against, and accredited by, international best practices.
- Develop graduates with the holistic aptitudes and core competencies sought by all top industries, irrespective of specific vocational skills.
- Continue to seek feedback from local industry through a system of program advisory committees (PACs), and to adjust program offerings and content so that HCT graduates would be work-ready immediately upon graduation.
- Equip graduates with lifelong learning skills and technology prowess so they would be able to upgrade their skills throughout their careers.

Balancing Quality With Demand (1988–1994)

As their first priority, HCT's leaders focused on establishing a reputation for program quality. While enrollment levels, the diversity of offerings, and the cost per student were basic considerations, the quality of the learning experience was considered paramount. This pursuit of excellence became the driving force for the system's development and change. In the early years, admission was highly selective and no effort was spared to ensure that students had access to world-class learning resources, equipment, facilities, and faculty, totally free of cost.

HCT made extensive investments to encourage top secondary school graduates to attend HCT rather than traditional universities. The goal was for employers to consider it preferable to hire HCT graduates. Selective enrollment ensured that early adjustments to the curriculum, assessment, and management processes of this fledgling institution would not be adversely affected by too large a number of students. It also allowed this young institution sufficient time to evolve into a system that would meet the UAE's unique requirements. An important early adjustment was the introduction of a foundation year, which was designed to prepare public secondary school graduates, who came from schools where Arabic was the primary language of instruction, for instruction in English. The foundation year armed students with the general education and active learning skills they needed to succeed in 3-year career programs through which they would earn a higher national diploma.

In the beginning, HCT modeled its curriculum, human resources, and academic policies on those of the Ontario Colleges of Applied Arts and Technology. However, during the first year of operation, it became apparent that HCT would be wise to incorporate best practices of other world-class postsecondary systems for several reasons:

- Industry in the region, HCT's ultimate stakeholder, was strongly influenced by international practices. In particular, the engineering and accounting industries in the UAE typically followed U.S. and UK standards and codes. This included the key sectors of energy and construction. Skilled technicians and semiskilled operators predominantly came from South Asia. There was little Canadian influence on regional industry.

- The human resource managers of major UAE companies were likely to recognize vocational or educational credentials that followed the British system of higher national diplomas and higher national certificates.

- The system of education followed in UAE primary and secondary schools, coupled with Arabic being the language of instruction, meant that school leavers had very different skill levels and learning styles than students who entered North American tertiary education institutions. Significant transitional programs had to be designed before HCT could effectively deliver any western-designed curriculum.

These forces led HCT's leaders to mandate geographic hiring adjustments that affected faculty and academic manager recruitment. These adjustments gave HCT a balanced mix of professionals from the United Kingdom, the United States, Canada, and Australia, as well as some with educational or industrial experience in the Gulf region. These international best-of-breed faculty teams then began to refine the original curriculum, in close consultation with relevant PACs, which were made up of representatives from major local employers.

Employers' early feedback about graduate attitudes and intellectual skills helped shaped HCT's policies on attendance, punctuality, and student conduct. Work placement as a program component, systemwide common assessments, and international language proficiency tests such as IELTS (International English Language Testing System) became major directives for future practice. UAE civil service regulations and employer-screening practices prompted HCT to switch from a pass or fail grading system to a letter grade system.

By 1993–1994, thanks to strategic appointments of executives to lead the new colleges and support structure, HCT had a fast-evolving, unique academic system of higher education. To balance an increasing demand for new campuses throughout the country, caused by increasing demand for admission, the leaders introduced a system of centrally monitored checks and balances, with a strong quality assurance and quality control unit at its center. This system included Academic Central Services (ACS), along with streamlined administrative processes via central committees under the leadership of HCT's vice chancellor.

Designing Relevant and Benchmarked Programs

From the outset, HCT's mission mandated that curriculum leaders design and continually refine programs with two primary objectives:

- Programs must be relevant to the needs of local industry so that HCT graduates could be employed at entry-level technical jobs with minimal need for retraining.

- To ensure quality and to maintain articulation paths that would allow HCT graduates to pursue graduate programs overseas, program outcomes must be benchmarked or accredited by relevant international institutions.

Every program cluster offered in each HCT college was expected to have a PAC composed of professional managers from potential local employers. PACs were to review curriculum, suggest changes, and advise on new career program opportunities, as well as foster interaction between HCT staff, students, and the relevant UAE professional community. The importance given to PAC feedback helped ensure that HCT continued to meet its first objective: producing graduates with skill sets that were locally relevant and sought after by employers.

International benchmarking and accreditation were encouraged at three levels:

- Specific programs sought relevant professional accreditation for international benchmarking. For example, all higher diploma and bachelor of applied science programs offered by the business division were accredited by the Association of Collegiate Business Schools and Programs (ACBSP), higher diploma programs in engineering were benchmarked by the Accreditation Board of Engineering Technology–Technology Accreditation Commission (ABET–TAC), and higher diploma programs in information technology were accredited by Edexcel for several years. Health science programs have also completed their professional accreditation with different international agencies.

- HCT has made significant strides toward institutional accreditation to ensure the quality of its management, administrative, human resources, and program delivery processes. HCT has applied for accreditation from the Northwest Commission on Colleges and Universities in the United States.

- Since 1998, HCT has had an internal quality assurance and audit process, which started as a program quality assurance (PQA) process and has now been extended to service quality assurance as well.

Mass Provider of Technician Training (1995–2002)

Although HCT followed a highly selective admission process during its first 6 years, its leaders maintained the overarching objective that HCT would be an open-access institution for every eligible UAE national student who wished to pursue tertiary education. By 1994, HCT had been established as a top-class higher education institution. With the number of secondary school graduates increasing every year, there was increasing pressure from the community for HCT to fulfill its open-access mandate.

In June 1995, after a year of structured consultation with community stakeholders and of internal curriculum discussions, HCT established certificate diploma programs that were open to all national school leavers who applied. This resulted in a dramatic shift in HCT's education paradigm and created considerable resource management challenges. In the 1995–1996 academic year, enrollment increased 80% over the previous academic year. In the 13 years since June 1995, enrollment increased from 2,300 students to more than 16,000 (HCT, 2008b).

Since its inception, HCT has responded well to the challenges of dramatic growth by adopting innovations in curriculum design and delivery and by aggressively recruiting faculty from more than 80 countries who are qualified to teach vocational programs whose students have basic levels of academic knowledge and English communication skills. HCT adopts technology to facilitate a flexible learning environment. Delivering courses through blended e-learning platforms has ensured effective utilization of HCT's resources and greatly improved student participation and learning. Close coordination with industry partners has also helped HCT create programs that equip graduates to meet industry needs.

Corporate Sponsored Training Programs: 1996–Present

HCT's operational costs are fully funded by the UAE federal government through its annual budget. Fixed investments such as land, facilities, and major equipment are the responsibility of individual local emirates. The federal government is committed to free tertiary education for all eligible UAE national secondary-school graduates. The UAE corporate sector has been keen to promote education opportunities for its employees. To meet the need for corporate training and consulting, in 1996 HCT established a commercial arm, the Centre of Excellence for Research and Training (CERT).

In its early years, in addition to running short continuing education courses for the community, CERT began to design, develop, and deliver academic programs customized to meet the needs of specific clients, such as the UAE armed forces, municipalities, oil and gas process industries, the aviation industry, and health-care agencies. These sponsored programs led to HCT credentials, including diplomas, higher diplomas, and bachelor's degrees, in specialist areas that were typically not available to general HCT students. These sponsored programs were a win-win for every stakeholder:

- For the client industries, the ability to design program outcomes helped reduce training and development time periods, so program graduates were able to quickly become productive employees. With a guaranteed number of UAE national graduates coming out of these programs, industries could plan and implement their own operations with confidence.

- Students in these programs were typically offered a good stipend, in addition to free tuition. These sponsored students were contractually guaranteed employment in the sponsoring company immediately upon graduation, removing any uncertainties they might have and enabling them to focus on their career paths even while studying.

- Because the costs of these programs were fully recovered from the clients, HCT has been able to expand its program offerings in specialist areas relevant to local industry.

As of 2005, CERT engaged in an ambitious plan to expand its operations and be actively involved in many other commercial education, training, and research opportunities in the UAE and the Gulf region. More than 1,000 students and trainees were engaged in sponsored programs and courses at HCT-CERT. Strategies that are being developed by CERT in 2008 may result in a significant increase in the number of trainees.

INNOVATIONS IN TEACHING AND LEARNING

From its inception, HCT has had consistent expectations for faculty and student participation in hands-on active learning. Curriculum design and assessment have been based on learning outcomes, and program delivery has always been learner-centered. Applied, hands-on, activity-based teaching and learning have been encouraged and form a basis for recruiting and rewarding faculty members. The "chalk and talk" lecture mode of delivery is strongly discouraged. Small classes (15 to 20 students) contribute to highly interactive and participative learning. HCT's learning environment and curriculum design help integrate the theoretical and laboratory components of courses: Traditional classrooms are set within labs, giving faculty total flexibility to teach a theoretical concept for a few minutes, then immediately get the students to apply and understand the concept through hands-on experiments in the same room.

Technology is an integral and essential part of teaching and learning in all HCT programs. Most HCT campuses are wireless-enabled, and students are required to purchase high-end laptops before registering. As a result, every learning space is a potential computer lab, and traditional computer labs have been eliminated. In addition, many learning spaces are equipped with electronic smart boards that enable faculty to display PowerPoint presentations, access Web sites, and write information that the students can then download. Through video conferencing facilities, students and staff are able to connect with experts from around the world. Faculty members are encouraged to put all course notes and course information on a WebCT platform, which students can access through the Internet. Online courses are designed and offered with two objectives:

- In the short term, to encourage directed, self-managed learning rather than traditional teacher-led learning.

- In the long term, to offer fully online degree programs that permit HCT diploma and higher diploma graduates in distant locations, who don't have easy access to HCT campuses, to continue their studies.

HCT has become a well-known center for pioneering work in electronic learning, bringing international e-learning experts and educators to together through major international conferences. It hosts a biennial conference, E-ducation Without Borders, and an annual E-Merging E-Learning conference. Project-based learning has become the norm. To ensure that learners are able to integrate and apply concepts across different courses taken in the same semester or year, interdisciplinary projects are often designed by a team of faculty, then formally assessed, as part of students' course work. Many programs include a final-year or final-semester graduation project that encourages students and faculty to solve real-life industry- and business-based problems.

HCT programs, particularly in engineering and allied health, increasingly incorporate field visits and industry-based, cooperative "sandwich" programs. Students alternate semesters in the college and the workplace, taking structured training for credit toward a diploma or degree. Work experience, clinical placements, or on-the-job training are mandatory parts of the programs. Students are given clearly defined goals and learning outcomes that are assessed by both the faculty supervisor and the workplace supervisor.

Outcomes-Based HCT Learning Model

With the introduction of several new program majors within a few years (from 1993 to 1997), it was critical that HCT ensure overall consistency in credential characteristics and program outcomes across different program majors. Since 1998,

HCT has made consistent efforts to develop a framework against which individual specialized programs could be developed and benchmarked. Continuing with its rich practice of building on best-of-breed global educational experiences and developments, HCT introduced outcomes-based education faster than many other leading international universities and colleges. It has created a clearly measurable and verifiable learning model (see HCT, 2008c) in which the curriculum and student efforts are well mapped and documented against target graduate outcomes for a specific credential or program major.

The learning model describes the standards expected of learners, the values and attributes they should be encouraged to obtain and maintain, and the learning environment in which essential dialogue between faculty and student should occur. Graduate outcomes are a mechanism for establishing the standards of credentials and the depth and breadth of knowledge of HCT programs. They can also help benchmark HCT graduates in the national and international tertiary sector. An HCT graduate who experiences a holistic learning experience is considered to be the truest expression of HCT meeting its mission.

The outcomes-based HCT learning model ensures that graduates acquire the knowledge, skills, and abilities appropriate to their graduating status. Graduate outcomes define the HCT graduate. HCT strives to make its graduates capable in communications and information literacy; critical thinking, problem solving, and interdisciplinary exploration; global awareness; information technology; self-management and lifelong learning; teamwork and leadership; and vocational competencies.

Credential characteristics developed as part of the learning model carefully distinguish among diploma programs (vocational training for technicians), higher diploma programs (a combination of theoretical and practical knowledge that permits technologists to serve as a link between theory-based designers and front-line technical staff), and bachelor's degree programs (a completion to undergraduate education). Credential characteristics for the diploma are as follows:

- Knowledge of the underlying concepts and principles associated with their field of study, and an ability to evaluate and interpret these within the context of that area of study.

- An ability to use tools and technologies appropriate for their field of employment.

- An ability to present, evaluate, and interpret both quantitative data (i.e., numeric data) and qualitative data (i.e., non-numeric, descriptive data).

- An ability to evaluate the appropriateness of different approaches to solving problems related to their area(s) of study and/or work.

- An ability to communicate the results of their study/work accurately and reliably, and with structured and coherent arguments.

- Knowledge of environmental and ethical issues relating to their field of study in the UAE context.

- An ability to undertake further training and develop new skills within a structured and managed environment both individually and as team member.

- Qualities and transferable skills necessary for employment requiring the exercise of personal responsibility. (HCT, 2008c)

HCT's academic leaders have learned from the mission and curriculum creep that have affected many polytechnics and 4-year colleges around the world. In many cases, this creep has turned vocational diploma programs into associate degree pathway articulation, then into undergraduate programs. The technical and applied character that distinguishes these polytechnics and 4-year colleges from traditional universities, and that enables them to offer unique provisions and services to the local community, gets gradually blurred.

EVOLUTION OF A QUALITY ASSURANCE MODEL

From HCT's inception, its leaders recognized that the system needed an academic central services (ACS) unit to coordinate and ensure design and delivery of programs at multiple campuses throughout the country. Programs were organized across the academic divisions: general education, engineering, information technology, business, health science, education, and communications technology. Deans and coordinators were appointed as part of the ACS unit, and they reported to the ACS director. A key function of the new ACS was to set minimum quality parameters for the design, delivery, and monitoring of every program in each college. The goal was for colleges to meet or exceed these parameters in order to assure employers of HCT graduates that the system was consistent throughout.

HCT's leaders gave ACS significant support, along with the mandate to set standards in curriculum design, key assessments, lab and library resourcing, and academic policies and procedures. Program teams, division academic teams, academic councils, and policy councils constituted the organizational framework approving new programs and policies. The ACS managers chaired most of these committees, which were formed by representatives from each college.

In 1992, ACS instituted systemwide graduate aptitude tests (GATS), three or four major written assessments that were a requirement for graduation from all HCT courses. Over the next 3 years, GATS became a part of HCT's regular assessments for key courses during the academic year, rather than being given immediately prior to graduation. Such key common assessments continue to be given primarily as spot-checks to ensure that the entire HCT system interprets course outlines in a consistent way. These assessments have taken different forms over time. High-stakes examinations, project work, oral presentations, practical work, and other appropriate assessments can now be part of key common assessments.

HCT's quality control system has evolved significantly. A program quality assurance (PQA) model was introduced in 1998 to ensure that each HCT program was designed and delivered according to common quality parameters. This internal QA audit ensured that each program team was engaged in a deliberate, documented, and measurable process of continuous quality improvement. PQA had two primary aims:

- To help colleges and divisional academic teams give students the best possible opportunities for academic and personal success.
- To provide a framework for colleges and divisional academic teams to report how they help HCT achieve its mission.

The PQA system was designed for quality assurance of both curriculum design and curriculum delivery. Thus, the unit responsible for implementing PQA had to monitor the work of deans at ACS and the work of college faculty. Consequently, a new unit, the Institutional Effectiveness Directorate, was created as part of the vice chancellor's office. The directorate focused on international program accreditation and sought appropriate international benchmarks.

Each college and its divisional academic teams (DATs) used HCT's PQA key criteria (KC) to evaluate the quality of its PQA processes and activities and then recommended how these could be improved. Colleges were required to demonstrate how they satisfied seven key criteria for each program:

1. Industry and community satisfaction with the program.
2. Professional and external benchmarking, status, and recognition of the program.
3. Alignment of program and course aims, design, and learning outcomes with HCT graduate outcomes.
4. Student performance in assessment and progression through the program.
5. Student and graduate satisfaction with teaching, learning, and assessment.
6. Optimization of resources and resource issues for the program and courses.
7. Alignment of course delivery and teaching, learning, and assessment strategies with KC 3.

Each college and DAT responds to the key criteria by answering three questions:

- What is our process?
- What is the evidence from our process?
- What program improvements can we make from analyzing this evidence

Each college was to document its responses to the seven KCs in a major PQA report for each of the programs that it offered, on a systemwide 5-year cycle. Evidence of PQA processes for KCs and evidence resulting from these processes became a part of the relevant divisional quality portfolio at each college.

An annual assessment of how well graduates meet the HCT graduate outcomes has operated in parallel with the PQA system. Each college demonstrates student achievement of the graduate outcomes in each of its programs through results from key common assessments in English, mathematics, and computing (and any other common, systemwide assessments required by divisional academic teams) and through outcomes-based assessments (including, where appropriate, associated assessment products and grades from the portfolios of final-year students).

HCT's QA system continues to evolve at a rapid pace. The system was extended to cover other college-supported services, including management and leadership, and HCT leaders continue to strongly encourage international accreditation and benchmarking of programs. As was stated earlier, business programs are accredited by ACBSP and engineering programs are benchmarked by ABET–TAC. Communication technology programs are accredited by the American Communication Association (ACA). HCT has been seeking new accreditation of information technology and health science programs. As a natural evolution of its internal QA, HCT has applied for institutional accreditation from Northwest Association of Colleges and Schools in the United States.

Future Challenges and Solutions

In a fast-evolving, dynamic society such as the UAE, it is a major challenge to prepare long-term plans for higher education. However, medium-term strategic plans are possible and are encouraged by the leaders. As Chancellor Sheikh Nahayan summarized in his 2002 address to HCT,

> Mature institutions such as ours share certain characteristics and qualities that enable them to experience success and forge their future. I would like to list some of these characteristics with you now: Mature organizations, especially academic institutions, avoid repeating past mistakes and are able to anticipate problems before they occur; mature organizations use technology wisely and effectively and espouse teamwork, creativity, and innovation. Mature organizations also have finely tuned fiscal management systems and firm resource allocation plans. And mature academic institutions have flexible course delivery strategies, strong student support services, an ongoing commitment to lifelong learning, active partnerships with the community, effective assessment procedures for students, faculty, and administrators, professional development plans for all staff, and relevant collegial relationships with their sister institutions. Many of these characteristics and qualities are already in place within our college system, but many others need to be developed and refined.

Since 2002, UAE national secondary school leavers applying for higher education have chosen HCT colleges over other national and private universities in the country and overseas. Demand for HCT enrollment has been further increased by an ever-growing population and the resulting growth in numbers of secondary school graduates. As a result, HCT must find innovative solutions to a combination of challenges:

- Because HCT's mandate is to provide open and free access to tertiary education for all eligible UAE nationals, it cannot levy student fees to recoup even part of its costs.

- At this stage of the country's development, UAE's higher education institutions must recruit most teaching faculty and administrators internationally. Providing housing, children's education, and other compensation is more costly than it would be for UAE nationals. Because HCT is highly selective, its human resources costs are higher than those of comparable technical colleges elsewhere in the developed world.

- To attract, recruit, and retain world-class faculty members, HCT must be able to offer compensation packages that are strong enough to encourage people to leave successful career paths in their home countries. HCT leaders are determined not to compromise the quality of education in order to meet the increasing demand for quantity.

- HCT's policy council has studied the solutions and approaches used by state-funded universities and colleges in other countries to solve their own, similar budgetary problems. It may be able to use combinations of the following solutions to help restore the balance between demand and supply: increasing federal and local government funding for HCT; acquiring private-sector contributions through grants, scholarships, and sponsored programs; recovering fees for direct costs such as textbooks, lab consumables, and computer usage and charging tuition fees of students who are repeating courses; and expanding and franchising HCT in other countries on a commercial basis and using the revenue to support HCT's operations in the UAE.

CONCLUSION

HCT is meeting the identified workforce needs of the UAE's business and industrial communities. Its graduates are competent in the use of the English language, and they have the computer and scientific skills needed for today's technology-driven world. Gulf region employers often regard HCT graduates as their preferred job candidates. By emphasizing quality and relevance, HCT has created a variety of programs that meet increasing and ever-changing requirements. Focusing on and measuring quality has made HCT a leading institution in the Gulf region, and Sheikh Nahayan's unwavering commitment to building a world-class institution has earned the UAE a high-level reputation among the world's postsecondary education systems. From its original Canadian roots, HCT has taken the best from the developed countries of the world, leading to a degree of success that the UAE can be very proud of.

REFERENCES

Abed, I., & Hellyer, P. (Eds.). (2001). *United Arab Emirates: A new perspective.* Bangor NSW, Australia: Trident Press.

Abu-Samaha, A. M., & Shishakly, R. (2008). Assessment of school information system utilization in the UAE primary schools. *Journal of Issues in Informing Science and Information Technology, 5,* 525–542. Retrieved September 25, 2008, from http://proceedings.informingscience.org/InSITE2008/IISITv5p525-542AbuSamaha440.pdf

Al-Sulayti, H. (2003). Education and training in GCC countries: Some issues of concern. In Emirates Center for Strategic Studies and Research (Ed.), *Education and the Arab world: Challenges of the next millennium* (pp. 271–278). London: I. B. Tauris.

Higher Colleges of Technology (HCT). (2008a). *About HCT: Mission.* Retrieved September 25, 2008, from http://www.hct.ac.ae/misc/aspx/about_us.aspx

Higher Colleges of Technology (HCT). (2008b). *HCT at a glance.* Retrieved September 25, 2008, from http://www.hct.ac.ae/misc/aspx/hct_at_a_glance.aspx

Higher Colleges of Technology (HCT). (2008c, May 27). *The HCT learning model.* Retrieved August 25, 2008, from http://www.hct.ac.ae/organization/aspx/learningmodel.aspx

Nahayan, N. M. (2002). *2002 annual conference address,* Higher Colleges of Technology, Abu Dhabi, UAE. Retrieved August 25, 2008, from http://crm.hct.ac.ae/events/archive/2002/chancellor2002.htm

14

Community College Development in Vietnam: A Global and Local Dialectic

Diane E. Oliver, Sandra Engel, and Analy Scorsone

Since it began in the late 1960s, Vietnam's community college movement has had long periods of dormancy and has faced numerous challenges. Although it has been gaining momentum since 2001, there are many uncertainties about its structure and whether many of its institutions will survive. The movement illustrates two themes that are relevant to higher education systems around the world. First, there is a link between a country's political climate and the characteristics of its higher education system. When political conditions facilitate exchange across borders, the ideas that are exchanged will include concepts about education. Second, education systems reflect the "dialectic between the global and the local" (Arnove & Torres, 2003, p. 1). Countries must deal with the impact of globalization—the movement of economies, technologies, people, and ideas across borders. The ways that a community college serves the needs of its local community are part of its country's larger response to globalization.

THE SOCIALIST REPUBLIC OF VIETNAM

Vietnam, which stretches from China in the north to the Gulf of Thailand in the south, is home to 83.5 million people, 90% of them ethnic Vietnamese and 50% of them under 25. The country is divided into 59 provinces and 5 municipalities and is governed by the Communist Party of Vietnam. The official literacy rate is 93.9% (Ashwill & Diep, 2004; U.S. Central Intelligence Agency, 2006). Reforms have opened Vietnam to the outside world and spurred economic growth. The U.S.–Vietnam bilateral trade agreement implemented in December 2001 was an important achievement for both countries. From 2000 to 2005, Vietnam's economy grew an average 7% annually, and per capita gross domestic product was USD 3,000 (U.S. CIA, 2006).

Vietnam has a long and difficult history of being ruled or colonized by outsiders—Chinese dynasties from 207 BC to the 10th century, the French in the mid-19th century to the mid-20th century, and the Japanese for a brief period during World War II. During the Cold War, North Vietnam was supported by China and the Soviet Union, South Vietnam, by the United States. After the Second Indochina War ended and U.S. troops were withdrawn in March 1973, the north overtook the south on April 30, 1975, and the country was reunified as the Socialist Republic of Vietnam.

The Community College Movement

In the Beginning

Vietnam's community college movement began in the late 1960s, when peace talks were under way and the Republic of Vietnam in the south was optimistically planning for reconstruction. "The concept of the community college, with a comprehensive curriculum responsive to the needs of the community was accepted with enthusiasm by the common people" (Yee, 1995, p. 142). Unneeded military installations and underused education facilities would be converted into community colleges, which would train demobilized military personnel for civilian jobs and relieve some of the pressure on the universities (Doan, 2000). Community colleges originated with a decree made by the president on August 15, 1971 (Thu, 1974; Thuy, 1971). Each college was to offer six core programs typical of U.S. community colleges: occupational, transfer, remedial, guidance and counseling, general education, and adult education (Thu, 1974).

The first two community colleges were established in 1971: Tien Giang (Upper Delta) Community College in the Mekong Delta, and Duyen Hai (Coastal) Community College in the Central Region (Doan, 2000; Thu, 1974). Duyen Hai Community College operated from 1972 to 1975. It had two divisions, career and transfer; many students in the transfer division went on to study at Saigon University and Hue University. The college enrolled about 800 students, and its main programs were fisheries and marine mechanics. Duyen Hai had a lot of autonomy but kept the ministry of education informed about its operations. If a problem arose, the college was required to respond (Oliver, 2002). Higher education in the south was modeled after the centralized French colonial system. "The decision-making reflected national policies which were, in reality, those of the French in the 1950s and to some extent the Americans of the 1960s" (Naughton, 1979, p. 104).

From Dormancy to Awakening

After North and South Vietnam were reunified in 1975, the Soviet model of higher education was adopted for the entire country. Community colleges were closed, private institutions were either closed or made public, most multidiscipline universities began to offer just one discipline, and separate research institutes were established. The next event that defined higher education in Vietnam was the 1987 implementation of *doi moi*, or renovation, which "refers to the process and consequences of pursuing an open-market orientation while maintaining the principles of socialism as interpreted by the [Communist Party of Vietnam]" (Le & Sloper, 1995, p. 3). According to Tran (1998), "higher education no longer had the sole purpose of supplying manpower for the state sector. It would now serve the market-based economy" (p. 170).

A 1993 United Nations Development Program (UNDP) assessment of Vietnam's education and training needs also had a substantial impact. One of the problems the report identified was poor coordination between higher education programs and the needs of research, production, and employment (Sauvageau, 1997). In response, the Ministry of Education and Training (MOET) proposed to establish new community colleges that would provide the training needed to support the country's economic transition and to convert pedagogical institutions throughout the country into community colleges (Sauvageau, 1997).

A collaboration with several Canadian community colleges and the Association of Canadian Community Colleges (ACCC) that began in 1990 had established a long-range vision for the country's higher education system. However, the 1993 restructuring of the system did not address this vision. The two most obvious results of the restructuring were that the pedagogical colleges were renamed junior colleges (Sauvageau, 1997) and that a provisional regulation decreed on March 30, 1994, became the legal foundation for establishing community colleges in Vietnam (Harvey, 2005).

The impact of the UNDP assessment illustrates the substantial influence that international agencies exert on education in developing countries. The World Bank advocates diversification of types of higher education institutions and their funding. Relevant to the development of community colleges, the World Bank (1994) stated that "in the most successful cases, non-university institutions offer training that responds flexibly to labor market demands and is linked with university programs through appropriate transfer mechanisms such as credit systems and equivalency provisions" (p. 5). Vietnam has been diversifying its higher education institutions and their funding. Tuition was instituted in 1987, and by 1994 it accounted for 22% of public universities' recurrent expenditures (World Bank, 1994).

Vietnam's community college movement began to come out of dormancy in the early 1990s through its exchanges with Canadian community colleges and as a result of the 1994 enabling regulation. In 1995, the United States and Vietnam restored diplomatic relations. In October of that year, the minister of education and training invited the president of Lansing Community College, Michigan, to visit Vietnam and discuss the development of a national community college system ("Memorandum of Understanding," 1996). This contact came about because a former member of the ministry of education had become a professor at Lansing; some of his former students had in turn began working at MOET, establishing a connection between the college and the ministry. At about the same time, MOET also invited ACCC to develop a joint proposal for community college development. Before these two community college projects could progress much further, though, the minister of education and training stepped down and MOET ended the projects.

A Pilot Program

Vietnam National University–Ho Chi Minh City (VNU–HCMC) was established in January 1995 through the consolidation of nine independent universities (see VNU–HCMC, 2000). In 1996, the university ran a pilot community college program in three remote and impoverished provinces—Tien Giang, Dong Tap, and Binh Thuan—with the intent of bringing education to young people who, because of the high cost of living in big cities, would not otherwise be able to get it. The program was designed to match the needs of the local areas. For example, in the Mekong Delta, the college would teach agriculture, fishery management, and forestry (Oliver, 2002). An important feature of the project was that successful community college graduates were able to transfer to universities affiliated with VNU–HCMC. MOET did not endorse the pilot program, but VNU–HCMC was able to proceed with it anyway: The university reports directly to the prime minister and could obtain the necessary funding from tuition and its existing budget.

In May 1996, Vietnamese academics, including the vice president of VNU–HCMC, visited community colleges in Kentucky. In exchange, the vice chancellor of the Kentucky community college system and representatives of the University of Kentucky visited Vietnam in April 1997. They met with university officials in Hanoi, Ho Chi Minh City, and Can Tho, and with community and technical college officials in Phan Thiet, Tien Giang, and Dong Thap.

But 2 years after the May 1996 visit, MOET still had not certified the pilot community colleges or provided them with any funding, so, in 1998, the colleges closed and their 3,000 students were transferred to other colleges. The senior academic who had led the pilot project identified three things that prevented MOET officials from supporting the colleges: a lack of understanding of the community college concept, concern that graduates would not have received a good quality education, and fear that the reputation of the sponsoring university would be damaged if the community colleges were unsuccessful (Oliver, 2002). The lack of articulation agreements between the community colleges and the universities to which they would transfer, all of which had different entrance requirements, appears to have been another significant reason why the colleges were closed. In addition, most of the academics in MOET were trained in the Soviet higher education system, in which institutions focus on topics with a narrow scope and great depth. They could not understand the fundamental concept that community colleges offer a broad scope and practice-oriented curricula. This lack of understanding continues to present a problem for the community colleges.

Six Community Colleges

After the VNU–HCMC program ended, Vietnam's community college movement was kept alive primarily through the efforts of Can Tho University (CTU), whose leaders had excellent international relations skills and a sustained interest in having community colleges in the Mekong Delta. One CTU rector, who had received his PhD in the United States, failed to convince MOET officials to establish a community college in the Mekong Delta. He then discussed his ideas about community colleges with the Netherlands (Oliver, 2002). The Netherlands does not have community colleges, but the education and training offered by its universities of professional education and its regional education centers are based on similar ideas (Teekens, 2002).

According to Teekens (2002), in 1995 MOET asked the government of the Netherlands to provide assistance for core programs at six pilot community colleges in Vietnam. Three would offer a food-processing program, the other three, a mechanical engineering program. The first of these colleges opened in Hai Phong in December 2000. Five others, in Ha Tay, Quang Ngai, Ba Ria-Vung Tau, Dong Thap, and Tien Giang, began operating in 2001. A long-range objective was to enable students to transfer to a sponsoring university.

In addition to funding, the Netherlands provided technical training to Vietnamese community college faculty members. In 2003, an apparent lack of agreement with MOET led the Dutch to withdraw their funding. The six community colleges continued to operate but did not have the equipment needed to establish the proposed core programs in food processing and mechanical engineering.

THE VIETNAM–CANADA COMMUNITY COLLEGE PROJECT

On August 3, 2001, MOET approved the establishment of Tra Vinh Community College (TVCC). The college was sponsored by CTU and received substantial assistance from the Canadian International Development Agency, in cooperation with ACCC and a consortium of Canadian institutions led by the Saskatchewan Institute of Applied Science and Technology. The Tra Vinh People's Committee, which had been highly supportive, established TVCC on August 29, 2001, and construction began (Pham & Harvey, n.d.). One reason why the TVCC project was accepted by MOET was that a Vietnamese technical team and representatives of both the Tra Vinh People's Committee and MOET made a well-planned study visit to a Canadian community college in 2001. It is almost impossible for people in Vietnam to imagine what a Canadian or U.S. community college might be like, so exchanges that have allowed them to see such colleges have been of great importance to Vietnam's community college development.

Tra Vinh is one of the poorest provinces in Vietnam. In 2001, rice farming with labor-intensive methods accounted for most of the economy, although aquaculture and some industrial capacity were emerging (Harvey, 2005). Approximately 85% of Tra Vinh's 985,000 residents lived in rural communities. A particularly important reason for developing a community college there was that only 10% of the population had completed secondary school and "women, rural residents and the Khmer minority (representing 30% of the provincial population) have traditionally been under-represented in the education system" (Pham & Harvey, n.d., p. 2). The Tra Vinh People's Committee planned to diversify the province's crops and expand its service, manufacturing, and commercial sectors. It believed that the community college model would provide the training needed to support economic development.

The first courses to be offered were agriculture, aquaculture, information technology, office education, electrical construction, and building construction (Pham & Harvey, n.d.), and it was assumed that TVCC would focus on 3-year college diplomas. Article 28 of the 11th Draft Education Law of 2004 stated that the college would grant an upper secondary education certificate to those who completed a 3-year college program and a certificate of technical education to those who completed a program of 1.5 to 2 years, including practical working experience. A Tra Vinh Province labor market analysis that was conducted in October 2002 suggested that college graduates would probably have difficulty finding employment. The greatest demand was for short-term training in agriculture and aquaculture production.

Like Vietnam's other rural provinces, Tra Vinh Province had to reconcile the needs of its labor market with political pressure to offer a college-level diploma and a certain degree of academic prestige. TVCC dealt with this challenge by offering articulation between postsecondary vocational programs and college-level programs. Students could earn a postsecondary vocational certificate through 6 months, 1 year, or 2 years of training. A student who had graduated from a 2-year vocational program could complete a further 18 months of training and be awarded a 3-year college diploma. TVCC also offered a continuing education program that enabled former students to return to the college later and upgrade their skills or their certification. MOET approved this pilot program in March 2005 (Harvey, 2005).

In November 2004, TVCC opened four satellite training centers in accessible locations. These centers offer short-duration courses designed to meet the needs of rural adult learners. TVCC and Nong Lam University in Thu Duc established an articulation agreement whereby TVCC graduates could transfer to the university's programs in agriculture, aquaculture, and post-harvest technologies. This was a notable development, because MOET had previously resisted transfer between community colleges and universities.

TVCC has established an impressive community college model with the financial support and highly professional assistance of the Canadian agencies and partners. Although other community colleges could learn from this model, exchanges of information among higher education institutions in Vietnam have not been common practice. The Canadians also provided TVCC staff and faculty with excellent training in needs assessment, strategic planning, and curriculum development. This training will help TVCC continue its progress. The types of knowledge and skills that TVCC has developed through its Canadian partners do not generally exist at Vietnam's other community colleges.

CAN THO UNIVERSITY AND THE KIEN GIANG COMMUNITY COLLEGE PROJECT

In May 2001, CTU officials met with representatives from each of the 12 Mekong Delta provinces to discuss higher education development in the region. CTU introduced the community college concept and recommended that each province establish its own community college. To overcome the negative perceptions that had resulted from a lack of understanding about the community college role and from the traditional preference for a bachelor's degree over technical–vocational diplomas, CTU's officials focused on distinguishing between college and university. They emphasized that, because universities serve state-owned organizations, large companies, and foreign-owned companies, community colleges are essential for developing private industry, training entrepreneurs, and developing small to medium-sized businesses.

Shortly after this meeting, the Kien Giang Provincial People's Committee (2001) submitted a community college proposal to MOET. With a population of more than 1.5 million, Kien Giang is one of the larger provinces in the Mekong Delta. Its demographics are quite different from Tra Vinh's. According to the proposal, two thirds of the province's districts are in remote rural and island regions whose residents are too poor to send their children to big cities to be educated. The socioeconomic situation and a shortage of trained workers were two of the compelling justifications for establishing the community college. It was estimated that Kien Giang Community College (KGCC) would enroll between 3,600 and 4,500 students.

CTU had a strong relationship with Texas Tech University's Vietnam Center, one of whose staff members was evaluating the suitability of the U.S. community college model for Vietnam. In June 2001, CTU asked the Vietnam Center to find a U.S. partner for KGCC. Mohawk Valley Community College (New York) agreed to take on that role, with the continued involvement of Texas Tech. The Kentucky Community and Technical College System joined the partnership in March 2002. In April 2002, the Kien Giang People's Committee received approval from MOET to establish the community college.

In November 2002, KGCC's U.S. partners, in cooperation with CTU and MOET, held a 2-day seminar that was attended by seven of Vietnam's eight community colleges. CTU and MOET announced that they would form an association of community colleges. It is not easy in Vietnam to obtain approval to establish a formal organization, so the association never came into being. However, MOET and CTU officials continue to meet periodically to work on systemic challenges, an approach that seems to be effective. By May 2003, when KGCC and its U.S. partnering institutions signed a memorandum of understanding, Richland College of the Dallas County Community College District (Texas) had joined.

Because the U.S. partners did not have a funding source to support the KGCC project, they realized that it would be necessary to take an incremental approach, rather than trying to help develop an entire community college, as had been done in Tra Vinh. KGCC was asked to prioritize the programs that it wished to develop, and the rector singled out the area of information technology (IT). One important factor in facilitating communications and exchanges of ideas during this formative period was that the partner from Mohawk Valley Community College worked at KGCC as a Fulbright Scholar from February to June 2003 (Engel, 2003).

In October 2003, the U.S. partners met at Mohawk Valley Community College to draft a grant proposal, and in 2004 a major milestone occurred with the award of grant from the U.S. Agency for International Development and the Association Liaison Office for Cooperation in Development to upgrade KGCC's 2- and 3-year IT programs (Kentucky Community and Technical College System, 2004). This project involved work by U.S. community college faculty in Vietnam and KGCC faculty in the United States. It was excellent for faculty development, served to make the partnership even stronger, and clearly demonstrated the great value of exchanging people and ideas.

As of the 2005 academic year, KGCC had 2,024 full-time and 2,975 part-time students. The primary 3-year programs were IT, accounting, electrical engineering, and food processing technology. The 2-year programs were in aquaculture, IT, accounting, and animal husbandry. KGCC also offered short-term and vocational training.

Moving Toward a New Era

In November 2005, MOET and the Kien Giang People's Committee cosponsored an important conference on Vietnam's community colleges, organized by KGCC's rector and held in the capital city of Kien Giang Province. The objectives were to create dialogue and to facilitate the drafting of a permanent regulation authorizing the operation of community colleges in Vietnam. KGCC's U.S. partners had arranged for speakers from the United States, Canada, and Thailand. Representatives of the U.S. embassy in Hanoi and U.S. consulate in Ho Chi Minh City attended, as did members of Vietnam's provincial people's committees, representatives of NGOs, and others. Importantly, more than 100 Vietnamese higher education leaders attended (Whitus, 2005).

The original 1994 decree establishing community colleges was amended on August 8, 2002. The new legislation "recognized that community colleges played a pivotal role in tertiary program articulation, especially between the vocational and college programming levels that were delivered in the colleges themselves" (Harvey, 2005, p. 89). Particularly significant was the discussion concerning decentralization of program decision making to the people's committee level.

In January 2006, participants at a conference at Ba Ria-Vung Tau worked on the draft of a permanent regulation for Vietnam's community colleges. The participants included officials of nine community college and two MOET representatives. Most of the ideas, opinions, suggestions, and papers from the November 2005 meeting were considered in preparing this final draft, which was submitted to MOET a few days after the conference.

These conferences are among many indicators that Vietnam now accepts community colleges as an important way to meet its socioeconomic and higher education needs, especially in the rural provinces. Others are that the country now has nine community colleges, that the completion of a permanent regulation is impending, and that the government plans to establish community colleges in seven more Mekong Delta provinces by 2010. Another significant development is that in May 2006, MOET was poised to enact an official document allowing transfers between community colleges and universities.

CHALLENGES

The future development of Vietnam's community colleges faces substantial challenges. The country must establish its own community college model, which will involve clearly defining the colleges' missions and determining how community colleges can be adapted to meet local needs. The management of community colleges must be informed by strategic planning and quality assessment. Strategic planning has not been a strength of higher education in Vietnam, and quality assessment is just beginning to be addressed, as a result of recent progress toward establishing an accreditation system.

In Vietnam, as in other developing countries, knowledge itself is highly valued. Vietnam faces a particular challenge in developing community colleges: The strong influence that Confucian philosophy has on how education is viewed (Oliver, 2004) and the mindset that community colleges are inferior to universities. Even though employment surveys indicate that the community college is an excellent fit for human resource development, especially in rural areas, some provinces will not be satisfied with anything but a university. For example, My Tho, in Tien Giang Province, had a community college, but in January 2005, the Tien Giang People's Committee decided to turn the college into a university. Although other provinces may convert their community colleges, it is probable that at least some community college leaders and provincial people's committees will stay the course in developing their community colleges. The government has voiced the need to provide vocational, occupational, and technical training and has discussed increasing the autonomy and accountability of higher education institutions (VietNamNet Bridge, 2005). These developments are encouraging for the future of Vietnam's community colleges.

CONCLUSION

Vietnam's community college movement is stronger now than at any other time in the country's history. The political climate has affected Vietnam's higher education system, and the move toward a socialist market-oriented economy has resulted in dramatic changes that make community colleges even more relevant to addressing the country's socioeconomic needs. Normalized relations between the United States and Vietnam have facilitated higher education partnerships, and Vietnam's colleges are likely to benefit from partnerships with U.S. community colleges that want to work with international partners on projects that broaden the perspectives of their faculty members and students. Canada's community colleges will probably continue to provide professional expertise and support to Vietnam's community college development.

REFERENCES

Arnove, R. F., & Torres, C. A. (Eds.). (2003). *Comparative education: The dialectic of the global and the local.* New York: Rowan & Littlefield.

Ashwill, M. A., & Diep, T. N. (2005). *Vietnam today: A guide to a nation at a crossroads.* Boston: Intercultural Press.

Doan, H. D. (2000). *Foreign-trained academics and the development of Vietnamese higher education since doi moi.* Unpublished doctoral dissertation, University of Nottingham, England.

Engel, S. (2003, January 12). Vietnam so much more than a war. *Utica Observer-Dispatch.* Retrieved March 27, 2006, from http://www.uticaod.com/archive/2003/01/12/opinion/14010.html

Harvey, D. J. (2005). *Policy recommendations for community colleges in Vietnam.* Unpublished master's thesis, University of Saskatchewan, Saskatoon, Canada.

Kentucky Community and Technical College System. (2004). *U.S. institutions and Kien Giang Community College partnership program: Information technology workforce development* (USAID/ALO grant). (Available from Kentucky Community and Technical College System, 300 North Main Street, Versailles, KY 40383)

Kien Giang Provincial People's Committee. (2001). *Kien Giang Community College founding project.* (Available from Kien Giang Community College, 217 Chu Van An Street, Rach Gia Town, Vietnam)

Le, T. C., & Sloper, D. (1995). Higher education in Vietnam: The door opens—from inside. In D. Sloper & T. C. Le (Eds.), *Higher education in Vietnam: Change and response* (pp. 1–25). New York: St. Martin's Press.

Memorandum of understanding on cooperation between the Department of Higher Education, Ministry of Education and Training, Viet Nam, and Lansing Community College, Michigan, U.S.A. (1996, May). (Available from Lansing Community College, 1113-Multicultural Center, P.O. Box 40010, Lansing Michigan 48901-7210)

Naughton, P. W. (1979). Some comparisons of higher education in Vietnam: 1954–1976. *Canadian and International Education, 8*(2), 100–116.

Oliver, D. E. (2002). *The U.S. community college system as a potential model for developing countries: The case of Vietnam.* (UMI No. 9918255)

Oliver, D. E. (2004, Summer). Higher education challenges in developing countries: The case of Vietnam. *International Journal of Educational Policy, Research, & Practice,* 5(2), 3–18.

Pham, T. K., & Harvey, D. (n.d.). *The Tra Vinh Community College model: Integration of vocational, college and university education and training delivery to meet local and regional needs.* (Available from Saskatchewan Institute of Applied Science and Technology, 119 4th Avenue South, Saskatoon, SK, Canada, S7K 5X2)

Sauvageau, P. P. (1997). *Higher education for development: A history of modern higher education in the Socialist Republic of Vietnam.* Boston: Boston University. Retrieved May 13, 2001, from http://www.gis.net/~psauvage/DISSERTATION/htm

Teekens, H. (2002). The establishment of six pilot community colleges in Vietnam: Educational innovation in higher education. In K. Epskamp (Ed.), *Education in the South: Modalities of international support revisited* (Nuffic Paperback 3). The Hague, Netherlands: Nuffic.

Thu, N. X. (1974). *Organizational structure and governance of public universities in Vietnam.* (UMI No. 7505672)

Thuy, N. V. (1971). *Proposal for a model core curriculum for the first two undergraduate years in institutions of higher education in Vietnam.* (UMI No. 7222294)

Tran, H. P. (1998). *Vietnamese higher education at the intersection of French and Soviet influences.* (UMI No. 9918255)

U.S. Central Intellligence Agency. (2006, January 10). Vietnam. In the *2000 world factbook.* Retrieved March 17, 2006, from http://www.cia.gov/cia/publication/factbook/geos

VietNamNet Bridge. (2005, November 6). *15 nam nua, GD dai hoc VN dat dang cap khu vuc.* [In 15 years Vietnam higher education will reach to the regional level]. Hanoi, Vietnam: Author.

Vietnam National University–Ho Chi Minh City (VNU–HCMC). (2000). *Prospectus.* [Brochure]. Ho Chi Minh City, Vietnam: Author.

Whitus, J. (2005, December 14). *Community colleges making history and international friends in Vietnam* [News release]. Retrieved August 13, 2008, from http://www.kctcs.net/newspublications/newsreleases.cfm?nr_id=127

World Bank. (1994). *Higher education: The lesson of experience.* (World Bank Stock No. 12745). Washington, DC: Author.

Yee, A. H. (1995). *East Asian higher education: Traditions and transformations.* New York: International Association of Universities and Elsevier Science.

EUROPE

15

Further Education in Denmark

Stuart A. Rosenfeld, Cynthia D. Liston, and Hanne Shapiro

enmark's system of vocational education and training (VET) has influenced a number of innovations in U.S. education policy, including youth apprenticeships, national skill standards, and middle colleges. In 1999, after an extensive review of vocational education programs around the world based on rigorous criteria, the Carl Bertelsmann Foundation in Germany awarded Denmark its prestigious prize for best program, a program that the foundation said, "represents a further development of the dual system and conveys a more extensive theoretical background than the German system of VET, as the young people spend more time in school" (Bertelsmann Foundation, 1999). Since then, Denmark has continued to improve its VET system with a series of educational reforms.

As the following timeline shows, VET in Denmark dates back to technical schools established by medieval guilds in the 17th century. Evening apprenticeship programs that began in the 19th century evolved into Denmark's present-day classroom- and workplace-based diploma, certificate, and degree programs.

1600s	Denmark's first technical schools were established by medieval guilds in the mid-17th century to train dock workers, carpenters, and clothing production workers.
1870	Denmark had 50 technical schools.
1889	The 1889 Apprenticeship Act allowed the government to regulate the technical education system through standardized syllabuses, texts, and examinations.
1910	The number of technical schools had grown to 170.

1921   The 1921 Apprenticeship Act created a "social partnership" among employers, unions, and schools.

1956   When skilled labor was in great demand, all previous restrictions to entry into technical apprenticeship programs were abolished. Instruction shifted from evening to day classes, new course requirements were added, and colleges were expected to choose areas of technical specialization.

1977   The Basic Vocational Education Act of 1977 was enacted in response to rising unemployment, a shortage of apprenticeship positions, and criticism that students were being forced to choose careers too early. The act reorganized the technical education system so that students would have a year of school-based education followed by an alternative to the traditional apprenticeship.

1991   The system was streamlined. Programs were consolidated, reducing their number from 300 to about 90.

1993   The minister of education launched the Education for All program to reduce the high dropout rate among Danish youth.

2000   The number of tracks was reduced to seven, six technical and one commercial, with almost 100 specializations within those seven tracks.

2003   The Stepwise to Qualifications plan of 2003, designed to increase flexibility, required each vocational–technical student to develop a personal education plan based on assessments of prior learning.

2007   Act No. 561, an amendment to the Act on Vocational Education and Training, was adopted. The government's Globalisation Council began implementing the globalization strategy published in 2006 by the Danish government to increase wages and skills to achieve social cohesion and economic competitiveness. Among the goals were to achieve an 85% completion rate for upper secondary students by 2010 and 95% by 2015.

Overview of Vocational Education Pathways

Denmark requires 1 year of preschool plus 9 years combined of primary and lower secondary education. The education system is primarily public, but the state covers 85% of the cost of attending private school (Shapiro, 2004). Although most students do complete the 9 years of compulsory education and all students have the option to attend 10th grade, there have been policy measures to encourage more students to go directly from 9th grade into an upper secondary program. Following the 9 compulsory years of basic schooling, 45% of students enter general upper secondary education (gymnasium), which offers academic programs preparing graduates for further studies if they choose to go on (Ministry of Education, 2008c). The majority of students, however, enter one of two VET tracks: 29.7% enter VET, and 17.8% enter vocationally-oriented upper secondary education (Ministry of Education, 2008c). (What distinguishes these two tracks is that VET programs are those providing recognized qualifications for practice within a specific trade.) Because most of the vocational programs last 3 to 4 years, they approximate the K–14 program of study that some U.S. policy experts have advocated.

The head of the department of vocational education describes the four main objectives of the Danish VET system as follows: (1) to involve all stakeholders, including government, social partners, students, and faculty; (2) to be flexible enough to attract and accommodate more students; (3) to be inclusive enough to ensure the integration of immigrants and weak learners; and (4) to be adaptable enough to meet the challenges of the globalizing world (Ministry of Education, 2008b, p. 4).

Key Characteristics of Danish VET

One of the key characteristics of the Danish VET system is its national system for assessing quality. Each school must have a quality plan, monitor quality, and make its strategy on ensuring quality public on the Internet. The Statistical Office of the Ministry of Education, in collaboration with the social partners, maintains a comprehensive collection of statistics and indicators to monitor program and labor market outcomes. Central curricular goals are based on competencies and outcomes corresponding to actual workplace competencies, which integrate practical, theoretical, methodological, and personal skills. Denmark's quality assessment strategies are outlined in *The Danish Approach to Quality—in Vocational Education and Training* (Ministry of Education, 2008a).

Lifelong learning is also at the core of the system, with credit transfer an important element. With the most recent reforms, the system provides substantial options for offering pathways and linkages horizontally and vertically. Personal education plans and validation of prior learning are also central to ensuring that the system can accommodate different students and their different needs. VET programs encourage lifelong learning by offering students the option of qualifying for a vocation upon completion of a program or postponing the decision and seeking further education. Recent legislation on the assessment and recognition of informal and nonformal learning plays a central role in this strategy (see Seyfried & Souto Otero, 2006). For a fuller description, see *Denmark's Strategy for Lifelong Learning: Education and Lifelong Skills Upgrading for All* (Ministry of Education, 2007).

Governance and Structure

The backbone of the Danish VET system is a tripartite governance structure that involves the ministry of education, social partners, and colleges and businesses, as well as trainees, across all levels. The ministry of education is responsible for general VET policies, approving qualifications, and for quality assurance. The social partners are represented by a number of councils and committees that act at local and national levels to provide advice on matters such as qualifications, labor trends, duration and evaluation of programs, availability and development of apprenticeship, and so forth. Colleges and businesses cooperate with each other on program planning, and each are involved in monitoring students' education plans.

The Danish VET system consists of approximately 115 colleges. Some of these are solely technical, others are commercial, and others yet are combined, primarily as a result of college mergers. Policy objectives and the framework for learning outcomes (competency standards) are formulated at the national level, while responsibility for operational planning for the programs of study, specialized content, and teaching methods rests at the local level. Although the overall elements of education plans are governed by the Act on Vocational Education and Training, the colleges are responsible for local planning for specific VET qualifications in cooperation with local training committees. Each college has its own board of directors and manages its own budget.

With the reforms of the upper secondary vocational qualification system during the past decades, the system has evolved from a rather prescriptive system based on detailed regulations to a framework-governed system. This implies greater co-responsibility for schools and school boards in financial accountability, as well as details of curricula, execution of programs, and quality control. These are part of strategy to ensure that the system continuously responds proactively to changes in the labor market and the wider society without necessarily amending the overall legislation as well as being more responsive to local conditions.

Dual Training

The main principle of the Danish VET system is that of dual training, whereby education and training is provided alternately in a college and in a company under an apprenticeship. Programs range from 18 months to 5.5 years and consist of two parts: a basic course, which is broad in scope, and a main course, which provides specialized training for a specific trade. The duration of the program and whether the student begins in either a college or a company depends on the individual student profile. VET programs have been consolidated into seven access paths, each of which has its own basic entry course that is fairly broad in scope: technology and communication, building and construction, crafts and technique, food production and catering, mechanical engineering, transport and logistics service industries, and commerce (including trade, office, and finance). Within each of these seven areas, there are many possible specializations for students to pursue.

All VET students have a personal education plan with a contract drawn up between teacher and student. Based on an assessment of the students' prior competencies, the education plan creates a pathway toward students' goals and interests. This plan is entered into a national Web tool called "Elevplan," which also contains the student's logbooks, papers, notes from college, and a scorecard showing progress toward the outcomes listed in the curriculum framework of their program. The system contains all learning activities, which include expected competencies and outcomes, which allows for closer collaboration between student and teacher in tracking progress and planning. It also allows employers to follow their apprentices' progress, although relatively few employers use this tool to enroll them online.

To participate in the sandwich apprenticeship program, each student must find an employer, occasionally more than one, and both sign a contract for the duration of the training program. Employers have to be approved by the trade committees to provide apprenticeships and must submit formal reports that become part of the students' portfolios. The portfolios, which include all formal communications between employer and school, follow students throughout their education. The classroom instruction becomes increasingly specialized over time, tuned to the particular occupation chosen. Students finish with a series of competency exams.

Costs of education and training in the colleges are borne by tax revenues distributed by the government. However, employers are required pay students' wages, which are at least half of minimum wage, during both the workplace and classroom parts of the program. Every company with more than one employee must pay into a collective training fund, and, as an economic incentive, those firms that take apprentices are reimbursed for 90% of the apprentices' wages during their in-school periods and 80% of their travel expenses through the fund. In 2003, each employer paid DKK 370 (approximately USD 60) every 3 months for every full-time employee-equivalent. In 2003, the fund paid more than DKK 2.9 billion (approximately USD 468 million) in reimbursement to companies with apprentices (Centre for Educational Research and Innovation, 2003).

Denmark's model differs significantly from the better-known German apprenticeship model by integrating school-based theory and projects more thoroughly with practice gained through work experience. Danish vocational students spend between 30% and 50% of their education in school, whereas their German or Austrian counterparts spend roughly 20% of their education in school. Because it layers extended periods of college and work, this dual system is sometimes referred to as the "sandwich model."

HTX and HHX

One of the characteristics of a knowledge economy is greater demand and rewards for higher levels of education—among both students and employers. In the 1980s, Danish technical and business colleges began to offer programs to better prepare students for higher education. The HTX (technical) and HHX (commercial) upper secondary programs are special non-dual system tracks within the colleges designed to simplify and enhance transfer. Although students' choices between academic and vocational paths are made quite early, either track provides entry to higher education.

VET programs result in a nationally recognized certificate that gives students access to higher education, typically 2-year short-cycle programs also housed at technical or business colleges; HTX and HHX graduates may enroll in universities or in professional tertiary education. Thus, HTX and HHX programs allow students more choices within their programs—two thirds of all curricular content is compulsory, and one third is elective. It is even possible for students to obtain full or partial double qualification through electives from the HTX and HHX programs. Although these are special programs that serve a relatively small number of students, policies are being designed to make all vocational programs more flexible so that any student with the interest and competence is able to continue on toward higher levels of qualification.

Adult Programs

Danish vocational college students are typically younger than their counterparts at U.S. community colleges because Danes enter college at an earlier age. Danish VET students are on average 21 years when they begin the basic program and approximately 26 years when they start the specialized program. The average age for completing a vocational qualification is 28 years with large variations across programs; for example, students who obtain a qualification within social and health services are on average 34 years old upon completion.

Until recently, Denmark had a separate set of institutions for adult training called AMU Centers. Some 24 centers provided training to adult unskilled and semi-skilled workers and more advanced training for skilled workers. Under a 2001 reform, jurisdiction was moved to the ministry of education, and most AMUs merged into technical and commercial colleges. This has created a more coherent further education system that offers adults the same qualifications offered to youth and supports Denmark's vision for lifelong learning. However, in the actual implementation of the reforms, there have been examples that the new providers have not put sufficiently emphasis on needs of companies for workforce development of semi-skilled and skilled workers. A national pilot called Competence Centres in Learning Regions is an experiment with one-stop models to address the needs for literacy and higher skills in training for the labor market (see Teknologisk Institut, in press).

STRENGTHS AND WEAKNESSES OF THE DANISH VET SYSTEM

Pedagogy and Success Rates

One feature of the Danish VET system is its willingness to embrace new pedagogical techniques. Almost all learning that takes place at technical and business colleges is either hands-on or project-based. Students work in teams, are encouraged to be self-directed learners, and develop their own learning plans that assess what they already know and allow them to tailor their college-based course work accordingly. Challenged to meet the target of ensuring that all 95% of students complete upper secondary education by 2015, however, Denmark has been led to ensure more structured pathways for students with fewer resources and learning difficulties.

In addition, significant resources are put into faculty development and team-teaching concepts. At Danish colleges, faculty often work in teams and are expected to work together to develop students' hard and soft skills using innovative educational approaches and real-world projects. In many instances, they work as facilitators circulating among students who are doing collaborative work. Importantly, faculty members at the colleges are paid salaries comparable to those of their industry counterparts.

Standards for completion at the colleges are also uniformly high. In fact, it is testimony to the Denmark's commitment to a very well-educated labor pool that standards have remained high, despite pressures stakeholders might have felt to water down programs in order to increase what have become troublesome completion rates, as will be described later. Instead of lowering standards, new efforts are under way to increase educational flexibility and provide more structured pathways to increase success rates.

Programs, Resources, and Facilities

In 1995, Denmark embarked on a "Systematic Plan for Quality Development and Effective Assessment in the Vocational Education Sector." The strategy was based on decentralized programs aligned with local needs, a common approach rather than a standard definition of quality, and self-evaluation at all levels of the system (National Education Authority, 2000). A further reflection of Denmark's commitment to education is the high quality of educational resources and the physical environment. Technical and business colleges have Open Learning Centers, instead of libraries, where students can work on joint projects, use computers, and access printed materials. Experience with the centers, however, has been mixed. Their success has depended on the availability of teachers as resources and the ability of students to organize and plan their own work.

Adaptability and Meeting Special Needs

Those involved in vocational education in Denmark often complain of reform fatigue because of the near constant pace of changes in the system since the early 1990s. However, a 2005 report from the ministry of education (see Cort, 2005) indicated that there would be no sign of a slow down in the number of changes that would occur in the VET system as a result of the implementation of Denmark's globalization strategy (Danish Government, 2006). Furthermore, the ambitious goal to achieve a 95% completion rate for upper secondary education by 2015 focused attention on serving special needs and at-risk students (Shapiro, Gam, & Panton, 2005). An initial practical foundation program is aimed at youth not in upper secondary programs or employed who would have difficulty completing VET programs. Students in this program still take combined school- and work-based learning. "Production schools" are an option for students under 25 without disabilities who have dropped out and lack some of the competences to complete upper secondary education. Although these schools do not provide workplace qualifications, they help youth develop skills, particularly the social and personal skills they need to reduce the risk of their dropping out of the upper secondary system. Vocational schools also use the production schools for students who are at risk of dropping out of secondary education. After a period in production schools, these students often return to college more focused on their futures.

Clear Pathways and Ease of Transition

One of the ways Denmark expects to meet its completion rate goal is by helping students make a better transition into upper secondary programs. Many of the colleges have collaborative programs with the lower-level schools called bridge-building programs. Colleges pair their students with younger students and generally introduce them to the colleges and programs. The colleges also offer programs as part of counseling in lower secondary education, whereby students can spend a week in a program at a technical college to get the flavor of what it means to be in a vocational college. Other programs run by employers focus on those in the production schools to boost students' self-confidence and increase their ability to succeed. Another way that colleges provide clear pathways for students to continue along their education is through the personal education plans described earlier in the chapter.

International Focus

Another distinguishing feature of Danish education is its international focus. Most students are proficient in English, many in a second foreign language as well. There is also a long tradition in programs such as business and culinary for students to pursue an internship outside of Denmark. Various European Union (EU) programs provide support for study tours and work-linked training abroad for trainers, policymakers, social partners, and researchers. As a component of the government's globalization strategy, a number of bilateral agreements with non–EU-member countries have been in operation for some years, including the United States. This program has provided a number of opportunities for student and staff exchanges and for joint curriculum development. A number of Danish colleges and U.S. Trans-Atlantic Technology and Training Alliance (TA3) member colleges have hosted each others' faculty members for short periods of time.

New Developments and Challenges

There are a number of recent developments in the VET system worth noting. Some are overarching policy strategies in response to pressures such as globalization and immigration, while others are new legislative and pedagogical measures designed to recognize formal and nonformal learning and increase the quality and flexibility of the system, thereby making the dual system more attractive and accessible to young people and employers. Others being implemented aim to improve the inclusiveness of the VET system and improve completion rates.

Recognizing Nonformal Learning

Denmark recently implemented assessments of prior learning to improve career paths and options for students by assessing and recognizing an individual's competencies. This may take place by awarding credits for competencies acquired in the educational and training system or through job experience. The initiative is part of Denmark's goal of supporting lifelong learning, as well as enhancing the flexibility and efficiency of the system. With youth increasingly gravitating toward tertiary professional pathways, recognizing nonformal learning makes the VET system more attractive and flexible for more youth and adults who want to reenter the education system or are seeking ways to efficiently obtain a qualification as skilled workers.

Preparing for a Global and Knowledge Economy

Like other highly developed countries, production and services are increasingly moving outside of Denmark. Denmark responded early. In 1994, Denmark co-hosted a conference with the Organisation for Economic Co-operation and Development (OECD) titled "Employment and Growth in the Knowledge-Based Economy," which touched on most of the areas that would become priorities for technical and commercial education: information technologies (IT), intelligent products, mass customization, and global competitiveness (see OECD, 1996). The VET system has reacted by creating more flexible educational programs in new occupations within sectors such as IT.

Ensuring Sufficient Numbers of Apprenticeships

The practical training vocational students obtain in companies through apprenticeship contracts is a core element of the Danish system, and balancing supply and demand for training is a constant challenge. Numerous measures have been taken to improve the supply and demand for apprenticeships. Many colleges now have better data and full-time professionals to help new companies take on apprentices. The social partners also provide more counseling to the schools about apprenticeships. Contracts terms have been made more flexible (e.g., types and durations of placements), and quota systems have been used to help ensure that placements are available beyond the basic program. In recent years, the number of signed apprenticeships has grown from approximately 26,000 to 37,000 (Ministry of Education, 2008b).

Improving Completion Rates and Equity

Dropout rates are a significant problem for the VET system. Although about of third of students completing basic schooling enroll in VET, the dropout rate is high: Only around 70% complete the basic course, and 80% complete the main course. Furthermore, about 40% of all dropouts do not continue any education or training in the following 10 years. Furthermore, dropout rates are higher among men than women and among immigrants than among those of Danish origin (Ministry of Education, 2008b).

Reducing the number of dropouts is an important political priority. It was hoped that reforms in the 1990s to require students to develop their own education plans would improve completion rates, because students would have greater control over, and be more vested in, their education. However, promising reductions in the late 1990s turned out to be temporary. The government's globalization strategy is, however, addressing the issue anew (Danish Government, 2006).

The Danish educational system is also targeting new efforts toward what it calls practically-oriented young people. These are youth who have learning disabilities, have experienced social or cultural exclusion, or have unrealistic expectations about what and how quickly they can learn. Often they have bad experiences during primary and lower secondary schooling. A variety of strategies have been developed to offer stepwise qualifications for students who initially lack the skills or interest to obtain a full vocational qualification:

- Short VET programs have been designed so that students can train in sectors where employment for those with minimal training is good.

- The majority of VET programs offer partial qualifications, whereby students may obtain a partial qualification, work for a period of time, and return to school at a future date to continue their studies and work toward the full qualification.

- The *mesterlaere* is an apprenticeship pathway in which the entire basic course takes place in a company, an option designed for students who do wish to continue school.

- The pretraining option allows young students (15–18) and employers to size each other up for 3–6 months before signing a training contract.

- EUD+, similar to the partial qualifications strategy, is a program for students under 25 to complete a basic course and the first part of a main course in a company or similar setting then be employed for 6 months before receiving a qualification.

- Finally, the VET system allows trainees to add academic qualifications to their vocational qualifications, an option designed to encourage VET students to pursue further and higher education.

These strategies allow students to try out concrete occupational experiences in their field of study earlier in educational programs so that they have a better sense of whether the choice is a good fit. They also provide increased opportunities for training in fields in demand in the labor market.

COOPERATION BETWEEN DENMARK AND THE UNITED STATES

Denmark and the United States have a long history of cooperation among colleges and college systems and have frequently looked to each other for innovative ideas and programmatic improvement. In 1995, two Danish colleges attended a meeting of an ongoing alliance of southern community colleges called the Consortium for Manufacturing Competitiveness, which, with their assistance, evolved into the Trans-Atlantic Technology and Training Alliance (TA3), now jointly managed by Regional Technology Strategies (RTS) in North Carolina and CIRIUS in Denmark.

At the national level, a delegation representing the U.S. Department of Education in 1999 was so impressed by Danish education that it put into motion a plan to establish a formal bilateral cooperation agreement between the two governments. Purely on the basis of scale, it appears to be an unbalanced relationship: The Danish system, one of the world's most innovative and successful, offered lessons for U.S. education policy and vice versa. In December 2000, in a ceremony in Washington, DC, a memorandum of understanding was signed by U.S. Secretary of Education Richard Riley and Danish Minister of Education Margrethe Vetager. In 2001, under the auspices of the steering committee, the U.S. Department of Education awarded a grant to RTS and the Danish Technological Institute (DTI) to compare the way the two countries prepare their workforce for IT.

Various states have also looked to Denmark for advice. North Carolina sent a high-level delegation to Denmark in 2003 that, on its return, produced the monograph, *Learning from Denmark* (Public School Forum, 2004). In January 2006, researchers from DTI visited western North Carolina community colleges to learn about their industry and community services and programs and their external programs in regional economic development and innovation.

Case Studies

We conclude this chapter with three brief profiles of vocational colleges in Denmark. The first is a large comprehensive college in southern Denmark. The second is a small specialized technical college in northern Denmark, and the third is a large urban commercial (business) college in Copenhagen.

EUC Syd in Sønderborg

Located in the southern rural portion of the Jutland peninsula of Denmark, next to the country's border with Germany, EUC Syd began as a college in Åbenrå in about 1920 and opened its doors at its Sønderborg campus in 1939. The college, like all vocational colleges in Denmark, is governed by a board of directors and an executive committee composed of representatives of unions, companies, the county, and the municipality. The 12-member board is structured so that five represent employers, five represent employees, and two represent local communities. Strategy groups form as needed around particular pressing problems (e.g., ways to attract young people to the college). Local education committees of employers, employees, and school staff address curriculum issues.

Today EUC Syd is among the largest of Danish technical colleges and encompasses both technical and commercial (business) educational programs. In it its current form, EUC Syd has existed since 1994 as a merger between four educational colleges in Southern Denmark. It is a self-governing institution with an annual budget of approximately DKK 300 million (or USD 43 million). EUC Syd provides a range of studies, courses, and learning opportunities for over 3,000 full-time students and 6,000 part-time students. It also runs an AMU that offers management and specialized technical training for incumbent workers in industry.

All faculty members are required to have industry experience. They are able to remain knowledgeable about the latest methods and technologies through their industry courses and frequent interaction with industry managers. Faculty constantly works directly with industry representatives to develop new courses to meet changing work requirements and generally produce four or five new courses each year. Examples of special programs to meet regional industry needs are those in mobile phones/telecommunications, medical equipment, and electronic security.

Despite this specialization according to local industry clusters, the college is very comprehensive in its breadth of geography and scope of programs, similar to many U.S. community colleges. EUC-Syd offers everything from culinary and cosmetology to electronics programs and has ongoing exchange programs through TA3 with Guilford Technical Community College in North Carolina and Bellingham Technical College in Washington. Among relatively recent developments at the college is the creation of distance learning options for learners and recruitment of more foreign students into technical programs taught in English.

Technical College of Jutland in Hadsten

Near the opposite (northern) end of the Jutland peninsula lies the Technical College of Jutland in Hadsten. It is a highly specialized technical college, offering only four vocational programs: carpentry, electronics engineering and automation, plastics processing, and industrial refrigeration and air conditioning. The latter two programs are unique in Denmark to this college, and as such it is the so-called national college for those areas and attracts students from across the country.

The college was founded in 1928 by an association of employers as a boarding school for VET. Today the college is a self-governing institution with very close relations to the trade committees. Approximately three quarters of the students live at the college while studying, and the college is following the U.S. campus philosophy with a 24-hour open door policy.

Today, the institution has a total of 3,300 apprentices, students, and in-service (incumbent worker) trainees annually. About 120 employees work at the college, and the annual budget is approximately USD 15 million. As mentioned, the college offers only four education and training programs but covers them comprehensively—vertically from the beginner's level through further and higher technical education to highly specialized advanced levels. Post-completion employment statistics for graduates exceed Denmark's overall 80% employment rate for VET completers. In 2004 the post graduation employment rate was 100%.

The college's traditional VET programs take 4 years to complete. Within two national programs—refrigeration and plastics—there is an option to take an additional higher technical education program that takes 2 years full time. The college has developed and offers e-learning programs within plastics processing technology and refrigeration. It has an e-learning network with colleges in Sweden, the United Kingdom, and France. Furthermore, all students are offered official computer license while attending college. The college is also very active in fostering innovation and entrepreneurship at the higher technical education level (diploma), aimed at students who wish to start up their own company or take over or be a partner in a company (often the young generation coming into a family business).

Niels Brock College

Founded in 1888, Niels Brock College is the second largest educational institution in Denmark and is located in the heart of Copenhagen, the country's capital city. It has six departments with nearly 35,000 students, more than 1,000 employees, and more than 200 various subject areas to choose from. Niels Brock offers a variety of business programs (such as finance, marketing, computer science, international business, and business administration) for youth and adults, as well as for private and public sector employees. Some of the college's programs are classified as short-cycle higher education programs, meaning that they do not follow the dual system apprenticeship model but are not part of the universities. Students in these programs often are required to hold leaving certificates from HHX or HTX upper secondary programs.

The college's name commemorates Niels Brock, a wealthy merchant who was one of the founders of the Danish vocational business education movement. The founders intended to provide vocational education for young self-made businessmen. Today Niels Brock gives high priority to the internationalization of education. The school actively engages in student and teacher exchange, and it permanently hosts visiting teachers from abroad. For example, it has an ongoing exchange program with Howard Community College in Maryland. An increasing number of courses are offered in English. The faculty comprises permanent staff as well as external part-time teachers from the business world in Denmark and abroad.

References

Bertelsmann Foundation. (1999). *Vocational education and training of tomorrow* (vol. 1). Gutersloh, Germany: Bertelsmann Foundation Publishers.

Centre for Educational Research and Innovation (CERI). (2003). *Education at a glance.* Paris: Organization for Economic Cooperation and Development.

Cort, P. (2005, September). *The Danish vocational education and training system.* Copenhagen: Danish Ministry of Education, National Education Authority. Retrieved May 19, 2008, from http://pub.uvm.dk/2005/VET

Danish Government. (2006, May). *Progress, innovation and cohesion: Strategies for Denmark in the global economy.* Retrieved September 30, 2008, from http://www.globalisering.dk/multimedia/Pixi_UK_web_endelig1.pdf

Ministry of Education. (2007). *Denmark's strategy for lifelong learning: Education and lifelong skills upgrading for all.* Copenhagen: Author. Retreived October 9, 2008, from http://pub.uvm.dk/2007/lifelonglearning/lifelong_learning.pdf

Ministry of Education. (2008a). *The Danish approach to quality—in vocational education and training* (2nd ed.). Copehagen: Author. Retrieved October 9, 2008, from http://pub.uvm.dk/2008/vetquality2/helepubl.pdf

Ministry of Education. (2008b). *The Danish vocational education and training system* (2nd ed.). Copenhagen: Author. Retrieved October 9, 2008, from http://pub.uvm.dk/2008/VET2/The_Danish_VET_System_web.pdf

Ministry of Education. (2008c). *Facts and figures 2007: Key figures in education 2007* (Statistical publication no. 3). Copenhagen: Author. Retrieved October 9, 2008, from http://pub.uvm.dk/2008/facts/facts_and_figures_2007.pdf

National Education Authority. (2000, April). *Quality work in the Danish VET system* Unpublished manuscript, Danish Ministry of Education, Copenhagen.

Organization for Economic Co-operation and Development (OECD). (1996). *The knowledge-based economy.* Paris: Author. Retrieved October 9, 2008, from http://www.oecd.org/dataoecd/51/8/1913021.pdf

Public School Forum. (2004). *Learning from Denmark.* Raleigh: University of North Carolina, North Carolina Center for International Understanding.

Seyfried, E., & Souto Otero, M. (2006). *National overview of methodologies and systems for validation of non-formal and informal learning in Denmark.* Retrieved October 9, 2008, from http://dfs.dk/inenglish/priorlearning/validation.aspx

Shapiro, H. (2004, January). *Denmark: The upper secondary vocational education and training system. Background report.* Unpublished manuscript, Danish Technological Institute, Copenhagen.

Shapiro, H., Gam, S., & Panton, T. A. (2005, November). *Retention in vocational education in Denmark: A best practice study.* Copenhagen: Danish Ministry of Education. Retrieved May 19, 2008, from http://pub.uvm.dk/2005/retention/retention_in_vocational_education.pdfTeknologisk Institute. (in press). *Final evaluation of the national initiative: Competence centres in learning regions.* Århus, Denmark: Author.

Teknologisk Institut. (in press). *Final evaluation of the national initiative: Competence centres in learning regions.* Århus, Denmark: Author.

16

From Demand-Led Skills to the Entrepreneurial College in England

Geoff Hall and Hugh David

Further education (FE) colleges in England work within a complex and changing policy environment. In this chapter, we outline how the context for these colleges has developed recently, describe the potential problems with the current configuration of these colleges, and explain the important role that these colleges have in further developing FE policies for the 21st century and exploiting the entrepreneurial opportunities that will arise. Since the late 1980s, a consensus has been reached that a high-skills, high-technology paradigm is essential for achieving growth in a globalizing world (see Castells, 1992; Lucas, 1988). The United Kingdom (UK) has shown strength in terms of providing high-level skills, but, like the United States, its labor market is heavily influenced by academic and professional qualifications (Whitley, 1999, pp. 100, 102). Furthermore, the UK government became aware of its weakness in providing low-level and intermediate skills, compared with its international peers (see, e.g., Department for Education and Skills [DFES] et al., 2003; Organisation for Economic Co-operation and Development [OECD], 2002). Because the government was concerned that this weakness would compromise the UK's ability to maintain its competitive position in the world economy, it has taken a number of steps to strengthen FE at all levels.

In the past 5 years, the UK has undertaken a dramatic reconstruction of the vocational educational and training (VET) system, proposing a national skills strategy in 2003 and subsequently creating a network of sector skills councils to articulate the skills needs of employers and reform the framework of vocational qualifications. A review of skills was commissioned in 2005; the final report issued in 2006 proposed the creation of a new demand-led system of public funding that would help the suppliers of training respond to the demand articulated by employers through the skills councils and at the same time meet government objectives of raising the UK's skills, particularly intermediate and low-level skills, to match those of its international peers.

The skills strategy is for the whole of the UK, but many of the education and training policies and initiatives discussed in this chapter cover England only, because education is one of the powers devolved to the four constituent countries by the UK constitution. England is the largest constituent country, accounting for 84% of the population of the UK. For simplicity's sake, where powers are devolved, only the case of England has been considered.

In June 2007, the UK's new Prime Minister Gordon Brown put in motion significant "machinery of government" changes that split DFES into two (Prime Minister, 2007). Responsibility for education up to the age of 18 was placed with the Department for Children, Schools and Families (DCSF), while education and training for those aged 19 and over, including at higher education institutions, was placed with the Department for Innovation, Universities and Skills (DIUS). These departmental changes were designed to allow DCSF to focus on providing "excellent education and… integrated support" for children and young people (Prime Minister, 2007, p. 5), while DIUS was to focus on the competitiveness strategy of the UK. The responsibilities of the two government departments is split according to the age of the student; FE colleges, however, straddle this divide.

Further education colleges in England work within a context of three different planning and funding philosophies. Provision for 14- to 18-year-olds will be planned and commissioned through local government (DCSF & DIUS, 2008, p. 19); education and training for adults is subject to the new demand-led system and the higher education that colleges provide is funded through the Higher Education Funding Council for England (HEFCE), although it has little to do with planning it (see the HEFCE Web site: http://www.hefce.ac.uk).

In this chapter, we first describe the process and dynamics that have brought this complex policy context into being, particularly the design and implementation of a demand-led system for adult VET over the 5-year period between 2003 and 2008. We then identify three potential policy fault lines.

- The first concerns the decline in intergenerational social mobility in the UK that Dixon and Paxton (2005) called attention to. The ability of colleges, through their local presence and reputation, to draw young people from disadvantaged backgrounds into higher education and on to high-status careers will, it is argued, be key to reversing this decline.

- The second is the focus of the Leitch Review (explained in the next section) on qualifications as a means of increasing productivity. Increasing emphasis on creativity and innovation, particularly in regard to services and the growing importance of informal, interorganizational, and transformational learning, all suggest that close links between colleges and local industry will provide an ideal vehicle for encouraging learning that underpins innovation and productivity (see Ashton, Green, Sung, & James, 2002; Billett & Somerville, 2004; DIUS, 2008; Engestrom & Kerosuo, 2007; Eraut, 2004; National Center on Education and the Economy [NCEE], 2007).

- The third is the market mechanism itself. We describe how the government is attempting to ensure that the education and training market that it has created is responsive to local needs and how this need for localness means that colleges themselves, with their commitment to their communities, will have a naturally growing role in ensuring the success of the whole enterprise (see DCSF & DIUS, 2008; Her Majesty's Treasury, 2007).

In the conclusion, we look further ahead at how the naturally evolving local role of colleges will need to embrace more entrepreneurial aspects if the opportunities to support the transformation of innovation and productivity in local industry and services using local creativity are to be realized.

Evolution of Demand-Led VET

The publication of the UK's first national skills strategy has led to dramatic changes in policy for the provision of adult skills over the past 5 years, and increasing productivity now lies at the heart of current UK skills policy (see, e.g., DFES et al., 2003; DIUS, 2007, Porter & Ketels, 2003). This policy development stems from endogenous growth theory and economic development theory, which both see productivity, in association with developing higher levels of skills and increased levels of technology, as being fundamental to sustaining above-average economic growth. In particular, the high-performing Asian economies have been successful in increasing economic growth by coordinating policies that have directed industry toward higher value-added manufacturing at the same time as increasing educational and skills levels, including through the development of learning in the workplace (e.g., Ashton et al., 2002; Ashton, Sung, & Raddon, 2003). As a result, and in response to the Lisbon 2000 economic reform agenda, the government commissioned the UK's first national skills strategy, which was published in July 2003 under the title *21st-Century Skills: Realising Our Potential* (DFES et al., 2003).

The overriding goal of the skills strategy was to "ensure that everyone has the skills they need to become more employable and adaptable" (DFES et al., 2003, p.12). The aim of the skills strategy is twofold. A network of sector skills councils covering all major sectors in the economy was created to help employers articulate their skill needs more effectively. Furthermore, the suppliers of training, including colleges; the public funding that supports these suppliers; and the qualifications framework through which the public funding is made available were all to be reformed so that the supply side would respond dynamically to the newly articulated demand.

The next stage was to work out how the national skills strategy was to be implemented. In 2004, Sandy Leitch, a former chief executive of Zurich Financial Services, was commissioned to lead a review to (1) examine the UK's optimum skills mix in order to maximize economic growth and productivity by 2020 and (2) consider the different trajectories of skill levels the UK might pursue. Leitch's interim report was published in 2005, his final report in 2006. After the publication of the interim report, the scope of the review was widened to include social justice, as well as specification of the policy framework that would support the implementation of the skills strategy. The significance and impact of the addition of social justice will be considered in the next section of the chapter.

The final report, *Prosperity for All in the Global Economy—World Class Skills* (the Leitch Review) focused almost exclusively on the level of skills required to match competitors' skill levels, as measured by qualifications, and spent little time considering the types of skills that might be required, as was the approach taken by NCEE in *Tough Choices or Tough Times* (NCEE, 2007). The Leitch Review was essentially a set of targets, backed by a demand-led system to deliver these targets (see Leitch, 2006, p. 3). The proposed demand-led system follows closely the World Bank's recommendations for opening up markets, which identify clear regulation as an important aspect of markets (see World Bank, 1997, p. 62). For a market in education and training, qualifications provide a regulatory structure that is readily handled (e.g., Young, 2003, p. 228), and this convenience has proved irresistible. The responsibility for approving qualifications has been placed in the hands of the employer-led sector skills councils (see DIUS, 2007, pp. 39–41; Leitch, 2006, p.139), thus enabling qualifications to become the crucial regulatory building block used to create a system designed to respond to employers' needs.

Concurrently, the supply side was being reformed through the Success for All program, whose goal was to "raise the effectiveness of further education colleges and training providers" so that they would be ready to rise to this challenge (DFES et al., 2003, p. 14). This process of reform was continued through the Agenda for Change (Learning and Skills Council [LSC], 2005), the Foster Review (Foster, 2005), and the Further Education Act (UK Parliament, 2007).

The process of reform of the supply side has culminated in the creation of a funding system for England that from 2008 to 2010 will allow the center to pull the levers of priorities for different levels of qualifications from basic skills (called "skills for life") and the "foundation learning tier" through to the intermediate skills of the UK's Level 2 and Level 3 qualifications, so that colleges and training providers will respond to demand and deliver the outcomes that are the government's goals (LSC, 2007a). FE colleges in England thus stand on the brink of putting into action the grand conception lying behind the UK's aim of achieving world class skills. But all is not rosy in the garden, for three interlocking reasons: declining intergenerational mobility in the UK, the chosen method of regulating the market for training, and overreliance on the market mechanism itself.

Intergenerational Mobility

The Leitch Review concentrates almost exclusively on "economically valuable skills" (Leitch, 2006, p. 2) that is expected to increase social justice and social cohesion (Leitch, 2006, pp. 15–16), but it does not articulate how this will come about. Why was social justice added to Leitch's terms of reference? The answer lies in the publication of a book by the influential social think tank, the Institute for Public Policy Research: *Social Justice: Building a Fairer Britain* (Pearce & Paxton, 2005).

Editors Pearce and Paxton described the UK as "fundamentally divided by social class" (2005, p. xxiii) and by Dixon and Paxton (2005) as a country where intergenerational mobility had declined for those born in 1970 versus in 1958 and where the rapid expansion of higher education in the 1990s had "disproportionately benefited those from more privileged backgrounds" (Dixon & Paxton, 2005, p. 44). For the Labour Party, which had been in power almost 10 years and saw itself as a progressive political party, this was a serious charge. The result was the addition of social justice to the terms of reference for the Leitch Review.

Just as social justice was added to the Leitch Review without the substance of the review being altered, a review of FE colleges by Foster (2005), *Realising the Potential: A Review of the Future Role of Further Education Colleges,* prescribed that the core focus of colleges should be on skills and employability; but Foster also commented that "the Government recognizes that a primary focus on skills does not exclude . . . promoting social inclusion" (p. 27). The Foster Review remained committed to colleges becoming more specialist vocational trainers, able to play their part in a more competitive training market as envisaged by Leitch, despite Foster's recognition that colleges play an irreplaceable role in making higher education accessible to adults and to those from lower socioeconomic groups.

The local reputation and accessibility of colleges is the key issue here. Researching reasons why participation in higher education can remain persistently low in areas with high concentrations of disadvantage, Gates, Coward, and Byrom (2007) found that a key stumbling block is not so much financial barriers or low aspiration as lack of knowledge among young people about how to make their aspirations happen, reflecting the inability of many parents to offer strategic advice on careers linking school with college, university, and a career. There is a consequent tendency among young people to stick with what they know and to stay local when moving onto higher education (Gates et al., 2007). Older students are also more likely to need to stay local, because they are more likely to have jobs and responsibilities. That colleges are better able to attract students from low-participating neighborhoods than are universities is confirmed through statistical data on higher education enrollments (e.g., HEFCE, 2008, p. 30;

Higher Education Statistics Agency [HESA], 2007, Table T1b). Expanding the range of local higher education opportunities in colleges is therefore a crucial part of the mix to increase intergenerational mobility, rather than restricting the role of colleges to that of vocational trainer.

In this context, it is useful to compare higher education in the English FE college system with the U.S. community college system. According to the American Association of Community Colleges (AACC), in 2005–2006 there were 2.4 million full-time and 4 million part-time students in undergraduate credit courses (AACC, 2008). In comparison, there were 40,445 entrants (first years) for foundation degrees in England in 2007–2008 (HEFCE, 2008, p. 11). Foundation degrees in England are primarily in vocational rather than academic subjects and are equivalent to the first 2 years of a 3-year honors degree. A direct comparison between England and the United States is difficult because U.S. colleges and universities operate a credit accumulation and transfer system, but England's do not. But taking into account the number of enrollments for foundation degrees and similar-level qualifications in English colleges (see Quality Assurance Agency, 2007), attrition and achievement rates (see HEFCE, 2008, pp. 42–43), and the number of associate degrees (equivalent to the first 2 years of a 4-year honours degree) awarded in U.S. community colleges (Snyder, Dillow, & Hoffman, 2008, Table 177), we estimate that per capita achievement of higher education at the foundation degree level in England is running at approximately a third that for associate degrees in the United States.

One reason why per capita achievement of sub-bachelor degrees is lower in England than in the United States is the range of subjects offered. In the United States, associate degrees cover a wide range of academic and vocational subjects. The largest category, accounting for a third of associate degrees, is liberal arts and sciences, general studies, and humanities; the second-largest category is health professions and related sciences; the third-largest category is business, management, and marketing (Snyder et al., 2008, Table 259). These three categories account for two thirds of associate degrees awarded. This strong focus on academic progression and managerial and associate professional career routes is not reflected in the range of foundation degrees available in England. The main categories, accounting for 48% of entrants, are in education, business, and administration and creative arts and design. Education programs are focused on childhood education and business programs on management and accounting, but neither program is as concentrated as U.S. associate degree programs (HEFCE, 2008, pp. 17, 19, 23). Foundation degrees in England are thus much less connected with academic progression and high-status careers than are associate degrees in the United States.

While Foster (2005) recognized that higher education in colleges had a narrow focus of subjects, he did not consider it necessary at that point to recommend that the range of higher education offered within colleges should be extended. Rather, he commented that the primary focus on skills did not exclude facilitating progression from colleges to universities. But subsequently, and in an important development, the Further Education and Training Act (UK Parliament, 2007) granted colleges the power to award foundation degrees in their own right rather than on behalf of universities. These new degree-awarding powers will in due course significantly raise the status of FE colleges in England and in turn may open up the exciting possibility that the range of subjects that foundation degrees can cover will be extended to include progression routes onto mainstream bachelor's degree courses at universities.

Thus we have seen that the process of implementing the national skills strategy has taken a route that may be subject to the criticism that it does not take sufficient note of factors that may be influencing the decline in intergenerational mobility. One of the most important of these factors in a labor market such as the UK's, which is dominated by academic and professional qualifications, is the de facto restriction of access to higher education for those born in more deprived circumstances compared with their more fortunate peers, which is evident in England. Colleges, with their strong links to the local community, will in the future have an increasingly important role to play in increasing access to higher education and intergenerational mobility (see, e.g., LSC, 2007b, p. 16).

ORGANIZATIONAL LEARNING AND QUALIFICATIONS

A second potential criticism of the approach that Leitch has taken is his reliance on qualifications as adequate to capture the type of skills and organizational learning that will be important for the UK's economic future. The Leitch Review acknowledged that qualifications were only a proxy and imperfect measure of skills (Leitch, 2006, p. 28); nevertheless, qualifications were taken as the cornerstone of the proposed policy framework, because of their convenience as a means of regulating Leitch's quasi-market solution to the UK's skills deficit. While the Leitch Review was concerning itself with the mechanics of implementing a demand-led system, other countries have been considering the type of skills that will be central to economic success in the 21st century.

For example, Singapore has identified a top-level strategic need for creativity (Ashton et al., 2002, p. 24) and has supported this through a centrally led program called Critical Enabling Skills Training (CREST) to "enable workers to constantly acquire and apply new knowledge and skills and to innovate", for which "delivery is through a network of (private sector) providers with very different learning designs" (Ashton et al., 2003, p. 27). In the United States, the National Center on Education and the Economy considers that most of the population will require high literacy, which incorporates math, science, literature, history, and the arts to support a "deep vein of creativity" to keep the United States an economic world leader (NCEE, 2007, p. 6).

Innovation and creativity are thus seen as a growing force in future economic success, and it was partly in recognition of this that DFES was separated into DCSF.

In 2008, DIUS was involved in publishing a white paper on innovation, *Innovation Nation* (DIUS, 2008), and a strategy for the creative industries (DCMS et al., 2008). While some of the initiatives proposed in these two documents, such as the creation of a major program of apprenticeships in the creative industries (DCMS et al., 2008, p. 8), are consistent with Leitch's approach, it should not be assumed that innovation and creativity are the same as so-called high skills, much less qualifications. Keating, Medrich, Vollkoff, and Perry (2002) commented on the lack of correlation between creativity and innovation on the one hand and the general level of skills on the other in Singapore, the UK, Germany, and Japan. The Confederation of British Industry [CBI], which is the premier representative group for employers in the UK, observed that "only a third of training offered by employers leads to a recognized qualification" (CBI, 2008, p. 8) and that employees are the main beneficiaries of "Train to Gain," rather than employers. This is a significant statement because Train to Gain is the centerpiece of the new demand-led system designed to respond to employers' needs, with public funding planned to double to £1 billion between 2007–2008 and 2010–2011 (see Leitch, 2006, pp. 75–76; LSC, 2007a, p. 44).

There is a growing body of research showing that the process of organizational learning that underpins productivity improvements is more informal, social, interorganizational, and, on occasion, subjectively driven (see, e.g., Billett & Somerville, 2004; Engestrom, 2001; Engestrom & Kerosuo, 2007; Eraut, 2004) than is suggested by a simple model of encouraging and capturing individual learning through the qualification system, especially if, following Vuorinen, Jarvinen, and Lehtinen (1998), productivity is taken to include improvements in the quality as well as the quantity of output when the concept is applied to the service industries. Engestrom, for example, detailed the process of "expansive learning among professionals from different medical organizations in Helsinki working together that leads to the development of the concept of a care agreement for those with complex medical needs, to facilitate improved coordination between all the professionals from multiple institutions involved in a particular case" (2001, pp. 149–150).

For local industry, personal individual motivation seems to be a strong motivation to generate change. Billett and Somerville (2004) gave a range of examples (e.g., funeral homes, aged care facilities, small businesses), where change and the associated learning were driven by individuals' identities, subjectivities, and intentions, rather than driven by national programs focused explicitly on concepts like productivity. It is also important that organizational learning and high performance is underpinned by supportive management development (see, e.g., Ashton & Sung, 2002, pp. 73, 95; Ellstrom, Ekholm, & Ellstrom, 2008, p. 95; Eraut, 2004, p. 271).

When advising the UK government on improving competitiveness, Porter and Ketels (2003) argued that whereas local industry accounts for the majority of employment in the United States but adds low value, the focus of UK policy should be on the creation of high-value globally focused clusters. That argument has moved on to that represented in *Innovation Nation,* in which innovation thrives at all levels and across all sectors and where "increasing the performance of the UK's service sectors would have a major impact in closing the productivity gap between the UK and other leading nations" (DIUS, 2008, p. 13). Once again, now that the focus of activity has moved local, FE colleges become crucial partners, and the UK government is keen "to encourage individual FE providers to showcase their expertise in implementing innovative business solutions, particularly for SMEs [small and medium-sized enterprizes]" (DIUS, 2008, p. 59).

Such activity is unlikely to be measured in terms of qualifications. We have seen how the Leitch Review has paid insufficient attention to how to address the UK's decline in intergenerational mobility and has insufficiently considered the nature of skills that will be important in the 21st century. In both cases we have seen that colleges, because of their strong links with local communities and local employers, are well placed to play a significant if not crucial role in implementing solutions to these challenges. Indeed, the importance of locality is playing an increasing role in the UK government's thinking, as epitomized by the concept of "place-shaping" which is central to a report on the future of local government in the UK (Lyons, 2007).

THE IMPORTANCE OF LOCALITY

Leitch's demand-led system is based on the World Bank's recipe for market liberalization, a heavily decontextualized approach (see, e.g., Nolan, 2001, p. 3). Whitley (1999), for example, argued that work systems and the training systems that support them are socially and culturally situated. This is particularly true of local labor markets, and colleges have a long track record of understanding the needs both of local employers and of the local populace. The Leitch approach, in contrast, has inherent weaknesses stemming from its lack of localness, and the UK government is now seeking to address these weaknesses. This is most evident in the renewed emphasis on local democratic accountability.

Currently, education and training (except for higher education) for those aged over 16 is funded in England through LSC (UK Parliament, 2000), but this will soon change. LSC is a government body set up by an act of parliament, which is accountable to the central government. After the separation of DFES into DCSF and DIUS, this funding will be split. Funding for 16- to 18-year-olds will be distributed via local authorities, as set out in the white paper, *Raising Expectations* (DCSF & DIUS, 2008, p. 19). "Local authority" is the name given to the local tier of democratically elected government in England. Funding for adults will be distributed via a new body called the Skills Funding Agency. This agency will be centrally accountable but will be need to work closely with regional planning bodies called Regional Development Agencies, which are not democratically elected but will be subject to scrutiny by local authorities (Her Majesty's Treasury, 2007, p. 95). In this rather convoluted way, locally elected government will control or influence how the funding for education and training below the higher education level for those aged 16 and over is spent. Whether this approach will be sufficient to instill local accountability and responsiveness into the demand-led system for the provision of skills to adults, time will tell.

CONCLUSION

It is a truism that the world does not stand still, and nor does our understanding of it. The high-skills, high-technology paradigm of growth emerged in the 1980s through endogenous growth theory and economic development theory as a way of understanding the high levels of growth in the high-performing Asian economies that could not be explained through the "Washington Consensus" of neoliberal economics (Williamson, 1990). In turn, the long-term, above-average GDP and per capita growth of Chile of 3.8% between 1975 and 2004 (United Nations Development Programme, 2006, pp. 331–334) challenges the high-technology paradigm: Chile's growth has relied mainly on developing resource-based industries such as agriculture, fishing, mining, and tourism rather than moving up the valuechain (Schurman, 1996, p. 84). Whereas Lucas (1988) focused only on highly substitutable goods and services, Porter and Ketels (2003) were not hopeful of improving productivity in local industry, and Vuorinen et al. (1998) showed how productivity remains an essentially manufacturing concept with as yet too little understanding of how it should be applied to service industries. In this way, large sections of the economy have been effectively sidelined in mainstream economic thought.

The Leitch approach to skill formation for the 21st century retains an essentially late 20th-century outlook. A gathering momentum toward innovation and creativity as the source of economic competitiveness, the development and recognition of the new forms of organizational learning that underpin productivity improvements (particularly in the service sectors), and the reemergence of locality as an important political, social, and economic dimension all point to a subtly different picture of the future path toward economic prosperity. The challenges of reducing inequality and improving intergenerational mobility remain, connected with, but also in many ways more intransigent and even more localized than, the economic challenges.

The strengths of English colleges are their understanding of the educational needs of their local populace; accessibility and local reputation; longstanding links with local employers and understanding of local industry; commitment to social inclusion; and resourcefulness, innovation, and creativity. Leitch's conception of the organizational demand for learning as being well represented in this complex world by a hierarchy of qualifications, to which individuals will subscribe for reasons solely of economic gain rather than developing self-confidence, self-esteem, or intellectual independence (e.g., Coffield, 2008, pp. 58–60), can feel at times like a Procrustes bed for colleges. The colleges' strengths are real and resonate strongly with the emerging economic and social agendas. There is a wide and increasing range of techniques that can be used to engage and inspire both employers and individuals. These include skills competitions potentially leading to participation in the WorldSkills International competition (www. worldskills.org), student talent shows, weekend junior academies for 14- to 16-year-olds, innovation mornings to generate knowledge exchange between local companies, and master classes where leading industrial exponents demonstrate their craft. Building on such approaches, the entrepreneurial college of the future has great opportunities to develop expertise in interorganizational working, supportive management development, coaching and mentoring, and promoting and supporting the flow of ideas and innovative practices throughout the fabric of the local economy, while also successfully including the creativity of the hitherto marginalized in these endeavours.

References

American Association of Community Colleges. (2008). *Students at community colleges.* Washington, DC: Author. Retrieved May 15, 2008, from http://www2.aacc.nche. edu/research/index_students.htm

Ashton, D., Green, F., Sung, J., & James, D. (2002). The evolution of education and training strategies in Singapore, Taiwan and S. Korea: A development model of skill formation. *Journal of Education and Work, 15*(1), 5–30.

Ashton, D., & Sung, J. (2002). *Supporting workplace learning for high performance working.* Geneva: International Labour Office.

Ashton, D., Sung, J., & Raddon, A. (2003). An integrated and employer-based workforce development programme: The case of Singapore. In *Raising employer demand for skills: Lessons from abroad: Part 3* (pp. 21–30). London: Department for Trade and Industry.

Billett, S., & Somerville, M. (2004). Transformations at work: Identity and learning. *Studies in Continuing Education, 26*(2), 309–326.

Castells, M. (1992). Four Asian tigers with a dragon head: A comparative analysis of the state, economy and society in the Asian Pacific Rim. In R. P. Appelbaum & J. Henderson (Eds.), *States and development in the Asian Pacific Rim* (pp. 50–70). Beverly Hills, CA: Sage.

Coffield, F. (2008). *Just suppose teaching and learning became the first priority.* London: Learning and Skills Network.

Confederation of British Industry. (2008). *Taking stock: CBI education and skills survey 2008.* London: Author.

Department for Children, Schools and Families (DCSF), & Department for Innovation, Universities and Skills (DIUS). (2008). *Raising expectations: Enabling the system to deliver.* London: Department for Children, Schools and Families.

Department for Culture, Media and Sport, Department for Business, Enterprise and Regulatory Reform, & Department for Innovation, Universities and Skills. (2008). *Creative Britain: New talents for the new economy.* London: Department for Culture, Media and Sport.

Department for Education and Skills, Department for Trade and Industry [DFES], Her Majesty's Treasury, & Department for Work and Pensions [DWP]. (2003). *21st century skills: Realising our potential.* London: Her Majesty's Stationery Office. Available from the Department of Children, Schools and Families Web site: http://www.dcsf.gov.uk

Department for Innovation, Universities and Skills. (2007). *World class skills: Implementing the Leitch review of skills in England.* London: Author.

Department for Innovation, Universities and Skills. (2008). *Innovation nation.* London: Author.

Dixon, M., & Paxton W. (2005). The state of the nation. In N. Pearce & W. Paxton (Eds.), *Social justice: Building a fairer Britain* (pp. 21–61). London: Politico's Publishing, Institute for Public Policy Research.

Ellstrom, E., Ekholm, B., & Ellstrom, P.-E. (2008). Two types of learning environment. *Journal of Workplace Learning, 20*(2), 84–97.

Engestrom, Y. (2001). Expansive learning at work: Toward an activity theoretical reconceptualization. *Journal of Education and Work, 14*(1), 133–156.

Engestrom, Y., & Kerosuo, H. (2007). From workplace learning to inter-organizational learning and back: The contribution of activity theory. *Journal of Workplace Learning, 19*(6), 336–342.

Eraut, M. (2004). Informal learning in the workplace. *Studies in Continuing Education, 26*(2), 247–273.

Foster, A. (2005). *Realising the potential: A review of the future role of further education colleges.* London: Department for Education and Skills.

Gates, P., Coward, S., & Byrom, T. (2007). *Young participation in higher education in the parliamentary constituency of Nottingham North.* Nottingham, UK: University of Nottingham. Available from http://www.nottingham.ac.uk/education/research/projects/index.phtml

Her Majesty's Treasury. (2007). *Review of sub-national economic development and regeneration.* London: Author. Available from the HM Treasury Web site: http://www.hm-treasury.gov.uk

Higher Education Funding Council for England. (2008). *Foundation degrees: Key statistics 2001–02 to 2007–08.* Bristol, UK: Author.

Higher Education Statistics Agency. (2007). *Performance indicators in higher education in the UK 2005/06.* Cheltenham, UK: Author.

Keating, J., Medrich, E., Vollkoff, V., & Perry, J. (2002). *Comparative study of vocational education and training systems: National vocational education and training systems across three regions under pressure of change.* Leabrook, Australia: National Centre for Vocational Education Research.

Learning and Skills Council. (2005). *Agenda for change.* Coventry, UK: Author.

Learning and Skills Council. (2007a). *Better skills, better jobs, better lives: Our statement of priorities.* Coventry, UK: Author.

Learning and Skills Council. (2007b). *The status and reputation of the further education system.* Coventry, UK: Author.

Leitch, S. (2005). *Skills in the UK: The long-term challenge.* London: Her Majesty's Treasury.

Leitch, S. (2006). *Prosperity for all in the global economy—World class skills.* London: Her Majesty's Treasury.

Lucas, R. (1988). On the mechanics of economic development. *Journal of monetary economics, 22,* 3–42.

Lyons, M. (2007). *Place-shaping: A shared ambition for the future of local government.* London: Her Majesty's Stationery Office.

National Center on Education and the Economy. (2007). *Tough choices or tough times— Executive summary.* Washington, DC: Author.

Nolan, P. (2001). *China and the global economy: National champions, industrial policy and big business revolution.* Basingstoke, UK: Palgrave.

Organisation for Economic Co-operation and Development. (2002). *Education at a glance.* Paris: Author.

Pearce N., & Paxton, W. (2005). Introduction. In N. Pearce & W. Paxton (Eds.), *Social justice: Building a fairer Britain* (pp. ix–xxiii). London: Politico's Publishing, Institute for Public Policy Research.

Porter, M., & Ketels, C. (2003). *UK competitiveness: Moving to the next stage* (DTI Economics Paper No. 3). London: Department of Trade and Industry.

Prime Minister. (2007, June 28). *Written ministerial statement on machinery of government changes (27 June 07).* London: Author. Available from the Prime Minister's Office Web site: http://www.number10.gov.uk Quality Assurance Agency. (2007). *Higher education in further education colleges in England: Statistical bulletin (2005-06).* Gloucester, UK: Author.

Quality Assurance Agency. (2007). *Higher education in further education colleges in England: Statistical bulletin (2005-06).* Gloucester, UK: Author.

Schurman, R. (1996). Chile's new entrepreneurs and the "economic miracle": The invisible hand or a hand from the state? *Studies in Comparative International Development, 31*(2), 83–109.

Snyder, T. D., Dillow, S. A., & Hoffman, C. M. (2008, March 25). *Digest of education statistics: 2007* (NCES 2008-122). Washington, DC: U.S. Department of Education.

United Nations Development Programme. (2006). *Beyond scarcity: Power, poverty and the global water crisis* (2006 Human Development Report). New York: Author.

UK Parliament. (2000). *Learning and skills act 2000 c.21.* London: The Stationery Office. Available from the Office of Public Sector Information Web site: http://www.opsi.gov.uk/acts/acts2000a

UK Parliament. (2007). *Further education and training act 2007 c. 25.* London: The Stationery Office. Available from the Office of Public Sector Information Web site: http://www.opsi.gov.uk/acts/acts2007a

Vuorinen, I., Jarvinen, R., & Lehtinen, U. (1998). Content and measurement of productivity in the service sectors. *International Journal of Service Industry Management, 9*(4), 377–396.

Whitley, R. (1999). *Divergent capitalisms: The social structuring and change of business systems.* Oxford, UK: Oxford University Press.

Williamson, J. (1990). What Washington means by policy reform. In J. Williamson (Ed.), *Latin American adjustment: How much has happened?* (pp. 7–20). Washington, DC: Institute for International Economics.

World Bank. (1997). *World development report 1997: The state in a changing world.* New York: Oxford University Press.

Young, M. (2003). National qualifications frameworks as a global phenomenon: A comparative perspective. *Journal of Education and Work, 16*(3), 223–237.

17

Further Education in Ireland

Frank McMahon

Ireland is a small island off the western coast of Europe. It is divided into Northern Ireland, which is part of the United Kingdom (UK), and the independent Republic of Ireland. In the middle of the 19th century, the island's population exceeded 8 million. Beginning with the famine of 1845–1847 and continuing by means of emigration until about 1990, the island lost almost half its population. The population is now about 5.5 million; just over 4 million live in the Republic of Ireland.

The Republic of Ireland gained independence from the United Kingdom in 1922. Because there had been very little industrialization, it remained economically dependent on the UK for most of the 20th century, primarily by supplying agricultural products to the UK, which operated a cheap food policy. After joining the European Union in 1973, Ireland began to receive higher prices for its agricultural products. It also received generous development aid for infrastructure projects and for education and training. In 1973, the average income in Ireland was approximately 60% of the EU average; it has since risen to more than 100%. Unemployment, which in the 1980s was 18%, was at 5% in 2008. Ireland has one of the fastest-growing populations in Europe, and grew by 2% a year between 2002 and 2006 (Central Statistics Office, 2008). The term *Celtic tiger* has been coined to describe the Irish economy, which has outperformed the economies of almost all countries that are members of the Organisation for Economic Co-operation and Development (OECD).

EDUCATION IN IRELAND

From its foundation in 1922, the Republic of Ireland has had free primary education, the right to which is enshrined in the constitution. Before it introduced free secondary education at the end of the 1960s, many people left school after completing the primary grades. As a result, the levels of illiteracy and innumeracy are still very high in the 55–65 age cohort. According to OECD (2007), in 2005, only 40% of the 55–64 cohort had an upper-secondary education, while 77% of the 25–34 cohort did. These statistics capture how well the secondary education system has caught up in the past 3 decades. Similar progress may be seen in third-level education: In 2005, 17% of the 55–64 cohort and 41% of the 25–34 cohort had a third-level qualification.

A green paper published by Ireland's Department of Education and Science (DES) in 1998 illustrated the relationship between education level and employment in the 1997 labor force. In general, employment rates increased with the level of education, and unemployment rates decreased. For example, those with only a primary education constituted 16% of the labor force and 28% of the unemployed. Those who had completed a third-level education (27% of the total labor force), constituted 29% of the employed and only 11% of the unemployed (DES, 1998).

One of the earliest pieces of education legislation in the newly independent Republic of Ireland was the Vocational Education Act of 1930, which established local committees to control vocational education in each county and major city. The first concern of these vocational education committees (VECs) was to create technical schools that would provide a less-academic alternative to the existing secondary schools. Children who struggled academically could learn woodworking and mechanical drawing (in boys' technical schools) or home economics, shorthand, and typing (in girls' technical schools). In the 1970s, the technical schools became more academic, offering a leaving certificate (equivalent to a U.S. high school diploma); at the same time, secondary schools extended their range to include such nonacademic subjects as mechanical/technical drawing. As a result of this change in their roles, technical schools and secondary schools in some localities merged to become community colleges. Unlike their namesakes in the United States, Irish community colleges are second-level schools that educate 12- to-18-year-olds.

VECs also inherited responsibility for some specialist colleges that predated the 1930 act. Five of these colleges, the oldest of which was founded in 1887, were in Dublin. They offered courses in science and technology, art, commerce, "women's work" (dressmaking, cookery, and laundry), and music. In the 1930s, the City of Dublin VEC embarked on an ambitious development of its specialist colleges, adding a sixth college in 1941 and of the 22 second-level schools under its remit. The six colleges were combined in 1978 to form Dublin Institute of Technology (DIT), which flourished with a regional and a national intake of students. The second-level schools were subject to the vagaries of the demographics of their local areas. Some were without adequate student numbers by the 1970s and had to develop a new role for themselves by providing post–leaving certificate (PLC) programs. These were primarily 1- or 2-year vocational courses that served students whose leaving certificate performance was not good enough to win them a place in higher education. In Ireland, secondary education is referred to as "second-level" and higher education is referred to as "third-level"; the PLC programs are sometimes described as being at "two-and-a-half level." In recent years this in-between level has been called the further education (FE) sector.

In 1970, the government gave a major boost to technology education by founding the National Institute of Higher Education (NIHE) in Limerick and 12 regional technical colleges (RTCs) around the country. (Dublin was not included in this initiative because it already had the six specialist colleges.) Each RTC was organized into three schools—engineering, science, and business/humanities—that offered a range of 2-year national certificate programs and 3-year national diploma programs.

The NIHE in Limerick concentrated mainly on degree-level programs. In 1980, a second NIHE was opened, in Dublin. In 1986, the government appointed a committee to review technology education in Ireland. The committee recommended that the two NIHEs be given university status; in 1989, they were.

In 1992, the Irish parliament passed two acts that affected education. The Dublin Institute of Technology (DIT) Act merged the specialist colleges operated by the City of Dublin VEC and gave DIT the power to grant education and training awards. The Regional Technical Colleges Act provided a new legislative basis for the RTCs and dictated that the RTCs receive their awards from the National Council for Educational Awards (NCEA). These award practices continue to this day, although the Higher Education and Training Awards Council, which succeeded NCEA, has empowered some RTCs (now called institutes of technology) to make some awards of degrees and higher certificates. A 1995 DES white paper on education confirmed the roles of DIT and the RTCs but did not address the growing role of the VEC–controlled colleges. Although there was no legislative basis for doing so, these colleges were increasingly providing PLC programs.

THE FURTHER EDUCATION SECTOR

Ireland's FE sector grew without the support of a legislative framework, and the government is now trying to catch up. Many of the PLC programs developed since 1985 to fill spare capacity in second-level schools were highly successful, which encouraged VECs to designate some of their colleges as FE colleges. The number of students participating in PLC programs increased from 12,000 in 1989–1990 to more than 24,000 in 1990–2000. In 2000, DES established a steering group to examine the provision of PLC programs and "make recommendations . . . regarding the organizational, support, development, technical and administrative structures and resources in schools and colleges with large PLC provision having regard to good practice in related areas across the system and in other countries" (DES, 2000). (A "large PLC" was defined as one that enrolled more than 150 students in a single school or college.) The steering group included representatives of DES, VEC managers, and members of teachers' unions.

An interim report (McIver, 2002) from the steering group highlighted the problems that beset the FE sector, which arose mainly from its origins in the second-level sector:

- inadequate physical facilities and space
- inadequate equipment, especially computers
- lack of space for social interaction among students
- excessive teacher supervision of FE students
- excessive teaching loads
- inadequate management and administrative staffing

Improving these problems would involve reducing staff teaching loads; adding managers, administrators, and technicians; improving library and computing facilities; upgrading buildings; and increasing support services. Although DES and Ireland's Department of Finance has not yet provided the considerable funding needed to make such changes, the FE sector has continued to grow. By 2004, it had 28,588 students (DES, 2004).

OECD reviewed higher education in Ireland in 2004. Its report on the review (OECD, 2004) did not mention PLC programs as the terms of reference provided by the government of Ireland related to higher education only, not further education. Ireland's FE sector provides other programs in addition to PLCs. These include Youthreach, for early school leavers (3,258 students in 2003); training programs for young and adult travellers who have left school early (1,076 students); back-to-education programs for adults (16,155 students); and adult literacy and community education programs (2,277 students) (DES, 2004).

Participation in Higher Education

The advantages conferred by higher education have long been recognized in Ireland, and participation in higher education has gradually increased. In 1980, 20% of high school graduates went on to higher education; in 1986, 25%; in 1992, 36%; in 1998, 46% (White, 2001). In recent years, the numbers have continued to grow, and now more than 60% proceed to higher education.

In Irish universities, and particularly in teacher training colleges, a significant majority of students are female, whereas more gender balance exists in technological colleges. Apprentices, who are not considered to be full-time students, are almost all male. Ireland's technological colleges offer 2-year programs (higher certificates), 3-year programs (ordinary degrees), and 4-year programs (honors degrees). The universities offer mainly honors degrees, with some provision for ordinary degrees.

Apprenticeship

Ireland has long used the apprenticeship approach to train skilled craftspeople. In an apprenticeship program, a young person is formally attached to and receives training from a company or an individual in the profession the person wants to learn. When the Republic of Ireland became independent in 1922, its technical education system involved long apprenticeship to a master (often 7 years) and attendance at day-release courses in technical schools. As O'Connor and Harvey (2001) pointed out, this system had two disadvantages: Classes were available only in urban areas, and class attendance was voluntary.

The Apprenticeship Act of 1931 gave the government the power to designate trades and to establish committees to make rules for apprenticeships in each trade. These rules covered the duration of an apprenticeship; conditions of employment, including pay rates; and arrangements for training. The apprenticeship committees could ask VECs to provide courses for apprentices. While this act improved the apprenticeship system, it did not address an important weakness—that time served in an apprenticeship was considered more important than demonstrable competency was.

A new industrial training authority, known as AnCO from the Irish form of its name, was established in 1967 to introduce more formalized training into both the on-the-job and classroom phases of apprenticeship. RTCs became an important resource for the classroom phase, as did the availability after 1973 of EU funding for building and operating training centers. In 1991, FÁS, the training authority that succeeded AnCO, introduced a 7-phase standards-based apprenticeship system. Phases 1, 3, 5, and 7 are done on the job; Phase 2 is done in a training center; and Phases 4 and 6 are done in an institute of technology. For most trades, Phase 2 lasts 22 weeks and Phases 4 and 6 are each 11 weeks. Phase 1 (3 months), Phase 3 (minimum 6 months), Phase 5 (6 months), and Phase 7 (minimum 3 months) are undertaken on the job, and trainees are paid by employers.

The 7-phase system seems to be successful, and recruitment to apprenticeships has been stronger in recent years than it was in the 1980s and 1990s. In 1980, the number of apprentices was 21,498; in 1985, 15,968; in 1990, 12,987; in 1995, 10,772; in 2000, 24,028; in 2005, 28,602; and in 2007, 28,500 (Skills Initiative Unit, 2008). Some areas of apprenticeship have been hard hit by the rate of innovation in industry, making some traditional skills obsolete. For example, changes in printing technology have resulted in the amalgamation of the trades of printing, bookbinding, and origination into a single trade (print media) and a reduction in the number of apprentices annually from 180 to 30 (Dublin Institute of Technology, 2008).

Enrollment in the apprenticeship system has historically been dominated by men. Despite efforts to encourage female trainees, more than 90% of new trainees in 2005 were men (Skills Initiative Unit, 2008). This is to some extent because the occupations that have been designated as apprenticeship trades (electrician, construction, sheet-metal work, etc.) are traditionally male dominated, while traditionally female-dominated occupations, such as nursing and hairdressing, have not been designated.

National Qualifcations Authority of Ireland

The Qualifications (Education and Training) Act of 1999 led to the 2001 establishment of the National Qualifications Authority of Ireland (NQAI), which has three main tasks:

- Establish and maintain a framework for developing, recognizing, and awarding qualifications based on standards of knowledge, skill, or learner competence.

- Establish and promote the maintenance and improvement of awards standards for nonuniversity institutions in the FE and higher education sectors.

- Promote and facilitate learners' access to, transfer among, and progression through education and training.

In October 2003, NQAI launched the 10-level National Framework of Qualifications (NFQ), which is designed to encompass all education and training awards up to the doctoral level. Ireland's education providers are committed to implementing NFQ and it is gradually gaining credibility among employers. NQAI is also committed to facilitating access, transfer, and progression. Its approach to policy development strongly emphasizes consulting with all stakeholders and publishing its draft policies on its Web site to encourage debate and comments (see www.nqai.ie).

Higher Education Initiatives in Europe

Irish education developed independently of other countries a 1999 European initiative: In June 1999, the education ministers of 29 European countries signed the Bologna declaration, committing to the creation of a European higher education area (EHEA) by 2010. All EHEA member nations would provide bachelor's, master's, and doctoral degree programs, and would share a framework for national qualifications systems. To increase student mobility within Europe, all universities in member nations would use the same credit accumulation and transfer system.

The ministers have met every two years since 1999 to review progress toward EHEA and to set new goals for achieving its creation. The number of countries participating has grown to 45, and it seems probable that EHEA will indeed be created by 2010. EHEA is expected to have a number of significant effects, including the following:

- Increased recognition of education and training awards would facilitate worker mobility, which would allow shortages of skilled labor in one member nation to be met by migration from others.

- The stipulation that EHEA bachelor's degree programs be relevant to the labor market would give member nations an economic advantage over countries that do not do as good a job of aligning university output with industry needs.

- Non-European students who have traditionally turned to universities in Australia and the United States would be more likely to turn to EHEA member nations, thus boosting the finances of European universities.

The signing of the Bologna declaration has already led to a number of changes in EU education, including the following:

- The EU has provided greatly enhanced funding for student mobility through its Eramus and Socrates programs.

- In 2005, Irish institutions of higher education were asked by the government to double the number of incoming and outgoing students in Erasmus and Socrates programs.

- Degree programs at many European universities have been accelerated. Countries where students have traditionally taken 5 years to earn a first degree (such as Finland, Germany, and Italy) have introduced new bachelor's degree programs, generally of 3 years' duration.

- Similar initiatives are in place for apprenticeship training through the so-called Copenhagen process, which aims to harmonize approaches to training in European countries.

CURRENT ISSUES FOR IRISH EDUCATION

Although excellent progress has been made in Irish higher and technical education to increase participation in the past 30 years, some important issues still need to be addressed. Since fees were abolished in the mid-1990s, higher education in Ireland's universities and institutes of technology has been almost free. That policy, which, it is claimed, results in most of the benefit going mainly to middle-class families rather than poorer families, is regularly called into question. OECD (2004) favored reintroducing fees in order to improve the higher education system's finances. The government continues to oppose higher fees. It was the current opposition party that abolished the fees when it was in power, so any change in the governing party probably wouldn't lead to the fees being reinstated.

Although Ireland's FE colleges are for the most part funded as second-level schools, they increasingly operate at a higher level. Articulation between the programs operated by the FE colleges and programs in universities and institutes of technology is not well developed; certainly, it does not compare favorably with arrangements between community colleges and universities in the United States. NFQ has been well received and implemented in terms of higher education awards, but progression opportunities from apprenticeship and PLC qualifications to higher education remains a problem that must be addressed.

The nature of the binary divide between universities and institutes of technology is coming under strain. In particular, Dublin Institute of Technology occupies an anomalous position: Even though it has full awarding powers (up to doctoral degrees) and is a member of the European University Association and the International Association of Universities, it is not designated as a university in Ireland. Two other institutes of technology (Cork and Waterford) have also sought redesignation as universities. In response to this latter problem, the government is considering the commission of a review of higher education policy to be undertaken in 2008 and 2009. The terms of reference of such a review have not yet been published, but it seems unlikely to address articulation between further and higher education.

REFERENCES

Central Statistics Office. (2008). *Population and labour force projections 2011–2041.* Dublin: Author.

Department of Education and Science. (1995). *Charting our education future: White paper on education.* Dublin: The Stationery Office.

Department of Education and Science. (1998). *Green paper: Adult education in an era of learning.* Dublin: The Stationery Office.

Department of Education and Science. (2000). *Learning for life: White paper on adult education.* Dublin: The Stationery Office.

Department of Education and Science. (2004). *Annual report 2003.* Retrieved April 28, 2008, from http://www.education.ie/servlet/blobservlet/dept_annual_report2003.pdf

Dublin Institute of Technology. (2008). *Student enrolments on apprentice programmes* [Internal report]. Dublin: Author.

McIver. (2002, March). *Interim report of the steering group of the PLC review established by the Department of Education and Science.* Retrieved April 28, 2008, from the Teachers' Union of Ireland Web site: www.tui.ie

O'Connor, L., & Harvey, N. (2001). Apprenticeship training in Ireland. *Journal of Industrial Training, 25*(6), 332–342.

Organisation for Economic Co-operation and Development. (2004). *Review of higher education in Ireland.* Paris: OECD Publishing.

Organisation for Economic Co-operation and Development. (2007). *Education at a glance: OECD indicators 2005.* Paris: OECD Publishing.

Skills Initiative Unit. (2008). *Report to the Department of Education and Science.* Dublin: Author.

White, T. (2001). *Investing in people: Higher education in Ireland from 1960 to 2000.* Dublin: Institute of Public Administration.

18

Creating a Learning Village in the Netherlands

Coen Free

In the Netherlands, primary education is available for 8 years (children may begin at age 4) and compulsory for 7 (children must begin at age 5). In their last year of primary school, pupils are advised on what type of secondary education they should pursue. Attendance at junior general secondary education schools (MAVO) is compulsory for ages 12–16. There are four types of schools that offer middle-secondary, upper-secondary, and prevocational education:

- Four-year preparatory middle-level vocational education schools (VMBO) combine general and vocational education. VMBO graduates may enter the job market, continue for a fifth year of vocational education in a HAVO (see next bullet), or be admitted to a middle-level vocational education school (MBO).

- Five-year higher general continued education schools (HAVO) offer to educate students for admission to an HBO—a postsecondary institution of professional higher education. HAVO graduates may also seek admission to VWOs (see next bullet).

- Six-year university preparatory education schools (VWO) prepare students for admission to universities specializing in general studies and science education.

Colleges of senior secondary vocational education and training (VET) in the Netherlands can be compared with British colleges of further and higher education.

Postsecondary education in the Netherlands is available at three types of institutions. WOs (Wetenschappelijk Onderwijs), also called research universities, are general universities that specialize in science education. HBOs are universities of professional education that offer general programs as well as specialized education in specific fields, such as agriculture, fine and performing arts, and teacher training. HBOs prepare students for particular professions; their programs tend to be more practically oriented than programs offered by the WOs. The Open University offers university degree programs through distance education.

REDESIGNING VET

Vocational education in Europe is closely tied to—and significantly affected by—both society and the employment market. To ensure that VET meets the changing needs of students, employers, and the economy, European Union member nations, the Netherlands among them, are introducing major innovations. In the Netherlands, these reforms will not just be an exclusive, internal education process; they will link the country's VET system with related systems in the rest of the world.

The Netherlands' redesign for upper-secondary vocational education, called the Herontwerp MBO, will create completely new programs based on a number of government and societal ambitions. The reforms will

- Introduce a completely new, competency-oriented qualification structure.

- Introduce new educational concepts centered on learning and developing competencies.

- Realize flexible and demand-oriented upper-secondary vocational education that fits seamlessly with the regional employment market and evolves with the market's needs.

- Create a strong learning environment in which the student's career is at the forefront.

- Significantly reduce the number of dropouts and encourage social inclusion.

- Encourage students to transfer from VMBOs to MBOs and HBOs.

- Lead colleges to adopt new education and advisory concepts that apply social constructivism to learning that is problem-based, project-based, and task-based; and to increasingly use the possibilities offered by e-learning.

The Importance of Personnel

Personnel are critical to the success of the Netherlands' redesign of upper-secondary vocational education. Employees play many roles: There are inventors and helpers, pioneers and inhibitors, followers and faultfinders. As in any organization, employees of Dutch colleges recreate their organizations each day, enabling them to operate and implement small and large changes.

The human and cultural sides of the Netherlands' redesign of upper-secondary vocational education require a lot of attention. Staff members need to adapt to dynamic new demand-oriented teaching concepts that constantly inspire young people to pursue mastery learning and thereby perform and succeed at the highest possible levels.

Teachers play an important role: They must model a professional attitude, a high degree of expertise, and excellent professional skills for their students, just as masters in a traditional apprenticeship system do for journeymen. Employee structures must shift from a vertical department orientation to a college orientation, sharing knowledge and creating horizontal synergy. All faculty must not only accept, but seek responsibility for, their college's results, both as individuals and as team members. The colleges themselves must shift from an internal to an external orientation: The education and the business communities can no longer be separate but must work together and complement each other.

The purpose of the redesign is to create strong colleges in a strong region. To achieve this, colleges must work intensively and effectively to cooperate with all parties involved in their local societies and economies, creating strategic alliances and covenants. The schools must take an entrepreneurial approach and develop into social businesses.

Characteristics of the Ideal College

In redesigning upper-secondary vocational education, it is posited that colleges should have the following 10 characteristics:

1. The college functions like a community college, helping to unite society by offering effective paths to senior secondary (and higher) vocational education and general secondary education to all learners 16 and over, to all social classes, and to all racial groups. It also teaches students to function as good citizens in society.

2. The college is a real community of learners, where students and staff learn together, not for the diploma, but for life. Its professional culture encourages constant education innovation. The college is appealing, innovative, vital, and creative. Learning paths are oriented to individual students, are attractive and challenging, and bring enjoyment to learning and working. Almost no students drop out.

3. The college envisions a sustainable society, and it balances its social, economic, and ecological values.

4. The college is the axis of ongoing regional, societal, and economic renewal.

5. The college provides effective learning paths that create students whose excellent professional skills give them a strong starting position in the employment market.

6. The college educates large and increasing numbers of students who can easily move further in higher education.

7. The college cooperates with higher education institutions to provide associate's degree programs.

8. The college keeps people employable by providing customized learning paths in the areas of integration and reintegration, refresher training, further training, and retraining.

9. The college contributes to innovation in companies by equipping its students with the necessary knowledge of languages, technological knowledge, creativity, thinking skills, active skills, and a professional attitude.

10. The college is as a breeding ground for self-employed entrepreneurs, who have learned how to deal with market risk and to capitalize on their knowledge and skills in the market.

Adapting to a Knowledge-Based Economy

The concept of knowledge is changing, and so are the concepts of school, student, and teacher. Technologies are succeeding each other rapidly, which is leading to a flood of information. Learning to find your way in new and ever-expanding fields of knowledge is far more important than memorizing as many facts as possible or being able to monotonously repeat job-specific procedures. The new concept of learning is characterized by the transition from passive consumption of teaching to active forms of learning.

The innovative use of technology and plugging into the learning skills and learning styles of the Internet generation (net generation) will have a huge influence on the didactics, the education theory, the content, and the structure of education. Thus the school as an institute and as an organization will also have to be redesigned. Students in the Dutch education system have had to repeatedly overcome the barriers placed before them by the exams they have to pass and the exit qualifications they have to acquire at various stages. Instead of development, the focus of Dutch education has been on creating obstacles to effective and efficient career development.

Placing the student's career and the introduction of competence-developing learning at the forefront has a major influence on the overall organization. It requires completely different management and direction. Learning processes and guidance should be customized as much as possible. Flexible education demands flexible management. You can offer students customization only if it is supported by the structure and the underlying processes. Changing structure and process requires a great deal of attention for synergy and cross-linking in the organization. Services, project agencies, and departments cannot and may no longer operate like islands with strictly separated and monitored boundaries. Management must be based on constant change, on external focus, and on results. This also has an affect on the organization financially. Therefore, there is a great need for systems and indicators to continually test innovations and quality. In short, a redesign affects the whole operation.

To effect this level of change, a college needs a clear strategy for innovation. Education institutions that do not plan for the future will be left standing on the wrong platform, waiting for the wrong train, with only the past to hold onto. A strong, realistic, and challenging innovation strategy that responds to the demands of a rapidly changing society also stimulates and excites parties interested in the school organization. The school can then emerge as a 21st-century learning and working environment and a valued partner in knowledge creation for the region. Koning Willem I College has developed just such an innovation strategy, which it calls "the learning village." The remainder of this chapter is devoted to examining the basic principles and philosophies underlying the learning village model, which is still being developed. No comprehensive example exists for us to follow as we develop this model, but we have drawn inspiration from organizations such as the University of Cambridge in England; community colleges in Phoenix, Arizona, and Kansas City, Missouri; Città della Scienza in Naples; and our own K–12 school. What we do already have is a number of basic principles to draw on.

Koning Willem I College

Overview

The Netherlands has 46 colleges of further education providing MBO programs, almost all with very similar programs and structures. Koning Willem I College, in the city of 's-Hertogenbosch in the south of the Netherlands, is regarded as one of the best and most innovative colleges in the country. It is the only community college in the Netherlands and the only college with a campus. In keeping with the belief that knowledge is best created and shared through a lifelong learning process, the college educates students from kindergarten through college. By the most recent count, 400 K–12 students are enrolled, and 20,000 students attend at the community college level (8,000 full time, 6,000 part time, and 6,000 noncredit). (See http://www.kw1c.nl.) Koning Willem I is playing a leading role in the redesign of the European and Dutch education systems. It is the founder of School voor de Toekomst (School for the Future); the founding member and base of the Dutch Consortium for Innovation, sister to the League for Innovation in the Community College; and a founding member of the European Federation for Open and Distance Learning.

The Learning Village Concept

Many of today's world citizens actively take part in a fast-paced and modern life, travel the world, and embrace technology. Yet many still have a great need for order, simple and comfortable solutions, and a return to the safety and security of yesterday. Absolute bliss may be surfing the Internet and text messaging by mobile phone in a sunny, nostalgic village square in the shadow of the rustling leaves of an oak tree. Many see college as a large-scale diploma factory, but most people think of a village as a cozy, friendly community. In this spirit, Koning Willem I uses the village as a metaphor for its redesign.

But the learning village is not just a physical space, a collection of buildings. The learning village also occupies intellectual space and cyberspace. Although neither is tangible, they do have a considerable influence on lives and on our learning processes, so they also affect the school. Teachers will no longer be, nor will they have to be, the only source of content and information. For centuries, the physical learning environment was determined by the didactics of teaching verbally to a selected group of students on the basis of a fixed program. This form of education was and continues to be bound to a specific location, characteristics, and time. However, it is no longer necessary to bring teachers and students together physically; the virtual classroom of the mind or cyberspace is never closed.

This is a fundamental shift from a culture of collective transfer of knowledge to a culture of individual learning, where learning does not occur solely by attending lectures at a school. Furthermore, today's students seek a learning environment that serves different functions. They seek a learning environment where they can go to develop themselves, meet others, and enjoy or experience something. The latter fits in with the trend of the experience economy, which means that today's consumer constantly wants to experience something and discover something authentic, so obviously a college must be a place you enjoy coming to frequently. Inspiring learning, working, meeting, and leisure environments are preconditions for this, and this is what we intend for the learning village to achieve. So, rather than a physical organizational concept, the learning village is a new learning, working, and living concept.

Education Theory and the Learning Village

Imagine a teacher from 200 years ago (when the blackboard was invented) arriving in our education system. He would be impressed by the techniques and the technology. But once in the classroom, he would simply start to teach. The only difference is that he would now have to write on a white board with black marker, instead of on a blackboard with chalk. Research has shown that students remember only 20% of what they read and hear. But they remember 80% of what they experience and as much as 90% of what they explain to somebody else. That is what the didactics will have to focus on. The theory and the teaching no longer occupy center stage. Instead, the student's personality and learning needs are at the forefront. Four forms of education that possess this potential are competence-developing, project-based, task-based, and problem-based learning.

The things that governments, business and industry, and educational institutions consider useful are becoming less and less meaningful to students, which is one of the main reasons why students drop out. Involvement is a condition for learning. You cannot create involvement automatically by teaching a lesson on a subject, no matter how interesting it is. You create involvement by linking in with the knowledge, ambitions, and qualities of the students, and, in particular, by taking them seriously.

The Dutch professor Monique Boekaerts of Leiden University supports her Leids Didactisch Model (Leiden Instruction Model) this way (see Boekaerts, 1995). Everyone has goals in life. Goals that arise from one's own personality structure have a motivating effect and bring about positive emotions and positive energy (award system). Goals that do not arise from one's own personality structure usually have a discouraging effect and bring about negative emotions and energy (punishment system). People draw value and meaning from needs, goals, motivation, and security. Students draw value from the following three goals:

- meaningful learning (context-oriented, interesting);
- personal balance (being successful, self-satisfaction); and
- social balance (feeling like they are being taken seriously, being able to make their own choices, which equals autonomy). Students who are frustrated in their learning objectives express this through maladjusted behavior: not actively participating, acting up, pestering, skipping class, and vandalism.

Virtually all students are motivated when they take up a course of study. This is based on three needs:

- the psychological need for competences (subject-specific and learning to learn);
- the psychological need for social relationships (fellow students, peers, and teachers who provide assistance and support); and
- the need for autonomy (negotiation model).

As far as educational theory is concerned, we have largely skipped the developments of increasing independence, increasing diversity, and, in particular, the increasingly changing ability of young people to learn. We worry about the future of education, and look for renewal of content, design, and didactics, but there is (too) little attention paid to the most powerful and most crucial renewal factor: the students themselves.

Understanding the Net Generation

Another factor that the learning village model needs to take into account is that students today belong to what has been called the net generation. Young people growing up with cable television, computers, the Internet, and mobile telephones are developing their own new and unique learning style that contrasts sharply with standard didactics and education theory. Education is still based on printed texts and standardized methods, is still linear, and is still formal and teacher-driven. The way in which the net generation learns is just the opposite: Learning takes place via monitors, symbols, icons, sound, games, trying things out, and asking others questions; learning is not linear but associative. Children are already experienced at processing information before they start school. They are used to choosing from many sources of information and do not make those choices anywhere near as randomly or coincidentally as educators think.

Some researchers (e.g., Dutch sociologist Henk Vinken) are convinced that the Internet is nothing less than a wedge between two generations. Others (e.g., American sociologist Rushkoff) regard the net generation as a new type of living being, beings that are capable of thinking associatively as if many different windows are open at the same time and who are even able to find connections between these different windows. This is in contrast to their parents, the linear-thinking television generation, who desperately and often unsuccessfully try to find logic in a flood of information.

This net generation—the first generation in the history of humanity to educate its parents—distinguishes itself from previous generations by the frequent and effortless use of three devices: the remote control, the mouse, and the mobile phone. What these devices have in common is that they enable the user to decide which information is available and absorbed. By changing channels, clicking, and text messaging, children learn from an early age to make their own choices from the many data flows. This freedom to choose has a great influence on the way in which children deal with information and how they learn.

Today's children learn through exploratory play with the aid of technology. When they receive a new computer game, they start playing immediately and do not waste time reading the manual. If they do not know something, they press the Help button, go to a site for a code that gets them to the next level, or use the mobile to phone a friend for advice. And with the answer, which they will always get some way or another, they can carry on playing and learning.

The net generation learns by trying things out, by communicating, and by networking. When communicating, they are concerned with the heart of the information, not with the style or the form. This leads to new forms of communication, such as chatting and text messaging, and to new words and concepts. For the net generation, virtual and physical contacts overlap seamlessly. They can talk in a group while simultaneously communicating with other people by mobile phone. They communicate with anyone, anywhere in the world, whether they know them or not. In this self-created learning environment, they constantly make choices and decisions about which knowledge and information is useful and which information to delete. And this is really what they want at school as well.

Learning is also very goal-oriented. The net generation learns things that will be useful in the future. Essentially, thanks to all their digital voyages of discovery, they have skills and a learning style that are perfectly suited for learning processes and future working environments. The net generation also reads in a very different way than previous generations. Actually, they do not read, but they scan. This means that they focus on a combination of images, icons, colors, movements, sound, and short texts. They mainly focus on the signs that refer to the heart of the information. Often these are words they can click on. As they scan the screen, they soon have an idea of the relevance of the information and decide just as quickly to click on the next page in search of more relevant information. In a society in which all information is available in digital form, and in which the role of multimedia will only increase, the ability to scan is important for all knowledge workers.

Another skill developed by today's children with ease is multitasking. The net generation can do everything at once: talk on the phone, watch TV, answer e-mails, chat, send text messages, listen to music, and do homework. Multitasking is a skill that greatly accelerates the rate of information processing and stimulates rapid knowledge construction.

The net generation develops another skill through watching a lot of TV: dealing with discontinuous information. On closer consideration, their channel changing behavior is not so random at all. They prefer to follow three or four programs at once. They see interrupted—or discontinuous—pieces of information from each program. Their brains make logical connections between these pieces of information. This way of thinking and acting enables them to develop the ability to construct a meaningful whole from discontinuous information, as well as the ability to process more information than someone watching a single program could process in the same amount of time. This skill is important in a society in which you have to be able to obtain information from many different sources, use this information to form your own opinion, and do so quickly.

Yet another skill the net generation develops is a nonlinear, associative approach to processing information across many different degrees of difficulty. They develop this skill through the way they handle playing computer games and one that is at odds with the scholastic approach, where the systematic, linear, and sequential approach is taught from easy to difficult. There is still insufficient recognition of the idea that learning in the digital age truly does occur differently and can occur through the use of technology and by taking advantage of the net generation student's skills.

Knowledge Networks at Koning Willem I

Creating, sharing, and organizing knowledge is the core business of every educational organization. When people learn together, individuals learn for themselves, but the group also learns collectively. Collective learning, with collective processes and collective results, leads to changes in behavior and in work, and to innovation of processes and products. According to social constructivism, learning is a process of social interaction in which knowledge is constantly constructed and reconstructed. A school cannot create knowledge without the full participation of its students. Students are knowledge workers, who constantly learn with each other and with other knowledge workers—the school's staff and people they know in their professional lives.

Building on this concept, Koning Willem I College has five knowledge networks: the Center for Teaching and Learning, the Innovation Platform, the Central Examination Board, the Advisory Council of the Information and Communications Technology (ICT) Academy, and the Student Success Center. A knowledge network is not a committee or a working group; it is a learning community. Participants share a passion and a practice and face the same worries and issues. They explore questions, take a look at what each participant has to offer, and enter into discussions with internal and external experts. A knowledge network does not offer any ultimate answers, but is a powerful learning environment in which difficult matters are addressed. Participants must have a sincere interest in being part of the network, and must be willing to contribute to each others' development. They face difficult questions, discuss taboos, and identify surprise and disappointment. They bear disappointments and celebrate successes together.

As knowledge workers, students learn by working. They have jobs in the college's internal businesses (including its restaurant and travel agency) and in college businesses that serve external customers (including a hairdressing salon and the Service Center High Tech Metalelektro). Students set up and run mini-businesses that the community can make use of. There are many possibilities for students to work in the college's social traineeships. For example, sports students referee games and provide sports training sessions and clinics for young children; wellness and health-care students organize activities for people with limitations and serve coffee and read aloud in hospitals or nursing homes; ICT and multimedia students give Internet and computer lessons to elderly people and others who are new to the Internet. The learning village bustles with activity generated by its working students.

Addressing Learning Styles and Environments

Learning involves assigning new meaning to information and constructing new knowledge. It is an individual mental process that is stimulated through communication with others. Constructing new knowledge is the aim of the knowledge economy. In the industrial age, educational psychology was dominated by the theory of behaviorism, which regarded the student's brain as an empty vessel; the teacher used verbal instruction and the exchange of questions and answers to fill the vessel with standardized knowledge. The theory of social constructivism is better suited to the 21st century: that the learner develops insight and constructs knowledge as the result of interaction with the environment. People learn by reflecting on their experiences, then adapting their behavior accordingly.

Howard Gardner's theory of multiple intelligences and Edward de Bono's ideas about the development of lateral thinking and creativity are useful within social constructivism (see, e.g., de Bono, 2000, 2003; Gardner, 1993, 1995). Gardner favors a new kind of education system that enables students to learn by means of eight intelligences. de Bono has translated his views on creative thinking into the CoRT program, 64 lessons that use play to teach children, beginning at age 4, how to learn using both sides of the brain. The ideas of Gardner and de Bono are indispensable in the learning village, because in order to have equal opportunities children must not be treated equally in education. An important tenet of the learning village is that giving children equal education opportunities does not mean treating them equally; rather, it means treating them as individuals.

In a study on conditions that contribute to learning in the 21st century, Knoke (1996) identified 10 learning spaces, some physical and some virtual. These are spaces for instruction, documentation, information, communication, cooperation, research, simulation, multimedia, virtual reality, and e-learning. Koning Willem I's School for the Future draws on this concept, along with the others described in this chapter, to create a space for researching, designing, developing, and implementing new learning environments, and to serve as a knowledge and presentation platform. The School for the Future is also a place where college staff can work, take breaks, and communicate with one another in a relaxed atmosphere. The School for the Future School is a teachers' success center, to which college employees can turn with questions related to learning, innovation, and professionalization. The School for the Future is also the home base for the Innovation Platform, the Application Expertise Center, and the de Bono Expertise Center.

CONCLUSION

Realizing the learning village concept has been a voyage of discovery for Koning Willem I College. Those who learn in the village are on their own inspiring voyages, to good jobs or further education. The learning village concept gives students individualized education paths based on their own characteristics as learners. This concept is based on the principles of self-driven learning and mastery learning, as well as on an understanding of today's net generation and knowledge worker. At Koning Willem I College, students develop high levels of competence that prepare them for the international employment market and for international higher education. The college strives to ensure that every student earns a diploma that is at the level of the European starting qualification or higher and that these diplomas correspond to the student's own ambitions and qualities.

A student is never alone on the education voyage but travels with fellow students and staff members in the college and with businesses, institutions, and organizations outside the college. In serving its students, Koning Willem I College is a true community college—not an island, but a bustling center of learning that is constantly evolving. The college's main motive is its deep social commitment to serve the community—the society—to which its students belong.

Since its beginnings centuries ago, the city of 's-Hertogenbosch has attracted artists, scientists, thinkers, and visionaries who have left their mark on the city. Koning Willem I College continues this tradition in its own way: by being a source for and a model of knowledge and culture, by striving for perfection, by constantly giving new impetuses to society, and, above all, by being a strong, inspiring, and contemporary learning environment.

REFERENCES

Boekaerts, M. (1995). Self-regulated learning: Bridging the gap between metacognitive and metamotivation theories. *Educational Psychologist, 30*(4), 195–200.

de Bono, E. (2000). *New thinking for the new millennium.* Beverly Hills, CA: New Millennium Press.

de Bono, E. (2003). *Why so stupid? How the human race has never really learned to think.* Dublin: Blackhall Publishing.

Gardner, H. (1993). *Multiple intelligences: The theory in practice.* New York: Basic Books.

Gardner, H. (1995). *The unschooled mind: How children think and how schools should teach.* New York: Basic Books.

Knoke, W. (1996). *Bold new world: The essential roadmap to the twenty-first century.* New York: Kodansha.

19

Spain's Vocational Education System

Sandra de Bresser and David Roldán Martínez

Spain, in the southwestern part of Europe, includes most of the Iberic Peninsula, the Balear Islands in the Mediterranean, the Canary Islands, and two cities in the northern part of Africa, Ceuta and Melilla. At about 506,000 km², the mainland accounts for 85% of the total land area. In 2007, the country's population was about 40.5 million. Spain underwent major political, social, and economic change in the late 1970s as it made the switch from dictatorship to parliamentary monarchy. Under the 1978 constitution, the country was organized into three types of territories: autonomous communities, provinces, and municipalities, each a full legal entity.

The constitution also laid the foundation for decentralizing government authority. This ongoing decentralization has affected Spain's education, vocational training, and occupational training systems. Some autonomous communities have full authority over education; in others, education is still controlled by the central ministry of education and culture. Legislation enacted in June 1997 allocated control of vocational training to the autonomous communities, the central government, and social partners. It also established a general council for vocational training, which created a national system of vocational qualifications. Responsibility for occupational training is now shared by the national and local governments, as well as other public- and private-sector entities.

Social Change and the Education System

Until the 1990s, Spain's education system was regulated by the 1970 General Education Law (LGE), which provided for basic general education from age 6 to age 14. After completing basic general education, a student could begin Level-1 vocational training or enter a baccalaureate program. Earning a baccalaureate allowed a student to enroll in either Level-2 vocational training or a pre-university course, the completion of which would permit enrollment in a university. LGE also regulated adult education and established a special education certification program in arts and languages for those who could not complete regular schooling.

Since 1970, Spain has experienced major social, political, and economic changes that have transformed all facets of life. These have included the gradual evolution into a democracy, the integration of women into the labor market, a declining birthrate, increasing immigration, and a rise in the numbers of people living in large urban areas. Spain's relationship to the world has changed, too, as evinced by its joining NATO in 1984 and the European Community (now European Union [EU]) in 1985.

Not surprisingly, Spain needed education reforms in order to meet its new challenges, and, the first of these, the General Education System Reform Act (LOGSE), was passed in 1990. Because the LOGSE reforms affected the entire education system, they were introduced gradually and not completed until the 2002–2003 academic year. Other significant education laws passed include the following: the 1995 Organic Law for the Participation, Assessment, and Management of Learning Centres (LOPEG), which focused on quality assurance in education; the 2001 Universities Organic Law (LOU), which focused on increasing government funding for university programs; the 2002 Organic Law for Quality Education (LOCE), which focused on adult education; and the May 2006 Education Organic Law (LOE), which is being implemented 2007–2010.

With the implementation of LOGSE and, now, LOE, Spain's education system meets EU guidelines for education, providing citizens with the skills and knowledge Spain needs to promote workforce mobility throughout the EU and with lifelong learning opportunities. The new system has allowed Spain to respond to the social, technological, economic, political, and cultural changes of the last two decades of the 20th century, as well as to increase access to education. LOGSE extended Spain's compulsory education to 10 years, from age 14 to age 16, which ended the practice of having students with disabilities attend special schools, instead giving those students access to the regular education system. LOU also improved access to universities for economically disadvantaged students. With the advent of LOE, compulsory education is divided into primary and secondary levels. Primary education has one 6-year cycle for ages 6–12. Its goal is to provide all children with certain basic skills and capabilities.

Compulsory secondary education (ESO) has two 2-year cycles, for ages 12–14 and 14–16. Its objective is to build on the skills and capabilities acquired in the primary years and to prepare students to work in any of the EU countries or to continue their education. Spain also offers some noncompulsory secondary education programs. For example, social guarantee programs are available to 16- to 21-year-old students who have not earned a secondary school certificate and who have no vocational training qualifications.

After completing ESO, students may enter a 2-year baccalaureate course or a vocational education program. The objective of the baccalaureate course is to help students mature intellectually and personally and to equip them with the knowledge and skills needed to perform well in society. The course helps determine which route a student will follow to obtain a vocational qualification or a university degree. The baccalaureate is organized into three streams, each of which is linked to a specific university career: arts, science and technology, humanities, and social studies. Spain has both public and private universities (run by either secular or religious bodies), which have complete autonomy in deciding which academic courses they will offer. Universities admit students who have earned a baccalaureate and passed an entrance exam. The type of baccalaureate and the exam grades determine which university programs a student is eligible for.

Both mid-level and high-level vocational education programs, which last 1 or 2 years, are available. Mid-level programs are designed to guide students in the transition from school to workforce. They also provide continuing training for those who are already employed in certain areas. Higher-level programs prepare young people for the workforce and for university courses.

Intermediate specific vocational training programs are for students over 16. Depending on the field, programs last either 18 months or 2 years. They may be provided in an institution that is dedicated to this type of training or in other education institutions. In most cases, intermediate specific vocational training is offered by institutes of secondary education, which also provide second-level compulsory education and baccalaureate programs. Intermediate training is categorized according to occupational families and *ciclos formativos*, or education cycles. As of 2006, and with the introduction of LOE, there were three intermediate cycles: vocational education, art and design, and sports.

Vocational Education

With the approval in 1993 of the national vocational education program and the 1998 to 2002 development of NVTP (national vocational training program, which was created in 1986), vocational education in Spain underwent a dramatic change. The intention was to create an integrated system that would deliver highly qualified workers and help make companies more competitive. NVTP divides the vocational education system into three parts: initial regulated vocational training (IVT), occupational training (OCT), and continuing vocational training (CVT).

IVT

IVT provides basic professional education and training. It is targeted mainly to young people but is also available to adults. IVT has two levels. The lower level is available to students who have completed compulsory secondary education. The higher level is for those who have earned a baccalaureate. Responsibility for IVT lies with the autonomous communities. Programs vary according to the needs of local business and industry, and according to the specific culture and language of each region. IVT also encompasses social guarantee programs, which provide vocational training to students who have not passed the exams needed to complete compulsory secondary education. A student who completes a social guarantee program is awarded two certificates, an academic certificate issued by the training center and a certificate of occupational competency issued by the provincial authority.

OCT

OCT helps unemployed people reintegrate into the workforce by giving them occupational skills and competencies. Participants earn a certificate of occupational competency, which specifies the occupational profile, the theoretical and practical content of the training, the training route, the duration of the training, the training objectives, and the evaluation criteria. OCT certification also allows students to continue on to academic education.

Training is provided by both public and private education centers that have contracts or cooperation agreements with the responsible authority. OCT can involve distance learning as well as attendance. It can be broad-based (to provide more general knowledge and skills), occupational, transformational, or specialized by character. OCT candidates are selected by two organizations. The provincial body of the national employment institute identifies a candidate, then the training provider approves or disapproves the candidate.

CVT

CVT supports the social and occupational advancement of workers and improves employers' competitiveness. All training with the objective of improving the competencies and qualifications of the workforce is considered to be CVT. It can be provided by employers, labor unions, branch organizations, or the workers themselves. CVT is managed by the Tripartite Foundation for Training at the Workplace. There are also some public-sector initiatives with a similar aim but on a much smaller scale.

A Unified Vocational Training System

The 2002 Organic Act on Qualifications and Vocational Training (LOCPF) incorporated IVT, OCT, and CVT into a single system. The act established a national system for vocational training and qualifications (NVTP). The main aspect of this system is a national catalog of vocational qualifications, whose aim is to coordinate vocational training curricula with the needs of the labor market and to facilitate lifelong learning, worker mobility, and labor market unity. Defining benchmarks for competencies allows learners to earn recognized qualifications for their occupational skills, regardless of where and how they acquired the skills. The catalog sets forth the qualifications that are recognized nationally and describes the training that leads to those qualifications.

Training is organized into modules, which are themselves presented in a catalog. Having a national system ensures optimum management of issues related to vocational education qualifications.

In addition to the catalog of well-defined training modules and a network of vocational training centers with courses that lead to qualifications, NVTP has these additional objectives:

- Professionalize the workforce through closer cooperation between employers and education providers.

- Develop a system to provide counseling and job-bank services to people who are choosing a career or looking for a job.

- Guarantee the quality, assessment, and monitoring of vocational training by following the European Foundation for Quality Management model and bringing training in line with the occupational profiles it defines.

- Promote worker mobility by participating in EU initiatives to make vocational qualifications more transparent and portable.

- Provide training for people with special needs.

CHALLENGES TO THE EDUCATION SYSTEM

Spain's education system has both strengths and weaknesses. Its strengths include providing mandatory free education to a wider age range, integrating students with special needs into the regular school system, and offering vocational education specialties that target business and workforce needs. Its weaknesses include a lack of exams to guarantee that secondary students achieve a minimum level of literacy and the failure to prevent students who have not met grade-level requirements from progressing to the next grade.

Some of the system's problems were directly related to changes made by LOGSE. For example,

- Under the previous system (LGE), students who were not interested in or able to keep up with compulsory secondary education could switch to a vocational training program at age 14. Because LOGSE has extended compulsory education to age 16, these students must spend 2 more years in secondary education, where they may not be challenged or motivated and where they may hold up students who can handle a faster pace.

- Under LGE, students could move from lower-level to higher-level vocational education without taking an exam, making transfer among programs easy. Under LOGSE and LOE, students must complete a baccalaureate and pass an entrance exam to move on to higher-level vocational education. Very few students do so, which cuts off their options for continuing professional education and earning a degree, and forces them into the labor market at a younger age than LGE did.

Spain's education system also faces the challenges created by changing demographics. The birthrate has declined, but immigration has increased. In 2003, more than 1.6 million immigrants lived in Spain, 24.4% more than in 2002. In 2005, more than 2 million residents—almost 8% of the population—were legal foreigners (Instituto Nacional de Estadistica, 2008). The education system uses the social guarantee programs to meet the needs of new foreign-born students and of second-generation citizens.

CONCLUSION

Although there are a few similarities between Spain's education system and U.S. community colleges, they can not really be compared. In the United States, a single community college might offer a wide range of courses that serve many purposes, including vocational and professional training as well as university preparation. In Spain, different types of courses are typically offered in different institutions; these institutions might be organized according to tradition, financial resources and funding, or to target a group with specific education needs.

For example, baccalaureate courses might be offered within an institution that provides compulsory secondary education, or they might be offered at a vocational training center, whereas vocational training courses are offered within the regular education system. Therefore, it has not been our goal to compare Spanish and U.S. vocational systems but rather to explain the historical background of Spain's education system, illustrate the challenges it has been facing over the past decades, and the challenges it still faces today.

REFERENCES

Instituto Nacional de Estadistica. (2008). INEbase [Statistical database]. Retrieved July 17, 2008, from www.ine.es

OCEANIA

20

Australia's Vocational Education and Training Sector

Antoine Barnaart

Australia is the world's biggest island, smallest continent, and, in land area, sixth-largest country. In 1901, the six colonies that had been created in the 18th and 19th centuries federated and became the Commonwealth of Australia. The federal government is responsible for national affairs, and the governments of the six states and two territories have a broad range of responsibilities, including education and health.

With a population of 20 million, Australia is the only nation in the world to govern an entire continent. Its multicultural society is made up of indigenous peoples and of immigrants from some 200 countries (Department of Foreign Affairs and Trade, 2008a). It is one of the world's most urbanized countries, with most of the population living along the eastern seaboard and in the southeastern corner of the continent.

As a result of effective economic management and ongoing structural reform, Australia has one of the strongest economies in the world, with a competitive and dynamic private sector and a skilled, flexible workforce (see Department of Foreign Affairs and Trade, 2008b). Its stable economic, political, and social environment has led to increased investment from overseas in recent years. As a result of major diversification in its export base, Australia is now not only a commodity exporter, it also has sophisticated manufacturing and service industries (see Department of Foreign Affairs and Trade, 2008a).

DEVELOPMENT OF VOCATIONAL EDUCATION AND TRAINING

Australia's vocational education and training (VET) system began to develop in the late 19th century through the creation of mechanics' institutes, schools of mines, and schools of arts that were designed to develop workers' skills in a fairly narrow band of trades (see Department of Employment, Education and Workplace Relations [DEEWR], 2008a). After federation in 1901, the states and territories continued to be responsible for technical education. For the most part, technical education evolved gradually and played a relatively small part in Australian education. Most increases in funding and support occurred during times of crisis, such as the Depression of the 1930s and World War II. The federal government provided the states with financial assistance for technical education during World War II and during postwar reconstruction, but during the 1950s and 1960s, financing was primarily the responsibility of the individual states and territories (National Office of Overseas Skills Recognition, 2002).

In the 1970s, Australia's industries and workforce were changing. New service industries, including communications and finance, were replacing the traditional manufacturing, mining, and agricultural industries. Increasing numbers of women were joining the workforce and seeking postsecondary education or training programs (see Training.com.au, 2008). Recognizing the urgent need for an inquiry into the country's technical education system, the government created the Australian Committee on Technical and Further Education (TAFE). The committee's report, *TAFE in Australia: Report on Needs in Technical and Further Education* (Kangan, 1974), familiarly known as the Kangan report, defined the roles and mission of the TAFE system. Its release put the system on the national agenda. Acceptance of the report by the government gave TAFE access to commonwealth funds for both recurrent purposes and capital works, although technical and further education was still delivered through publicly funded colleges in each state and territory.

Reforming the VET System

In the 1980s, Australia's service and other industries continued to expand, requiring TAFE colleges to broaden their scope of training beyond the traditional trades that serviced the resource, manufacturing, and construction sectors. Networks of private training providers emerged to meet the needs of the service industries (see Training.com.au, 2008). Also in the 1980s, a large decline in the value of Australia's natural resources and primary production export base triggered a recession. The economy needed to be restructured toward service industries and higher-value manufacturing industries. Leaders of national employer and employee organizations became concerned that Australia's skills development system could not meet the needs of a modern economy operating in a world market. It became obvious that the existing TAFE system needed changing and that change had to be driven by the needs of industry. This led to a 15-year period of education reform led by the Australian government and industry.

Before this period of reform, the six states and two territories ran their own VET systems, which differed in a number of fundamental aspects: policy priorities, course design and learning materials, nomenclature and qualifications, physical infrastructure, and levels of investment. The lack of consistency resulted in poor transportability of qualifications across the country; duplication of the effort involved in developing VET learning resources, limited or uneven involvement of industry in determining VET outcome, and reduced opportunities to assure the international education market that Australia's VET system was of consistently high quality. The federal government commissioned reports by Deveson, Finn, and Carmichael, which recommended expanding the training systems, increasing young people's participation in training, and developing a consolidated national system (see Training.com.au, 2008).

In 1992, the states, territories, and federal government agreed to establish a national training authority and a cooperative federal VET system that would operate with strategic input from industry. The new Australian National Training Authority (ANTA) operated under government statute and reported to an industry-based board. This board advised the Ministerial Council, now called the Ministerial Council for Vocational and Technical Education (MCVTE), a council of federal, state, and territory ministers that were responsible for VET. The board advised MCVTE on national VET policy, strategy, priorities, goals, and objectives, and on the VET plans that the states and territories developed each year to detail how they would meet national VET priorities, goals, and objectives.

ANTA operated from 1992 to 2005, administering national programs and the federal government's funding of the national VET system. Its key accomplishments were developing, managing, and promoting the national training framework; establishing a strong industry training advisory structure; introducing VET in schools; and developing training packages. When ANTA was abolished in June 2005, its responsibilities were transferred to Australia's Department of Employment, Education and Workplace Relations (DEEWR), formerly called the Department of Education, Science, and Training. DEEWR has retained the core national VET structures that had been implemented in the previous 10 years, albeit with some modifications.

As a result of the reform that began in the 1990s, Australia's VET system is now both national and strong. It is led by industry and government, supported with delivery by both public and private VET providers, and underpinned by a solid, quality-assured national training framework.

Registered Training Organizations

A significant characteristic of Australia's VET system is the amount of flexibility and choice students have when deciding where and how to undertake their education, training, and assessment. VET is now delivered not only by public or state-funded TAFE colleges, but also by a broad range of government-recognized providers, known as registered training organizations (RTOs). Students can now receive VET entirely on an RTO campus, entirely in the workplace, or in a combination of the two. Public RTOs (TAFE colleges) provide most VET, but many other organizations have also become RTOs. These include secondary schools, enterprises, industry organizations, private

VET providers, community organizations, and universities. Each RTO is registered by a state or territory government. Because registration has a national effect, an RTO has to register in only one state or territory.

When the early VET reforms first made it possible for diverse organizations to become RTOs, many registered. Over time, as some organizations learned that complying with the Australian Quality Training Framework (AQTF) could be costly and difficult, the number of new RTOs decreased. Some organizations ceased operating as RTOs because they concluded that they did not have the expertise to provide training and assessment or that being an RTO distracted them from their core business. Australia now has more than 4,400 RTOs, of which 3,100 are private providers. Public RTOs deliver VET to more than 1.7 million Australians, and approximately 2.2 million students undertake training with private RTOs, although private RTOs tend to deliver a much larger number of short courses (see National Centre of Vocational Education and Research [NCVER], 2007).

The reformed system has increased partnerships between RTOs and industry. Businesses benefit from high-quality services provided by RTO training and assessment specialists. RTOs benefit from access to advanced technology and by receiving help with VET delivery and assessment from skilled industry personnel. Furthermore, the wide range of RTOs gives VET students flexible education opportunities regardless of age, employment status, or reason for using VET. It also presents governments with the challenge of ensuring that, whatever type of RTO awards a VET qualification and no matter where in Australia that RTO is, the qualification is of consistently high quality throughout the country. Such consistency gives industry and the people of Australia full confidence in the national VET system.

Australian National Training Framework

A core part of the VET system was the Australian National Training Framework (ANTF), which has three key components: training packages, the Australian Qualifications Framework (AQF), and AQTF. ANTF is now called the National Skills Framework, and it incorporates AQTF and the training packages with a linkage to AQF (see DEEWR, 2008b). Training packages are used to evaluate whether a student has acquired the skills and knowledge needed to perform effectively in the workplace. Each package includes competency standards for each level of qualification and guidelines for assessing learner competence. Training packages do not prescribe how an individual should be trained. RTO instructors develop training for students based on their needs, abilities, and circumstances.

Training packages are designed to meet the training needs of specific industries or industry sectors. They are developed by national industry skills councils or by enterprises. Training packages complete a quality assurance process, then are endorsed by the National Quality Council and placed on the National Training Information Service.

There are 75 endorsed training packages; 3 of these were developed by enterprises for their own unique needs. Training packages have a set date for review—usually around 3 years after they are endorsed. (See the DEEWR Web site at http://www.dest.gov.au for a detailed description of training packages.)

AQTF is the basis of Australia's VET system (see ANTA, 2005). It specifies nationally consistent standards for ensuring the quality and integrity of the training and assessment services provided by RTOs. There are two sets of AQTF standards, one for RTOs and one for the state and territory authorities that register RTOs and accredit training. In 2006, AQTF was reviewed, and on July 1, 2007, AQTF 2007 came into effect, which is more streamlined and nationally consistent and has more transparent outcomes (see Training.com.au, 2008).

AQF covers the nationally endorsed qualifications issued by secondary schools, VET providers, and higher education institutions (see AQF Advisory Board, 2007). Because AQF includes senior secondary school certificates and university qualifications, it facilitates linkages and credit transfer among the three education sectors, thus promoting lifelong learning and a seamless and diverse education and training system. The VET sector has eight AQF qualifications: certificates I, II, III, and IV; diploma and advanced diploma; and vocational graduate certificate and vocational graduate diploma. A VET student who does not want to complete a full qualification can be issued an AQF statement of attainment, which recognizes learning completed. A statement of attainment may recognize partial completion of a course leading to a qualification, attainment of competencies within a training package, or completion of nationally accredited short course that may accumulate toward qualification through recognition of prior learning processes.

A New Mechanism for Obtaining Formal Input From Industries

Industry advisory bodies have been the key conduits of advice and information between the national VET system and industry. In 2003, the ANTA board decided to take a new approach to this exchange. It established 10 new industry skills councils (ISCs), which have progressively replaced the previous industry advisory bodies. The Australian government provides funding to ISCs to do the following:

- Provide industry intelligence and advice to Skills Australia, the government, and enterprises involved in addressing workforce development and skills needs.
- Actively support the development, implementation, and continuous improvement of high-quality training and workforce development products and services, including training packages.
- Provide independent advice on skills and training to enterprises, including matching identified training needs with appropriate training solutions.

- Work with enterprises, employment service providers, training providers, and the government to allocate training places (see Industry Skills Councils, 2008).

VET in Schools

As part of the national reforms, ANTA encouraged delivery of VET in the schools sector. The VET in Schools program is recognized throughout the country as a way to increase the number of school leavers who enter VET, particularly in areas where Australia has critical skills shortages. ANTA defined VET in Schools as follows:

> Vocational education and training should be included as VET in Schools if it is undertaken as part of a senior secondary certificate and its completion by the student provides credit towards a recognized VET qualification within the Australian Qualifications Framework. (DEEWR, 2008c)

Australian school-based apprenticeships are part of VET in Schools. They provide the opportunity for young people to gain VET qualifications and undertake employment while completing a senior secondary certificate. The student is both full-time student and part-time employee, with the same employment and training requirements as for other Australian apprenticeships.

Ongoing VET Reform

Reform in Australia's VET sector is a significant and ongoing challenge. Although there is a national system, education, including vocational education, is still a prime responsibility of the states and territories. The division between federal and state powers regarding VET can vary depending on the political status of the national, state, and territory governments. Getting all governments to agree on national VET strategies, reforms, and policies can be time-consuming and frustrating for policymakers.

In order to withstand significant political changes at the national, state, and territory levels, the core of the national VET system must be robust and relevant to a broad range of Australians and enterprises. A national VET system that is subject to frequent major change cannot function in the short term or be sustained in the long term. The National Skills Framework is a strong core that has withstood changes of government, substantial bureaucratic change with the transfer of ANTA responsibilities to DEEWR, and ongoing changes to industry advisory structures. Modifications and enhancements to the framework will occur on an ongoing basis, but the fundamental structure is relevant to Australia's VET needs and is a good model for other countries to consider when developing a national VET system.

Australia's national VET strategy, outlined in *Shaping Our Future: Australia's National Strategy for Vocational Education and Training 2004–2010* (ANTA, 2003) covers a long planning horizon. This strategy represents a commitment by all concerned levels of government to continue working with industry providers and other stakeholders to develop VET. The strategy has four key objectives:

- Industry will have a highly skilled workforce to support strong performance in the global economy.

- Employers and individuals will be at the centre of VET.

- Communities and regions will be strengthened economically and socially through learning and employment.

- Indigenous Australians will have skills for viable jobs and their learning culture will be shared. (ANTA, 2003)

In accordance with the Skilling Australia Workforce Act 2005, DEEWR produces annual reports for the national VET system. Each report assesses the system's performance that year and gives detailed information about the system's operations, achievements, and challenges. The current annual report and other relevant VET policy documents can be found on the DEEWR Web site (www.dest.gov.au).

REFERENCES

Australian Qualifications Framework Advisory Board. (2007). *AQF qualifications.* Retrieved June 4, 2008, from www.aqf.edu.au/aqfqual.htm

Australian National Training Authority (ANTA). (2003). *Shaping our future: Australia's national strategy for vocational education and training 2004–2010.* Retrieved June 4, 2008, from www.dest.gov.au/NR/rdonlyres/98206EC7-3B9A-4A58-991F-4F28010BF825/16445/national_strategy.pdf

Australian National Training Authority (ANTA). (2005). *Australian quality training framework: AQTF overview 2005.* Retrieved August 3, 2008, from http://www.dest.gov.au/sectors/training_skills/publications_resources/profiles/anta/profile/aqtf_overview_2005.htm

Department of Employment, Education and Workplace Relations (DEEWR). (2008a). *History of VET.* Retrieved August 3, 2008, from http://www.dest.gov.au/sectors/training_skills/policy_issues_reviews/key_issues/nts/vet/history.htm

Department of Employment, Education and Workplace Relations (DEEWR). (2008b). *The national skills framework.* Retrieved August 3, 2008, from http://www.dest.gov.au/sectors/training_skills/policy_issues_reviews/key_issues/national_training_system/how_nat_training_system_prov_train.htm#The_National_Skills_Framework

Department of Employment, Education and Workplace Relations (DEEWR). (2008c). *Vocational learning and VET in schools.* Retrieved August 3, 2008, from http://www.dest.gov.au/sectors/school_education/programmes_funding/programme_categories/key_priorities/vocational_education_in_schools/vocational_education_in_schools_initiative/vocational_learning_and_vet_in_schools.htm

Department of Foreign Affairs and Trade. (2008a). *Australia today.* Retrieved June 2, 2008, from www.dfat.gov.au/facts/aust_today.html

Department of Foreign Affairs and Trade. (2008b). *A competitive economy.* Retrieved June 2, 2008, from www.dfat.gov.au/aib/competitive_economy.html

Industry Skills Councils. (2008). *About us.* Retrieved June 2, 2008, from http://www.isc.org.au/display_main.php?id=about

Kangan, M. (1974). *TAFE in Australia: Report on needs in technical and further education.* Canberra, Australia: Australian Government Publishing Service.

National Centre of Vocational Education and Research (NCVER). (2007, August 13). *Did you know? A guide to vocational education and training in Australia.* Available from http://www.ncver.edu.au/vetsystem/publications/1790.html

National Office of Overseas Skills Recognition. (2002). *History of VET.* Retrieved June 2, 2008, from www.griffith.edu.au/vc/ate/content_vet_hist.html

Skilling Australia Workforce Act 2005. (2005). Available from the Commonwealth of Australia Law Web site: http://www.comlaw.gov.au

Training.com.au. (2008). *The history of VET.* Retrieved August 3, 2008, from http://www.training.com.au/portal/site/public/menuitem.3e365e26c4085888a392e5101 7a62dbc

21

Further Education in New Zealand

Jim Doyle

New Zealand consists of two main islands in the southwest Pacific, midway between the equator and the Antarctic. The land area is 265,000 km², the same as the state of Colorado. The population of 4 million is 15% Maori, 68% European, 9% Asian, and 7% Pacific Islander (Statistics New Zealand, 2006). Maori settlement dates to the 12th century; European settlement began in earnest in the mid-19th century. New Zealand is a British Commonwealth country, and its form of government—parliamentary democracy—and its education system follow British traditions.

POLICY CONTEXT

Since 1990, New Zealand's education system, particularly the postsecondary sector, has undergone sweeping changes that arose from wider government reforms that took place during the mid-1980s. In response to the oil shock of 1973, New Zealand adopted a policy of protectionism, increasing subsidies for agriculture, which accounted for the bulk of foreign exchange earnings. By 1984, the country was on the verge of bankruptcy. The election of a center-left labor government in July of that year marked a watershed in economic policy. Faced with a series of crises, the new government undertook the most rapid and sweeping reforms in New Zealand's history. The reforms included devaluing, then floating, the New Zealand dollar; replacing the complex progressive tax system with a simpler flat tax; introducing a goods and services tax; ending all agricultural and consumer subsidies; and ending import licensing and export incentives.

Reforms to the state sector involved three strategies: corporatization or commercialization, deregulation, and privatization. Commercial state enterprises that did not get privatized became state-owned enterprises. The public sector was significantly downsized, and the government implemented reforms that were intended to expose it to the realities faced by the private sector. New Zealand's economic reforms were designed to replicate free-market conditions within government departments, creating a clear division between providers of services (government departments) and purchasers of services (government ministers). These changes played a crucial role in the education system reform process that began in 1988.

Development of the New Zealand Polytechnic System

New Zealand's polytechnic system evolved from technical high schools that emerged in the latter half of the 19th century. These schools initially had a dual vocational and hobby focus (see Dougherty, 1999, p. 16), but they gradually became an alternative to traditional academic high schools. By 1939, New Zealand had 27 technical high schools that were attended by more than 13,000 full-time students each year.

In the years immediately after World War II, an increasing number of trades made it compulsory for their workers to have attended technical high school. Government ministers and other officials realized that in order to meet the demands of the postwar economy, technical schools must provide a higher level of education than they had before. The Technical Correspondence Institute (now the Open Polytechnic of New Zealand), which opened in 1946, provided distance learning in technical areas to returning servicemen. In 1956, the director-general of education recommended to parliament that technical high schools in the country's main urban centers be converted into senior-level colleges. The conversion took place during the 1960s, and by 1970 New Zealand had eight of these new technical institutes, as they were known.

Pressure to establish technical institutes in regions outside the main urban centers grew during the 1970s. In 1974, the government passed legislation enabling the establishment of community colleges with some features of the U.S. community college model. It was expected that incorporating a continuing education component would allow community colleges to reach a much greater number of people than they would by offering only vocational programs. Nine community colleges were established in the 1970s and 8 more in the 1980s, giving New Zealand a total of 25 technical institutes and community colleges.

In the mid-1980s, New Zealand's minister of education sought to remove perceived differences between technical institutes and community colleges by encouraging all of them to describe themselves as polytechnics. All but 2 of the 25 adopted the term. (In more recent years, about half of New Zealand's 20 polytechnics have become known as institutes of technology. The Education Act 1989 [sect. 162(1)(c)] recognized the term *institute of technology* as being equivalent to the word *polytechnic*.

After the election of 1987, the new government immediately embarked on a series of social reforms and published policy decisions related to tertiary education in 1989 (see

Ministry of Education, 1989a, 1989b). The latter policy decisions led to the Education Act being amended in 1990. This was intended to give tertiary education institutions "as much independence and freedom to make academic, operational, and management decisions as is consistent with the nature of the services they provide, the efficient use of national resources, the national interest, and the demands of accountability" (Education Amendment Act, 1990, sect. 160).

As part of the overall reform process, the department of education was replaced by a much smaller, policy-focused ministry of education in 1989. A new funding system was introduced in 1991 to serve all education institutions, including universities, polytechnics, and teacher training colleges. Education system reforms also included a new governance structure, a new strategic planning process, and the establishment of two key agencies, the New Zealand Qualifications Authority (NZQA) and Skill New Zealand.

According to Education Amendment Act 1990, NZQA's purpose was to "establish a consistent approach to the recognition of qualifications in academic and vocational areas" (sect. 247). NZQA would oversee the setting of qualifications standards and develop a national qualifications framework (NQF) for secondary schools and for postsecondary education and training. (NZQA's powers did not extend to universities, whose academic quality assurance is overseen by a committee of the New Zealand vice chancellor.)

NQF was to ensure that "all qualifications have a purpose and a relationship to each other that students and the public can understand [and that] there is a flexible system for the gaining of qualifications, with recognition of competency already achieved" [sect. 253(1)(c)]. NQF was designed to be standards-based rather than norm-referenced. Every qualification would consist of a set of *competencies* (standards), and learners would be assessed on their ability to demonstrate competencies. A student who achieved a particular competency would earn credits; by accumulating a predetermined number of credits, the student would earn a qualification.

On average, 10 hours of learning would equal 1 credit; 120 credits would be a year's work. Each qualification would be composed of a group of *unit standards* that described the required skills. NQF initially addressed 8 qualification levels. Levels 1–4 were for the national certificate; Levels 5 and 6, for the national diploma; Level 7, for the bachelor's degree; and Level 8, for postgraduate education. NQF was enthusiastically welcomed by industry leaders, who saw it as an opportunity to define the skill sets their industries required. Not surprisingly, university leaders rejected NQF, believing that it would lead to "atomization" of their holistic degrees and a rejection of the concept of excellence inherent in norm-referencing.

Skill New Zealand (initially called the Education and Training Support Agency) was created to administer the access training scheme, the apprenticeship schemes, the primary industry cadet scheme, and other activities and programs determined by the minister of education. The agency registered, negotiated training agreements with, and allocated public funding to industry training organizations (ITOs). The new system, which gave education institutions the independence to do their own strategic planning and to compete for students, was put into place in January 1991.

The funding system was relatively simple: The government paid institutions a subsidy for each equivalent full-time student (EFTS) enrolled, with the amount of the subsidy determined by the type and level of program the student was enrolled in. For example, the subsidy was higher for medical programs than for engineering; the engineering subsidy was higher than the business subsidy. The government paid all of an institution's subsidies once a month. Institutions were free to allocate the subsidies as they chose, whether to capital, payroll, or other costs.

Standard tuition fees were introduced in 1990 to offset the costs of the rapid expansion of the system, but the fees were repealed in 1992 by the newly elected government. Institutions could set their own tuition fees. Students were eligible to receive government-funded cost-of-living allowances, based on their parents' income. The government introduced subsidized student loans that could be used for tuition, up-front course fees and, for students who were not entitled to allowances, living costs. The loans are repaid through New Zealand's income tax system, with minimum repayments determined according to the borrower's income.

During the 1990s, the government increased the number of EFTS subsidies by about 5% per year, but at the same time, the subsidy rate was decreased by an estimated 5% each year. To make up for shrinking subsidies, institutions raised tuition fees. The government encouraged private establishments to provide training, which increased competitive pressures on state institutions. The subsidies available to private training establishments were significantly lower than those for state institutions, however, and the number of funded places was tightly limited, which somewhat relieved competitive pressures on state institutions.

For New Zealand's polytechnics, one of the most significant reforms was gaining the right to offer degree programs, which had previously been limited to universities. By the end of the 1990s, polytechnics delivered more than 100 degree programs. However, the Education Act (1989) requires that polytechnic degree programs be taught primarily by instructors who are engaged in research, which increases the cost of providing degree programs and thus makes it prohibitive for some polytechnics to do so. In the 1990s, the reform process led to many changes in the polytechnic sector. Total polytechnic enrollment doubled, reaching 60,000 EFTSs per year by the end of the decade. The number of degree programs grew to more than 100, with 10,000 students enrolled each year.

Being able to offer degree programs led a number of the larger polytechnics to seek university status. In New Zealand, use of the word *university* is protected by Education Act 1989 (sect. 254). An institution that wants to become a university must apply to the ministry of education and NZQA. If the minister of education decides that it is in the country's best interests to have another university, NZQA establishes an international panel that determines whether the institution displays the characteristics of a university. After being advised by NZQA, the minister consults with interested parties; if the determination is favorable, the minister recommends to the governor-general that the applicant become a university.

The Auckland Institute of Technology was New Zealand's first polytechnic to seek university status. It received approval from the minister of education in November 1999, just a week before the general election established a new government, and became the Auckland University of Technology in January 2000. Unitec Institute of Technology, also in Auckland, applied to become a university, but the new government did not want another university to be established. Unitec proceeded with its application for the next 5 years despite open opposition from the government. In 2006, Unitec's president retired and his successor made it clear that the pursuit of university status was no longer a priority for the institution. Wellington Polytechnic, believing that its prospects for becoming a university were slim, decided to merge with an existing university instead. It became part of Massey University in 1999.

While a few of the bigger polytechnics were able to become universities during the 1990s, growing competitive pressures were a hardship for other polytechnics. By 2001, three polytechnics had become insolvent. They were disestablished and their assets distributed to other polytechnics.

In 1998, the government decided to make the higher education market fully competitive. It increased the student subsidies given to private education providers to the same levels as those given to state institutions. In the belief that the tertiary education system could not grow much further and that increasing the number of funded places would therefore not present a high fiscal risk, the government removed restrictions on the number of places.

REGULATORY ENVIRONMENT: 1988–PRESENT

The State Sector Act 1988 designated the chief executive of a polytechnic as the employer of all staff and faculty. Each polytechnic's governing body therefore employs only one person, the chief executive. This practice was based on the principle that governance and management responsibilities should be clearly divided, with an institution's board of directors or council providing governance and its chief executive managing employment and other matters.

Under the Education Act 1989, each higher education institution in New Zealand is required to publish goals, objectives, and quantifiable performance measures. Each must present a formal annual report to parliament, and publish that report as a public document. The report must document how well the institution has performed against its stated objectives. It must also include a financial report that is based on full accrual accounting and that complies with standard accounting practices.

The Education Amendment Act 1990 allowed NZQA to delegate responsibility for overseeing academic quality assurance in the polytechnic sector to an organization of tertiary institutions that did not include universities. It chose the existing Association of Polytechnics of New Zealand (now the Institutes of Technology and Polytechnics of New Zealand). In 1993, this organization established the New Zealand Polytechnic Programmes Committee (NZPPC, now called ITP Quality) to oversee polytechnic quality assurance.

New Zealand's education reforms did not stop at academic education, but also addressed industry training. The Industry Training Act (1992) allows employer groups to establish training organizations to serve their industries. Within a few years of the legislation's passage, employer groups had created 53 ITOs that serve more than 85% of the country's workforce. ITOs are legally mandated to serve their own industries by setting skill standards, arranging for the delivery of training, receiving government funding for training, and providing strategic leadership. In keeping with the principle that services should not be both purchased and provided by the same organization, ITOs can set standards and develop qualifications but cannot provide training. Each ITO has a detailed contract with the government under which it receives government funding, then uses the funds to pay training providers to serve its industry. Most of the training leads to national qualifications developed by the ITOs.

With the general election of late 1999, New Zealand got a new center-left government and a new education policy. This government believed in moderating the destructive aspects of competition and wanted to make the tertiary education system more collaborative and strategic. To help reach its goals, the government established the Tertiary Education Advisory Commission (TEAC) in 2000. By November 2001, TEAC had produced four advisory reports. Following TEAC's most significant recommendation, the government established a new agency, the Tertiary Education Commission (TEC), in January 2003. TEC has eight members, who are appointed by the minister of education. The agency advises the minister and is charged with negotiating charters and profiles with, allocating funds to, and building the capability of tertiary education organizations.

A tertiary education strategy and a statement of tertiary education priorities are fundamental to New Zealand's education reform process. The *Tertiary Education Strategy 2002–2007* (TES) outlined six strategies, as follows:

1. Strengthen system capability and quality.
2. Contribute to the achievement of Maori development aspirations.
3. Raise foundation skills so that all people can participate in our knowledge society.
4. Develop the skills New Zealanders need for our knowledge society.
5. Provide education for Pacific peoples' development and success.

6. Strengthen research, knowledge creation, and uptake for our knowledge society. (Office of the Minister, 2002)

The Statement of Tertiary Education Priorities 2005–2007 (STEP) focused on

> ensuring that students and learners progress to higher levels of study through accessing tertiary education, which is of excellent quality and relevant to the needs of New Zealand. It will be provided by vibrant, highly capable and well-connected tertiary education organisations. It wants tertiary education organisations to build upon their areas of expertise, develop strong strategic links with their stakeholders, and complement their strengths with the strengths of others through partnerships and alliances. (Office of the Minister, 2005, p. 3)

STEP 2005–2007 included eight key change messages:

1. increased quality
2. greater system collaboration and rationalization
3. more future focus
4. improved global linkages
5. increased responsiveness to students and learners
6. greater alignment with national goals
7. stronger linkages with businesses and other external stakeholders
8. a culture of optimism and creativity (Office of the Minister, 2005, p. 5)

Furthermore, STEP 2005–2007 focused on four major connected themes:

- Investing in excellence in teaching, learning, and research.
- Increasing the relevance of skills and knowledge to meet national goals.
- Enabling students and learners to access excellent and relevant tertiary education and progress to higher levels of study and achievement.
- Enhancing capability and information quality in the tertiary system to support learning, teaching, and research. (Office of the Minister, 2005, p. 5)

Each TES and its accompanying STEP set forth the current government's vision for the tertiary education sector over a 5-year timeframe. Under this new policy, each tertiary education provider is required to prepare a charter and a profile, taking TES and STEP into consideration. A charter is a high-level document that describes an organization's role in the tertiary education system and how it aligns with the government's TES. It covers a long-term timeframe and provides the basis for the annual profile that each education provider must prepare. In this profile, the provider describes operating plans and proposed activities for the next 3 years; objectives, performance measures, and targets; the areas of activity for which funding is being sought; and how the organization will make its charter effective.

TEC's primary function is to steer tertiary education institutions toward achieving TES, with regard to STEP. The steering instruments it uses are charter and profile documents and funding. The funding model is designed to encourage increased participation. Funding consists of a combination of government subsidies based on EFTS enrollment numbers, tuition fees, and modest revenue from industry training.

Can the existing funding system, designed as it was to serve a demand-driven system, serve the needs of a system that is now looking to intervene on the supply side? Probably not, because the incentives in the existing system do not necessarily deliver on the priorities. The government can, through TEC, refuse to fund certain programs on the grounds of low relevance or quality, but it is not well placed to encourage the delivery of programs where the market demand is marginal. In any event, attention will need to be given to encourage participation by students in areas of low demand but high national priority. So, incentives will need to be devised to encourage institutions to engage in high-priority activities and to encourage students to enroll in such programs.

CURRENT DEVELOPMENTS

The government's 1998 decision to remove the cap on funded places led to a series of responses by some providers that produced the most significant policy issues facing the polytechnic sector for decades. That decision to remove the cap on funded places was based on the premise that future growth in tertiary education participation was likely to be modest, so the risk of a serious fiscal blow-out was low. This assumption was based on two observations: Participation in tertiary education had grown steadily over the previous two decades and was higher than the OECD (Organisation for Economic Co-operation and Development) average, and that participation in higher education had probably reached its natural limit.

Those assumptions gave an incomplete picture. Enrollment programs that offered degree-level qualifications had indeed reached a plateau, but potential growth in lower-level programs, especially ones that had no academic entry requirements, was almost unlimited. It is not surprising that some providers found ways to maximize these growth opportunities.

Providers identified community education as the area with the greatest potential for growth. Community education courses did not have entry prerequisites, nor did they necessarily have assessment requirements or lead to a qualification. These factors allowed providers to offer low-intensity, low-cost courses to a wide public. The potential for growth was almost unlimited, especially if the courses were free to students, and the government provided the same level of subsidies for community education courses as it did for higher-level programs that included intensive learning and assessment. This combination of low cost and relatively high subsidies resulted in healthy profits for community education providers.

By the beginning of 2003, community education courses enrolled more than 26,000 EFTS, up from 3,000 just 2 years before. The additional cost to the government was estimated to be more than USD 70 million. In July 2005, in the face of widespread political and public criticism, the government announced a series of decisions to divert spending from community education programs to higher education programs that were more in line with the government's strategy and priority areas.

The 1998 decisions to remove the cap on funded tertiary education places and to subsidize private providers at the same level as state institutions were driven by the government's belief that a highly competitive market environment would deliver optimum results. The center-left government elected in late 1999 opposed the market model, as its policies made clear, but it did not reverse the 1998 funding decisions despite its commitment to removing the more destructive elements of competition. Whatever the reason for its inaction, the 1999–2005 administration was happy to see participation increase and did not become concerned until the scale and nature of the increase became evident. The government failed to appreciate private education providers' ability to respond to market opportunities.

The Way Ahead

It is unlikely that any future New Zealand government will want to face the risks inherent to a deregulated, competitive market or to return to the type of tightly controlled education environment that existed before the 1990s. The universities were never in a position to compete in the education mass market, even if they wished to, and the experiences of the uncapped period basically passed them by. During this period the universities operated as they had for many decades, and it is safe to assume they will continue to do so.

In contrast to the universities, the future for polytechnics and institutes of technology is more likely to be influenced by change. While polytechnics will continue to provide degree programs, it is unlikely that the numbers of such programs will grow. It is extremely unlikely that any polytechnic will pursue university status. Polytechnics will be steered toward fulfilling their vocational missions and will not need to constantly grow in order to survive in a competitive education market. The aim will be to strengthen the links between polytechnics and their geographic regions, cementing the polytechnics' role as an integral component in regional economic development.

The structure for achieving this new environment of synergy between polytechnics and regional economic development has been put in place by TEC. The key element is the funding system. There is little doubt that the existing system, whereby funding is driven almost exclusively by the choices of hundreds of thousands of individual students, will be moderated. Those individual students are likely to be largely immune to high-level government strategies or priorities. The institutions, for their part, will continue to keep a sharp focus on that student market. The challenge facing the present and future governments will be to introduce a variation to the funding system that will steer institutions in the way desired and at the same time acknowledge the fundamental fact that students will make individual decisions based on what they believe is in their own best interests.

It is highly probable that the new system will involve some element of the appropriated funding being made available to TEC to (a) allow the smaller institutions in particular to operate without the relentless pressure to seek growth and thereby achieve critical mass and (b) encourage institutions to engage in high-priority activities that otherwise would not be delivered on pure economic or business grounds. In addition, TEC is likely to see the need for it to have access to funds that will enable it to facilitate some rationalization, of programs if not of institutions.

OBSTACLES, CHALLENGES, SUCCESSES, AND TRIUMPHS

The most obvious characteristic of the education reform process that was enacted by the Education Amendment Act 1990 and implemented in 1991 was the move from what had been a highly centralized system to a more devolved and competitive one. Competition was a key component, but relatively tight rationing of funding before 1999 acted as a strong counter-balance to excess. The environment was challenging to education institutions. Three polytechnics became insolvent, and at least two universities experienced serious financial difficulties.

The 1998 decision to remove the cap on funded growth dramatically changed the equation for tertiary education providers. For 4 years (1999–2002), the tertiary education sector experimented with a true market model, probably to a greater extent than any other country's education system had. The experience proved interesting. A number of institutions generated significant financial surpluses but strayed from their academic roots. Decisions that were successful from a business perspective were liabilities when measured against political and public opinion.

The challenge facing New Zealand's government and policymakers is to find a way back from the highly competitive environment toward a more collaborative and strategically focused one. While many leaders of education institutions will voice support for a less competitive system, they are likely to balk at any restrictions to their autonomy and freedom to act. The challenge of reconciling greater collaboration and less autonomy will be considerable and will take great skill and patience if it is to be successfully met. It is certain that the universities will be the most vociferous opponents of any move to reduce institutional autonomy.

Any look at the performance of New Zealand's tertiary education system since 1990 inevitably leads to the question, were the reforms successful? For the polytechnics, the answer is yes. Their enrollment more than doubled from 1990 to 1999, and the range and variety of their programs expanded enormously. The introduction of degree programs has improved academic quality assurance throughout the tertiary education sector.

The establishment of NZPPC in 1993 began a process of steady improvement in the academic quality assurance systems across the polytechnics sector. NZPPC adopted a formative or supportive approach to academic quality assurance, requiring each polytechnic to develop and document a comprehensive quality management system. The polytechnics themselves, through the national Association of Polytechnics of New Zealand, developed a set of 12 academic quality standards, which were approved by NZQA and became requirements in 2000. NZPPC adopted a system for auditing how well a polytechnic's quality management system meets the 12 standards. The audits are conducted by panels of external auditors. If the auditors find no significant noncompliances, the polytechnic is granted quality-assured status for 4 years. If they do find significant noncompliances, the polytechnic is granted provisional quality-assured status and must be audited again in 12 months.

PROFILES OF THREE POLYTECHNICS

New Zealand's polytechnic sector is highly diverse, making it difficult to describe any institution as average or typical. Polytechnics are located on both the North Island and the South Island. Some serve urban areas; others are in less-urban regions. Institution size varies. This section describes three polytechnics with a range of characteristics.

Manukau Institute of Technology is a large urban polytechnic located in Auckland, New Zealand's biggest city (population 1.2 million). In 2004, Manukau's EFTS enrollment was greater than 10,000, its operating revenue was USD 62 million, and its asset base was USD 75 million. Fifty percent of Manukau's revenues were from government subsidies; tuition fees accounted for 45% (Manukau Institute of Technology, 2004).

Manukau offers programs in applied studies, computing and information technology, electrical and computer engineering, further education, nursing and health studies, business, visual arts, maritime sciences, social sciences, technology, and Maori language and culture. The polytechnic's three main objectives are to offer a wide range of relevant education and training programs in a positive, innovative, and equitable learning environment; to appoint and develop staff to enhance the provision of high-quality education and training; and to manage resources efficiently and effectively in an equitable and entrepreneurial environment. (For more information about Manukau, see its Web site: www.maukau.ac.nz.)

The Eastern Institute of Technology (EIT) is on the east coast of New Zealand's North Island. It serves the Hawke's Bay region, which includes the twin cities of Napier and Hastings (combined population 100,000). The wider region has a population of 140,000; its economy based on agriculture, horticulture, and wine production. In 2004, EIT's EFTS enrollment was 3,600, its operating revenue was USD 23 million, and its asset base was USD 40 million. Fifty-nine percent of EIT's revenues were from government subsidies; tuition fees accounted for 30% (Eastern Institute of Technology, 2004).

EIT offers programs in arts and social sciences, business and computing, health and sports science, Maori studies, and science and technology. The institution's goals are to strengthen the capability and quality of its system; to help Maori people achieve their development aspirations; to raise the level of the foundation skills it provides; to teach the skills that New Zealanders need in order to participate in the knowledge society; to provide education that contributes to the development and success of Pacific peoples; and to strengthen research, knowledge creation, and uptake. (For more information about EIT, see its Web site: www.eit.ac.nz.)

Nelson Marlborough Institute of Technology (NMIT) is in Nelson City (population 40,000), at the top of the South Island. In 2004, NMIT's EFTS enrollment was 2,600, its operating revenue was USD 15 million, and its asset base was USD 28 million. Government subsidies accounted for 50% of NMIT's revenues; tuition fees, for 23% (Nelson Marlborough Institute of Technology, 2004).

NMIT offers programs in arts, business and computer technology, health and social sciences, technology and primary industries, and Maori language and culture. Its goal is to respond to the region's needs and opportunities by providing high-quality education and training in multiple areas, including art and design, media, tourism and hospitality, English language, business and computer technology, nursing and health sciences, early childhood education, counseling, social services, psychotherapy, special education, seafood production, agriculture, forestry, horticulture, conservation, animal care, wine production, aviation, and Maori language and culture. (For more information about NMIT, see its Web site: www.nmit.ac.nz.)

OVERVIEW OF PROVISION

According to the New Zealand Treasury (2008), in 2004, New Zealand had 20 polytechnics and institutes of technology. Polytechnics served every town with a population of 20,000 or more, and many towns with populations below 20,000. Enrollment totaled 200,000 individual students (equal to 95,000 EFTS); the average student age was 29 and rising. Revenues were about USD 600 million, 60% of which was from government subsidies. Tuition fees paid by New Zealand residents accounted for 20% of revenues and fees paid by international students for 11%.

The polytechnic sector currently employs more than 4,400 academic staff and 3,700 nonacademic support staff. Fifty-four percent of academic staff in polytechnics are female, compared to 42% in the university sector; 56% were full-time, compared to 61% in the university sector. The ratio of academic staff members to EFTSs increased from 1 to 14 in 1997 to 1 to 22 in 2004. (The ratio for universities in 2004 was 1 to 16.)

In 2004, 79% of students who completed qualifications in polytechnics received certificates, 11% received diplomas, and 10% received degrees. In the university sector,

18% of graduates earned certificates, 5% earned diplomas, 53% earned bachelor's degrees, and 24% earned postgraduate qualifications.

New Zealand's polytechnics offer an extensive range of qualifications in numerous areas. For information about these areas and other aspects of higher education in New Zealand, see the Web site of the New Zealand Ministry of Education (www.minedu. govt.nz) and the Education Counts Web site (www.educationcounts.govt.nz).

REFERENCES

Dougherty, I. (1999). *Bricklayers and mortarboards.* Wellington, New Zealand: Dunmore Press.

Eastern Institute of Technology. (2004). *Annual report 2004.* Hawke's Bay, New Zealand: Author.

Education Act 1989. (1989, September). *New Zealand legislation.* Retrieved September 16, 2008, from www.legislation.govt.nz/default.aspx

Education Amendment Act 1990. (1990). *New Zealand legislation.* Retrieved September 16, 2008, from www.legislation.govt.nz/default.aspx

Industry Training Act 1992. (1992). *New Zealand legislation.* Retrieved September 16, 2008, from www.legislation.govt.nz/default.aspx

Manukau Institute of Technology. (2004). *Annual report 2004.* Aukland, New Zealand: Author.

Ministry of Education. (1989a). *Learning for life: Education and training beyond the age of fifteen.* Wellington, New Zealand: Government Printer.

Ministry of Education. (1989b). *Learning for life two: Policy decisions.* Wellington, New Zealand: Government Printer.

Nelson Marlborough Institute of Technology. (2004). *Annual report 2004.* Nelson, New Zealand: Author.

New Zealand Treasury. (2008). *Estimates of appropriations for the government of New Zealand for the year ending 30 June 2008.* Available from www.treasury.govt.nz

Office of the Minister of Education. (2002, May). *Tertiary education strategy 2002–2007.* Wellington, New Zealand: Ministry of Education. Retrieved May 29, 2008, from www.tec.govt.nz/upload/downloads/tertiaryeducationstrategy-2002-2007.pdf

Office of the Minister of Education. (2005). *Statement of tertiary education priorities 2005–2007.* Wellington, New Zealand: Ministry of Education. Retrieved May 29, 2008, from www.tec.govt.nz/upload/downloads/step05-07.pdf

State Sector Act 1988. (1988). *New Zealand legislation.* Retrieved September 16, 2008, from www.legislation.govt.nz/default.aspx

Statistics New Zealand. (2006). *Census 2006.* Retrieved July 24, 2008, from www.stats. govt.nz/census/default.htm#2006census

CROSS-
CONTINENTAL

22

Three Styles of Community College Development: India, the Dominican Republic, and Georgia

John Halder

n this chapter I examine how three countries—India, the Dominican Republic, and Georgia—have begun to develop their own community college systems. Only a few years ago, community colleges were relatively unknown outside the United States. Although organizations like Community Colleges for International Development, as well as individual U.S. colleges, have worked with international colleagues for 3 decades, few countries had established community college systems. That begin to change around 1990, as educators around the world recognized the value of the community college concept and sought to adapt the U.S. model to their countries. Several factors spurred this change, including the following:

- A desire by U.S. community colleges to internationalize their faculties.
- The availability of funding for U.S. community colleges to undertake work overseas.
- Countries' pursuit of U.S. partners to support college development.

U.S. community colleges provide several types of education, including university transfer, further education, and workforce training. The U.S. model is based on the concepts of open access, financial accessibility, and credit transfer. No other higher education system in the world has as much flexibility to reflect and support societal mobility.

Because community college systems outside the United States emerge in different ways, under different circumstances, they must cast the U.S. model aside or adapt it

The author wishes to thank the following people for sharing information to assist with the writing of this chapter: Lali Ghogheliani, Robert Keener, Yvette Lopez, and Ardith Maney.

to their own circumstances. In many countries, community colleges emerge into an education landscape that is already occupied by universities, polytechnics, and technical colleges that have their own histories, political connections, and funding systems.

India's community colleges arose largely from grassroots initiatives in the early and mid-1990s, as educators and others were inspired to create "colleges for the people." By 2006, the community college movement had been officially accepted by the government, which introduced legislation to bring the growing number of colleges (160 as of this writing) under the umbrella of India's higher education system. In the Dominican Republic, community colleges were introduced largely as the result of the vision of one man, Leonel Fernández, who had studied and worked in the United States and was familiar with the U.S. education system. When he ran for the presidency in 1996, Fernández used the idea of "colleges for the people" as part of his political platform. Georgia's higher education system was in collapse after losing the support of the Soviet Union. The impetus for developing community colleges came from government officials, seeking ways to rebuild the system and to meet the country's 21st-century need for trained technicians.

India's Experience

Community Colleges for International Development (CCID) has worked in India for about 25 years. Its early activities there included Fulbright exchanges and hosting Indian education delegations sponsored by the World Bank, the University Grants Commission, and the U.S. Department of State. CCID has also sponsored U.S. community college delegations to India, conducted community college development workshops in India, and created working partnerships between higher education and the Indian business community.

The impetus for the development of community colleges in India was a 1990 chance meeting at a conference between Indian educator Adrian Almeida and Jean Cook, a professor at Sinclair Community College (SCC) in Dayton, Ohio. Following their meeting, Sinclair applied for a U.S. Agency for International Development (USAID) University Development Linkage Project grant to help Almeida create the Center for Vocational Education (CVE) in Madras (now Madras Community College). This 5-year project, which began in 1992 and was valued at $750,000, was co-directed by SCC and Eastern Iowa Community College District (EICCD).

The project initially brought 15 vocational–technical faculty members from eight U.S. colleges to Madras, where they worked with Indian partners to develop vocational training programs that would apply the U.S. open access model to serve school dropouts, the rural and urban poor, and women with limited opportunities. Ultimately, more than 25 U.S. faculty members participated. Even after the grant expired, educators had such a strong interest in CVE that they used their own colleges' professional development funds to travel to India. The building where the center was established was donated by the Catholic archdiocese of Madras, which also paid for updates and repairs.

In August 1997, CVE, SCC, and EICCD held a Training Options for Early School Leavers conference in Madras. More than 100 people from five countries attended. The conference promoted training and education for school leavers, giving attendees the inspiration to create workforce development and school-to-work programs.

India's community college movement is thriving, with an estimated 150 colleges in 17 states (MCRDCE, 2005). The Madras Center for Research and Development of Community College Education (MCRDCE), which was established by the Jesuits of Tamil Nadu, has kept up the momentum. The center provides consulting services, holds national workshops, provides networking and monitoring services, and acts as a resource center.

CCID and U.S. community colleges have provided ongoing support for India's community college initiatives. In 2000, they presented 1-day workshops, targeted at business, government, and educators, in Chennai, Trivandrum, Hyderabad, and Bangalore. The workshops focused on the development of relevant workforce training in India and the potential for workforce partnerships with U.S. colleges. CCID representatives also met with officials from two employers, Mahindra Motors and L & T John Deere, to discuss their workforce development needs.

Other support for community college development in India has included a 1995–1998 United States Information Agency university affiliations project, valued at $120,000, directed by SCC. The project strengthened literacy education in the United States and India and involved an exchange of faculty between Stella Maris College, a Catholic women's college in Madras, and SCC and EICCD. Its success led to discussions about establishing a community college under the auspices of Stella Maris College.

In the early 1990s, EICCD directed a 2-year U.S. Department of Education Title VI-B business linkage project to strengthen international business education at U.S. community colleges and to promote trade relationships between companies in India and the United States. EICCD led a trade mission of small and medium-sized U.S. businesses to India in the fall of 1996. In addition to developing trade, this project gave Indian educators an excellent look at the role that a community college can play in the economic development of its community.

Key factors in the rapid growth of India's community colleges include the following:

- The community college movement has been able to use as a foundation the many existing sewing schools, cooking schools, secretarial colleges, and other technical schools that the Catholic church had developed over decades.

- Early converts to the community college concept in India, where class and caste have been major barriers to education, leapt at the idea of open access for all. The idea of providing opportunities, especially for women and minorities, resonated with the church's mission to serve peace and justice.

- India has long had a high-quality university system that can hold its own against universities around the globe, but the country's technical colleges did not compare favorably. Many in India wanted to improve this sector of the education system and provide short-term, high-quality, relevant training.

In a country as large as India there will be many variations on the community college theme. It is clear that India's federal and regional governments are making a serious attempt to manage the growing number of community colleges and to determine how they should fit into the country's higher education structure. Course approval, funding, accreditation, and other issues are being addressed more centrally, and in many instances community colleges are being placed under the administrative purview of universities.

The Dominican Republic's Experience

Community college development in the Dominican Republic came about largely through the vision of one man, Leonel Fernández, who has been president from 1996 to 2000 and 2004 to present. Fernández, who lived in the United States during his middle and high school years and visited there during his first term as president, had been impressed by community colleges. He believed that the community college model could provide the Dominican Republic with high-quality short-term training. Companies looking for a capable labor force would locate in areas that offered such training, thus providing economic development. For young people who could not afford to attend private universities, community colleges would provide a way to learn skills that would allow them to get jobs and be a means for continuing their educations.

Fernández strongly believed that economic development begins with education, and that in order to compete in the 21st century, the Dominican Republic needed to focus on training its human capital. He incorporated this belief into his political platform when he ran for the presidency again in 2004. Subsequently, Fernández signed an agreement with Daytona Beach Community College (DBCC), Florida, to foster exchanges and work on a variety of projects together.

In 2004, Fernández met with a group of business leaders from the eastern province of Santo Domingo. Because their province lacked a qualified and adequately trained labor force, they had been trying for 10 years to develop formalized technical training. They had attempted to align themselves with the public university and with former government officials, but political interests prevented the project from getting off the ground. Because of Santo Domingo's industrial development, nearby airport, and free zones, Fernández thought it would be the perfect location for the Dominican Republic's first community college.

With a goal of opening the Dominican Republic's first community college in the fall of 2006, the challenges included finding the right location, clearing the site, and beginning construction, as well as working with local universities and other partners to develop a model. The government hired and trained staff and administrators, established a board of directors, and certified community college programs and course content; DBCC hosted delegations and provided expertise. The government and DBCC created time lines, analyzed obstacles, and devised solutions for opening the first community college.

DBCC served as the model for the new community college's organization, student services, and adult education and remedial programs. Courses and programs were also modeled on DBCC's but were adjusted to the Dominican Republic's needs. Tompkins-Courtland Community College (New York) and Portland Community College (Oregon) played an important role by hosting Dominican delegations that reviewed the colleges' programming diversity and studied other aspects of the U.S. community college model. The Dominican government plans to create four community colleges. Depending on what areas of expertise the colleges provide to their communities, they will be partnered with U.S. colleges whose programs are a good match.

The Dominican Republic's community college development depended on a populist leader who had definite ideas about education that he incorporated into his platform. His election to the presidency made it clear that there was a public mandate for the new colleges. Political support from the government followed. Business and industry have supported the initiative and will continue to play a key role in the choice of courses and programs offered at the community colleges.

GEORGIA'S EXPERIENCE

Georgia's development of community colleges, while still in its early stages, is part of a major program of education reform introduced by the government in the post–Soviet era. These reforms have reduced the number of university majors, departments, teachers, and students. Importantly, they follow the requirements of the Bologna process by giving all Georgian graduates and school leavers access to vocational and professional career education through the network of new community colleges.

After the breakup of the Soviet Union, Georgia's system of professional education began to fall apart. As in other Soviet-dominated territories, specialized schools called *technikons* had been the sole source of technical education. They were designed to produce large numbers of technicians, but in extremely limited and focused disciplines. In the new Georgia, technikons produced more graduates than were needed in many disciplines. Some graduates' skills were not needed at all because many Soviet-era businesses that had depended on technikons for workforce training had themselves disappeared. Georgia's technical education system no longer met the needs of business and industry, and it was clear that the country needed a new mandate for workforce development.

Beginning in 2005, dialogue among professors at the Georgian Technical University (GTU) in Tblisi, educators overseas, and members of the government and administration brought the community college concept to the attention of key Georgian policymakers. In the summer of that year, a delegation of Georgian higher education officials, which included teachers from GTU, visited four CCID member colleges: Kirkwood Community College and Eastern Iowa Community College, both in Iowa; Waukesha County Technical College in Wisconsin; and Moraine Valley Community College in the western suburbs of Chicago. In February 2006, officials from Georgia's Ministry of Education and Science attended CCID's 30th anniversary conference in Jacksonville, Florida. Meetings with U.S. community college officials assured the Georgians that they would have the support and resources needed to create a community college system. The assurances included the following:

- The four colleges visited by the 2005 delegation made a commitment to continue supporting Georgia's efforts.

- As a result of what they learned at the conference and from visiting Santa Fe Community College in Jacksonville, Florida, ministry officials were confident that they had a clear understanding of the scope of community colleges.

- CCID and Georgia's education ministry agreed to sign a memorandum of understanding in support of community college development.

The memorandum of understanding was signed in Tblisi in April 2006, by the minister of education and a CCID official. In remarks to the gathering, the U.S. ambassador to Georgia attributed the vitality of the U.S. economy in part to the training capabilities of U.S. community colleges. The ambassador heralded the beginnings of such a system in Georgia, created with U.S. assistance but designed to meet the unique needs of the Georgian economy.

The movement to introduce community colleges in Georgia gained political support from the highest sectors of the government and administration. On the occasion of a new factory opening, Georgia's prime minister spoke about how the new community colleges would train factory technicians in the skills needed for modern industry. Although many issues remained to be resolved—including student testing, the application process, teacher qualifications, and university transfer—it was expected that legislation to enable new community colleges would be introduced in parliament before the end of 2007.

The government decided to locate Georgia's first community college in Gori, a regional center northwest of Tbilisi. Because it is near the main east–west and north–south transportation corridors and is close to one of the two regions that claim independence from Georgia, Gori is considered to be strategically important. The government's goal is to modernize the economy and build careers for Georgia's young people so that they do not have to move away to find work. Gori's difficult economic conditions reflect those of small towns and rural areas throughout the country, where many people rely on subsistence agriculture for survival, making it an ideal place to establish a new model of market-responsive professional training.

Georgia began its reforms of primary and secondary education with funding from the World Bank. As is the case elsewhere in the world, the establishment of community colleges is being realized through a combination of government funding, building donations, in-kind contributions, and U.S. grant submissions. Significant funding was obtained in the spring of 2006, when USAID awarded a start-up grant to a GTU consortium, originally consisting of GTU and Muscatine Community College, Iowa, and later joined by Waukesha Technical and Community College (Wisconsin), Moraine Valley Community College (Illinois), and Kirkwood Community College (Iowa). The consortium will serve as the implementing agency for Georgia's community colleges. With the college at Gori as the pilot, CCID will continue to assist the government's efforts to open community colleges in 12 locations around the country.

Credit transfer is a key aspect of the community college model, and one that Georgia's officials and educators view positively. Many countries do not have the capability to incorporate credit transfer into their systems. Georgia will need to achieve much larger reforms to do so, but the commitment and dynamism it has exhibited thus far in changing its education system make it clear that the country will be able to achieve its goals for a community college system.

Conclusion

The U.S. community college model has been a beacon to other countries as they contemplate education reform. In some cases it has been so extensively adapted to fit local needs that an educator from a U.S. community college might not recognize it, but the core values of open access, relevance to workforce training, and credit transferability remain. The community college creates a gateway to the world of higher education for the underprivileged, thereby connecting potential with opportunity. Education reformers in India, the Dominican Republic, and Georgia have seen how the U.S. model can be adapted and are moving forward assertively. As with all adventures, the journey is as important as the destination.

References

Madras Center for Research and Development of Community College Education. (2005, December). *Marching with the marginalized.* Madras, India: Author.

Additional Resources

Many other countries around the world, in addition to the 23 profiled in this book, are interested and engaged in developing or enhancing community college, technical, or further education pathways to higher education for their citizens. The purpose of this appendix is to lead readers to a few excellent sources of information about countries not profiled in the chapters of this book, as well as additional information about some that are.

European Centre for the Development of Vocational Training (Cedefop)
http://www.cedefop.europa.eu

European Training Village
http://www.trainingvillage.gr/etv

Founded in 1975, Cedefop is a European agency, with offices in Greece and Belgium, established to promote vocational education and training (VET) throughout the European Union. Its mission statement is as follows:

> To ensure economic and social development it is essential that vocational education and training meets the needs of the citizen, the labour market and society. Building on a rich tradition of VET systems in Europe, governments and social partners devise policies for modern and innovative VET, which is a key element for employment, social inclusion and the competitiveness of the EU.

> Cedefop is the centre of expertise to support the development of VET and evidence-based policy-making. It provides advice, research, analysis, information, and stimulates European cooperation and mutual learning. Its networks allow the Centre to keep abreast of recent developments. Cedefop works closely with the European Commission, governments, representatives of employers and trade unions, as well as with researchers and practitioners. It provides them with up-to-date information on developments, experience and innovation in VET, and forums for policy debate. Cedefop shares its expertise through electronic and hard-copy publications, conferences and working groups.

One of the networks alluded to in the mission statement is Cedefop's European Training Village (ETV). Accessible from Cedefop's home page, ETV is a Web site that provides access to current, up-to-date information, data, and publications on VET throughout Europe, as well as forums for sharing and discussion. Of particular interest to readers of this book are the thematic overviews and thematic analyses of national VET systems. The thematic overviews are well-written country-by-country reports outlining the context and features of each country's VET system. The thematic analyses explore in further depth specific features of VET (e.g., institutional frameworks, skills and competency development, transfer, etc.). As of this writing, the following countries are featured in ETV (those in italics are countries featured in chapters of this book).

Austria	France	Italy	Slovenia
Cypress	Germany[1]	Latvia	*Spain*
Czech Republic	Greece	Lithuania	Sweden
Denmark	Hungary	Poland	*United Kingdom*
Estonia	Iceland	Portugal	
Finland	*Ireland*	Slovakia	

Cirius Denmark

http://www.ciriusonline.dk

Cirius Denmark is an authority within the Danish Ministry of Science, Technology and Innovation that supports the internationalization of education and training in Denmark. It serves as an information center and is responsible for a number of EU programs and initiatives, including Lifelong Learning and Youth in Action.

Eurydice Information Network on Education in Europe

http://eacea.ec.europa.eu

Eurydice is a Web site managed by the Education, Audiovisual and Culture Executive Agency, which is responsible for the management of certain parts of the EU's programs in the education, culture, and audiovisual fields. Among the wealth of information included on this site are detailed descriptions of how European education systems are organized and how they function, as well as comparative studies covering various aspects of education systems.

International Labour Organization

http://www.ilo.org

Using the search string "technical and vocational education and training" on the ILO Web site yields access to thousands of documents covering VET around the world. One document that will be of particular interest to readers of this book is *Technical and Vocational Education and Training for the Twenty-first Century: UNESCO and ILO Recommendations*. A PDF version of the document can be downloaded directly from the UNESCO Web site at http://unesdoc.unesco.org/images/0012/001260/126050e.pdf.

---

[1] The editors would like to offer special acknowledgment of Volker Rein and Ute Hippach-Schneider, who are scientists at the Federal Institute for Vocational Education and Training. At our request, Rein and Hippach-Schneider were willing to contribute a chapter on Germany. However, they had already written a thorough thematic overview for publication by Cedefop, which we urge readers to obtain from the ETV Web site at http://www.trainingvillage.gr/etv/Information_resources/NationalVet/Thematic/criteria_reply.asp

About the Contributors

Ahmet Aypay is an associate professor of education in Turkey and has been a consultant on vocational and technical schools for the Council of Higher Education of Turkey.

Antoine Barnaart is the former vice chancellor and CEO of the Northern Territory University in Australia. In the late 1990s, Barnaart presided over the structural and organizational revision of the TAFE system. He is a project director for a $20 million Australian Aid for International Development grant to modernize technical and workforce programs and capacity for several universities, polytechnical institutes, and municipal vocational training centers in the Chongqing, China, region.

George R. Boggs is the president the American Association of Community Colleges. He sits on the Washington Higher Education Secretariat and is the current president of the World Federation of Colleges and Polytechnics, the host of the fourth Congress that met in New York in February, 2008.

Philip Cary is the founding director of the DuocUC English program, one of Chile's largest higher education institutions.

Allen Cissell is the executive director of the East-West Community College Partnership at the Center for International Community College Education and Leadership. He has served with the U.S. Congress, the office of International Education, and the Office of Community College Liaison at the U.S. Department of Education. He has been working with the development of community colleges in Thailand since 2000 and was awarded a Senior Specialist Fulbright Scholarship in 2004.

Hugh David is a strategy analyst at New College Nottingham in the United Kingdom.

Sandra de Bresser is the director of the ICT department of Regio College in the Netherlands. She has also worked in the United States as the vice president of eXplio, an e-learning company with its headquarters in Belgium.

Jim Doyle has worked for more than 20 years in the New Zealand Institute of Technology sector, for 17 years as executive director of the Institutes of Technology and Polytechnics New Zealand. He has been a member of government-appointed committees and working groups including the Capital Charging Reference Group, Collaborating for Efficiency, and Governance Review. He is a member of the World Federation of Colleges and Polytechnics, which he chaired 2005–2006.

Paul A. Elsner has visited the Higher Colleges of Technology in the United Arab Emirates on several occasions and has written a definitive organizational study of the highly regarded HCT system. He serves as chancellor emeritus of the Maricopa County Community College District, one of the largest community college systems in the United States.

Sandra Engel is head of the humanities department at Mohawk Valley Community College in New York.

Glen Fisher is director of strategy and advocacy at the National Business Initiative in South Africa, where he focuses on sustainable development and the role of business in society. He was involved in the establishment of Khanya College; served as a researcher for the National Education Policy Investigation and the National Commission on Higher Education; and was a member of the Ministerial National Committee on Further Education. He was closely involved in the drafting of the new democratic government's green and white papers on FET and established the Colleges Collaboration Fund.

Coen Free is president of Koning Willem I College in the Netherlands and president of the Dutch Consortium for Innovation, a sister organization of the American League for Innovation. He is also founding member of the European Federation for Open and Distance Learning.

Mary Crabbe Gershwin is founder and president of Gershwin Consulting, a company focused on workforce development. Her clients include the Lumina Foundation, Ford Foundation, the U.S. embassy in Brazil, and the U.S. Department of State. Gershwin is leading a variety of initiatives to link U.S. community colleges with South American technical institutes.

John Halder is president of Community Colleges for International Development, Inc.

Geoff Hall is the CEO of New College Nottingham in the United Kingdom and has served as a chief analyst and policymaker for British funding authorities.

James Horton was chief operational officer and vice chancellor of the Higher Colleges of Technology system in the United Arab Emirates 2003–2005. He has also held positions as chancellor and president of major multicollege systems. He is currently president of Yavapai College, a system in one of the largest counties in Arizona.

Yasuko Iida is a professor at Tokyo Metropolitan University.

Tanom Inkhamnert is a member of the Thailand Higher Education Commission and president of the Project for Consortium on Doctor of Philosophy Programs at Rajabhat Universities. He previously served as the secretary general for the Office of Rajabhat Institutes Council, Ministry of Education, and as senior advisor to the ministry for the establishment of community colleges.

Judith T. Irwin is director of international education and programs at the American Association of Community Colleges. She has served as executive director of the American Council on Education's Business–Higher Education Forum, which includes 40 of the major Fortune 500 U.S. companies and the most influential research-based universities.

Tayeb Kamali is the vice chancellor of the Higher Colleges of Technology in the UAE and founder and chair of numerous international conferences on e-Learning and entrepreneurship convened in the UAE.

Steven Sai Kit Kwok has studied, with a focus on education and training, at the Chinese University of Hong Kong, New School for Social Research, Oxford University, Göethe Institut, and University of South Australia and has held full-time research positions at the Hong Kong SAR Government, the University of Hong Kong, and the Chinese University of Hong Kong.

Bertha Landrum has been with Maricopa Community Colleges in Arizona for 41 years, as a professor, director of research and development, dean of instruction, and, for 19 years, district director of business and workforce development. Since retiring from the position of interim vice chancellor for academic affairs, she has been consulting in the United Arab Emirates, Sri Lanka, and Indonesia.

Cynthia D. Liston is a senior policy associate at Regional Technology Strategies, Inc., in North Carolina, a nonprofit organization dedicated to researching, designing, implementing, and assessing regional development strategies.

Frank McMahon is director of academic affairs at the Dublin Institute of Technology.

Arturo Nava Jaimes has a PhD in physics, mathematics, and sciences, with a specialization in education. He has been president of several associations and has obtained national and international recognition for his contributions to higher technological education. Since 1991, he has been the national coordinator of technological universities in Mexico.

Diane E. Oliver is an assistant professor in the community college leadership program at National-Louis University.

Gerard A. Postiglione is a professor and head of the Division of Policy Administration and Social Science at the University of Hong Kong.

David Roldán Martínez is a telecommunications engineer at the Universidad Politécnica de Valencia (UPV) in Spain. He has published more than 10 books about IT and many articles on new technologies. Since 2004 he has been a member of the e-learning expert group at UPV and works as an application integrator for e-learning solutions.

Stuart A. Rosenfeld is the founder and president of Regional Technology Strategies, Inc., in North Carolina, a nonprofit organization dedicated to researching, designing, implementing, and assessing regional development strategies. He also founded and directs the activities of the Trans-Atlantic Technology and Training Alliance, an international consortium of community and technical colleges in the United States, Europe, and South Africa.

Geremie Sawadogo has extensive experience in West Africa as an intercultural trainer, international educator, and international development specialist with interest in workforce development issues. He is currently the program manager for global mobility at the World Bank. He has a special interest in workforce training infrastructure in postcolonial countries and has been an advisor and resource for the American Association of Community Colleges.

Analy Scorsone is the director of global studies and international partnerships for the Kentucky Community and Technical College System.

Marianne Scott is director of the National Business Initiative (NBI) in South Africa. Her career reflects her passion for the link between education, skills development, and the world of work. She worked in the mining industry before starting a career in teaching, becoming a principal of an FET college before coming to NBI.

Hanne Shapiro is the centre manager at the Danish Technological Institute.

Cristóbal Silva is a lawyer with experience in the design and management of educational projects oriented to technical and professional training.

Michael L. Skolnik is a professor emeritus of the University of Toronto. Until 2007 he held the William G. Davis Chair in Community College Leadership and directed the PhD program in community college leadership.

Joyce S. Tsunoda is emeritus chancellor for the University of Hawai'i (UH) Community Colleges. She retired in 2004 after 38 years of service including 20 years as community college system chancellor and 10 years as senior vice president for international education for the UH system.

David Valladares Aranda is director of the division of careers at the Universidad Tecnológica del Sur de Sonora in Mexico.

Marcelo Von Chrismar is rector of DuocUC in Chile.

Don Watkins is a professor emeritus of the City University of New York and vice president of the United States-China Education Foundation. He has been active in China since 1982.

Shelley L. Wood is the director of strategic partnerships at the Community College of Aurora in Colorado. She is tasked with building relationships with community, industry, and government partners to further the mission of the college and to coordinate grant proposals and projects.

Index

T